the
third
woman

Also by William Cash

*Educating William: Memoirs of a
Hollywood Correspondent*

the
third
woman

The secret passion that inspired
THE END OF THE AFFAIR

WILLIAM CASH

LITTLE, BROWN AND COMPANY

A *Little, Brown* Book

First published in Great Britain in 2000
by Little, Brown and Company

Copyright © William Cash 2000

A CIP catalogue record for this book
is available from the British Library.

ISBN 0 316 85405 0

Typeset in Bembo by M Rules
Printed and bound in Great Britain by
Clays Ltd, St Ives plc

Little, Brown and Company (UK)
Brettenham House
Lancaster Place
London WC2E 7EN

contents

acknowledgements

This is not another biography of Graham Greene; rather, it is an investigation into fact and fiction in the work of one of the most important writers of the twentieth century. Many of the quotations from Greene's letters to Lady Catherine Walston are here published for the first time. The Greene literary estate protects its copyright with 'vigour' and I am enormously grateful to Francis Greene, as his father's literary executor, for allowing me to use Greene's own words in helping to critically examine the most tumultuous period of Greene's life: the years from his first meeting with Catherine Walston in the winter of 1946 to the publication of *The End of the Affair* in September 1951.

The ability to quote from Greene's correspondence is essential for any attempt to penetrate the intimate and paradoxical secrets of what made Lady Walston the hidden spring behind much of Greene's most powerful creativity. It is impossible to paraphrase or summarise the emotions of a strongly felt letter, let alone a love poem, especially when the writing is of Greene's quality.

The existence of *Babbling April* (1925), Greene's tortured collection of undergraduate verse, caused him to remain shy about publishing poetry for the rest of his life. His love poems to Catherine Walston (often written as letters) display a very different level of artistic and emotional maturity. Indeed, they are arguably often a more reliable indicator of private truth than the complicated narrative of his letters. Again, I am greatly indebted to Francis Greene for allowing the quotation of extracts from

Greene's very rare private volume of poems to Catherine, *After Two Years*, including in its entirety, '*Il Pace*', written after their first trip to Italy in February 1948, and his unpublished love elegy, 'After Four Years' dedicated 'To Catherine February 6, 1951 in the plane from Indo-China to Paris'.

I referred to the following editions of Graham Greene's work: *Brighton Rock*; *The End of the Affair*; *The Heart of the Matter*; *The Ministry of Fear*; *The Quiet American*; London, The Bodley Head and Heinemann Collected Edition 1974; *The Third Man*, London, Heinemann 1950; *A Sort of Life*, London, Bodley Head 1971; *Ways of Escape*, London, Bodley Head 1980; *The Lost Childhood*, London, Eyre and Spottiswoode 1951; *The Complaisant Lover*, London, Heinemann 1959; also, the privately printed editions of *A Quick Look Behind*, 1983 and *Sylvester and Orphanos*. Poems from *After Two Years* are taken from the original handwritten poems that Greene gave to Catherine Walston, which are held at Georgetown University, USA. The quotation from Michael Korda's *Charmed Lives: A Family Romance* is from the London, Allen Lane 1980 edition. Extracts are also quoted from Ernie O'Malley's *On Another Man's Wound* (Anvil Press) and Cyril Connolly's *The Unquiet Grave* (Penguin).

In helping me to access and study the original manuscript of *The End of the Affair* as well as the 1,200 or so hand-written letters and poems held in the Greene–Walston Collection at Georgetown University, I would like to thank the entire staff of Special Collections at the Lauinger Library, in particular: Nicholas B. Scheetz, Manuscripts Librarian, who graciously put up with me and my band of researchers invading the fifth floor reading room over the summer of 1999; George Barringer, whose knowledge of prehistoric-age computer programs greatly helped with the transcribing of the letters; Lynne Conway, for not requiring me to fill out a new request form for every letter and folder (as an unauthorised biographer was slowed down); and Scott Taylor, for diligently carrying out my copying requests and always addressing me as 'Professor Cash'. Sadly, I do not hold any professorial or university chair, but it was a nice feeling at the time.

Instead of footnotes, I have preferred to state the date and place of the writing of each letter (with a few exceptions, to avoid the book reading like an appointment diary) because 'location' was such an integral part of their inter-continental romance. Thankfully, the Greene–Walston affair took place before the age of AT&T international calling cards.

I would also like to thank the excellent staff of other libraries holding Greene archives whose help was invaluable. At the John J. Burns Library at Boston College, Dr Robert O'Neill generously allowed me to see all the papers I requested, with only a few exceptions. His back-up staff – in particular John Atteberry and John Russell – were highly efficient. The Harry Ransom Humanities Research Center at the University of Texas at Austin also holds a vast collection of Greene's private papers, in addition to the private papers of Evelyn Waugh which were also extensively researched. Greene would approve that one of the most helpful custodians of his papers at the University of Texas (of all places) is Chris Farrington, a full card-carrying Marxist who ended up at Texas after graduating as a mature student from Sussex University.

My other main source is original interviews. Without the assistance and generosity of the following this book could never have been written. In particular I want to thank Vivien Greene, the only Mrs Graham Greene, for her candour in the face of so many questions that took her back to a painful period of her life. Also Caroline (Lucy) Bourget, Greene's daughter, who filled in several missing parts of the jigsaw and presented a fresh perspective on Greene's family life in the late 1940s. Although Yvonne Cloetta has given very few interviews about her thirty-one years with Greene, she proved a model subject. She made our time together so much easier by simply laughing whenever the subject of Gram's (as she pronounces Greene's name) subversive and double-faceted nature arose. Lady Longford remains a percipient and witty expert on post-war London literary society.

Michael Meyer talked of Greene in the 1950s with the informal frankness that marks true friendship. Lady Selina Hastings was a source of not only invaluable information but also encouragement, having been through many similar vicissitudes in her excellent biography of Evelyn Waugh. On the subject of Waugh, I would also like to greatly thank Auberon Waugh, literary executor of his father's estate, for permission to quote from Waugh's novels, diaries and letters. The Greene–Waugh friendship was not forged until the late 1940s, and Waugh's monocle offers a fascinating side-view from which to watch the evolving Greene–Walston affair.

Others who must be thanked are Piers Paul Read, for his astute and intelligent analysis of the paradoxes of Greene's Catholicism; Lucy Rothenstein; Cormac O'Malley; Professor Richard English; Alan Williams, Ben Pimlott, Antony Powell, Father Cyril Barratt SJ, Noel Barber SJ and the archive staff of the Jesuit House in Leeson Street, Dublin; Diana Crutchley; Jocelyn Rickards and her husband Clive Donner; Hon. Elizabeth Montagu; Brian Wormald; Paddy Kelly in Achill; Sir Arthur Marshall; Terry Holloway; David Short; Rev Hugh Brewer; Leslie Wordell; Gitta Bittorf; Caroline Bullock; the McDermott family in Rye; the old alumnae office staff at Barnard College; the Rye Historical Society; the Berkhamsted police; and the Hon. Oliver Walston for wishing me 'well' with my project whilst producing his own documentary about his mother (although I have 'drawn from' Catherine Walston's diaries, he did not allow me to quote from them).

On the accommodation front, Sir Christopher and Lady Meyer in Washington were most generous in providing me with a welcome and civilised 'official' alternative to a Holiday Inn. Victoria Grey also kindly helped out. In London, Charles Dean proved, as always, a true and uncomplaining friend (with a few entirely justifiable exceptions). Richard and Vivian King, at both Ropley and Mount Street, were unfailingly kind. Allan Scott was a great support. In Cambridgeshire, Beth Norman and Kevin Armstrong invited me to stay at Harston House (I slept in Greene's mother's room overlooking the old fountain) whilst I researched Newton Hall and Thriplow. Grania Lyster also put me up. James Huddleston was a generous host in the South of France. In Shropshire, my mother was a saint and my father a source of invaluable advice, in particular with regards to the Jesuit world of the 1950s.

A very special thanks goes to Rebecca Wallwork, my outstanding research assistant, whose meticulous attention to detail and scholarly intelligence shows every indication of a brilliant academic career in Cambridge. I hope deciphering Greene's inky scrawls proves to be useful training for her Ph.D on Thomas Hoccleve, the fifteenth-century cleric, poet and philanderer. I must also thank Dr Richard Luckett of Magdalene College, Cambridge for recommending Rebecca to me, putting me up in college and for reading the manuscript. As always, I am grateful for his constructive critical advice. Catherine Jordan was of help in the early stage of this book. Norman Sherry gave me some helpful advice at the outset of this project. His comprehensive authorised biography is the benchmark by which all other Greene scholarship is judged. I look forward to the final volume.

My 'headmaster' and literary agent Gillon Aitken offered his wise, frank and expert counsel at every stage. Martin Soames and Nicola Thatcher gave excellent advice. I would also like to thank everyone at Little Brown & Company, in particular Richard Beswick, for his skilful and sharp editing, and Tamsyn Berryman, for her patience after the Midlands Electricity Board cut off the neighbourhood power supply at 9am on deadline day. As a result, I wrote the last sentence of this book in a sixteenth-century pub near Bridgnorth whilst locals watched the House of Lords being abolished on television.

Above all, I am eternally grateful to my girlfriend Louise, my true heart, for all her love, support, perceptive mind and toleration of my strange writing hours; and, once again, I humbly apologise for missing her play.

Upton Cressett,
Shropshire

November 1999

To Louise King,
with three years' love

For most men the road of life is a dead-end, leading to nowhere. But there are some who, even in childhood, realise that they are moving towards an unknown sea. At the very beginning of their journey they are amazed by the bitter violence of the wind and taste the salt on their lips. On they go on, until, at length, when the last dune has been surmounted, they find themselves in a world of spume and blown sand which seems to speak to them of an infinity of passion. That is the moment when they must choose their path. Either they must take the final plunge, or they must retrace their steps . . .

François Mauriac, prologue to *The Unknown Sea*
(Eyre and Spottiswoode, London, 1948)

point of departure

Is it really possible to fall in love over a dish of onions? That is the absurd question asked by Bendrix, middle-aged author and the narrator of *The End of the Affair*, shortly before leaving behind a half-eaten steak and a third of a bottle of wine, and walking out of Rules restaurant in Covent Garden with the wife of a dull senior civil servant whose life he has been using as copy in a book. They hail a taxi and direct the driver to a tawdry hotel (the sort that only has double beds) off Sussex Gardens, near Paddington Station, where they make love 'badly'.

But it was certainly not over a dish of fried onions at Rules that the acclaimed forty-three-year-old English novelist, Graham Greene, first fell in love with the thirty-year-old American beauty Catherine Walston, upon whom Sarah is partly modelled in *The End of the Affair*. If one agrees with Cyril Connolly that adultery is a 'form of murder' – because one murders the image of the rival husband or wife in the eyes of those whom they love – then the police file on Greene and Walston begins around a quarter to four on a biting cold winter afternoon, just before Christmas 1946, with a trail of heel- and footprints left behind on the snowy landing field at Cambridge Airport.

There were no witnesses – except perhaps a shivering ex-RAF petrol pump attendant – to what Greene later repeatedly referred to in his letters to Catherine as the most 'important

event' of his life. Only a few lonely shoe tracks in the hard crust
of snow: those of an expensive pair made by a French designer
like Dior; of another, more plain, pair of women's dress shoes;
and of a man's black Oxfords about size eleven. They were left by
the three 'Walston account' passengers as they walked to their
tiny four-seater Percival Proctor V aeroplane parked on the
frozen landing field.

Guests at Thriplow Farm, near Cambridge, and later at nearby
Newton Hall, would privately complain that Catherine Walston
rarely bothered with any formal seating plan. Often barefoot
and dressed in a silk shirt, Catherine usually sat next to her husband Harry. The weekend shortly before Christmas 1946,
however, it can reasonably be assumed that Mrs Walston chose to
sit herself beside the six foot two, gas-blue-eyed author of
Brighton Rock and *The Power and the Glory*. Opposite Greene
was Vivien, his wife of nineteen years and the mother of his two
young children.

As the fine claret flowed during lunch, the talk turned to
religion, sin, Ireland (where Catherine had a cottage), books
and Christmas stockings. Greene liked secret panels, hiding
places, private jokes. Had his attention not been captivated by his
hostess, he would have enjoyed knowing that on the wall of her
dining-room was a painting that could be slid away to reveal the
prize Jersey cow sheds of the 2,500-acre farm.

Although wrong about the painting being a Picasso, Evelyn
Waugh gave an insight into Thriplow life in a letter to Nancy
Mitford after a visit there with Greene two years later:

> I went to such an extraordinary house on Wednesday. A side of
> life I never saw before – very rich, Cambridge, Jewish, social-
> ist, highbrow, scientific, farming. There were Picassos on sliding
> panels & when you pushed them back plate glass & a stable
> with a stallion looking at one. No servants. Lovely Careolean
> silver unpolished. Gourmet wines & cigars.

But Greene's acute, slightly bulging eyes were far too diverted by the sight of what Mitford later described as a 'Ritz vision in mink' for him to take in such details. Exotic clouds of Chesterfield cigarette smoke encircled the striking figure of Catherine Walston. As they spoke, drank and laughed, Greene was suddenly reminded again what happiness felt like. Catherine was intensely direct and frank with men, especially those she wanted to sleep with.

Having always lived in fear of boredom, for now, at least, he had forgotten about such concerns as the tedious stack of reading waiting for him at his office at the publisher Eyre and Spottiswoode; his long-standing mistress, Dorothy Glover, back in London; his squabbling children in Oxford. If a sure sign of middle-age is the sudden realisation – as a critic of Boswell once observed – that the future has turned into the present, then Greene felt too alive at that moment to care.

Now that he was heading towards middle-age, with eleven novels or 'entertainments' published and his reputation assured, Greene had for some years been looking for a very different fulfilment: a new great love; an escape from the awful domestic future that loomed towards him – like a trap – at his family's Georgian terraced house in Oxford. The sheer thought of a slow train journey back to Beaumont Street with Vivien was in itself enough to make him reach for a drink.

Even if he and Vivien left right now, he thought to himself irritably, they wouldn't be back in Beaumont Street for hours.

'We must be getting back to give the children supper,' volunteered Vivien, almost reading his mind.

A Cambridge–Oxford train timetable was produced and studied.

'Why not fly back?' announced Mrs Walston matter-of-factly in her East Coast drawl. 'I'll fly with you . . .'

She paused.

'. . . and then fly back.'

Fly back?

Catherine dialled 56291, the number for Marshall's aerodrome in Cambridge. Extension '40' was the controller's ground-floor operations room, which dealt with private 'taxi' air charters.

Before the war, when the newly married Greene was living very modestly with Vivien in a thatched cottage in Chipping Campden, working on the two unreadable novels that followed *The Man Within*, he had sometimes been so 'short', as he put it later, that he had hardly been able to afford the train fare from Oxford to London. In his journal for the early 1930s, he wrote with a sense of self-pitying economy that a Tiger Moth bi-plane had been flying around fields in the local countryside, offering the 'cheapest ever prices' for pleasure flights over the Cotswold countryside. At the time, however, working around the clock on Benzedrine to complete *Stamboul Train*, he had no money for such thrills.

For Greene, to be flown back to Oxford in a private aeroplane by a wealthy American beauty with lustrous, knotty dark hair, smooth Anglo-Saxon cream skin, perfectly formed high cheek bones, and smelling of Guerlain scent, would have touched a sensitive nerve. Freud wrote that all train journeys are about death or sex. I have no idea whether he wrote a dream treatise about flying, but Greene himself always associated flying with a high level of excitement. Aged seven, when he filled out a questionnaire for the *Berkhamsted School Gazette*, he won second prize – twelve tubes of watercolour paint – for his 'confessions'. The first question, back in 1911, had been: What is your greatest aim in life? Greene's answer: 'To go up in an aeroplane'. (When asked again aged seventy-one, the answer was: 'To write a good book'.) In his autobiography, Greene recalled how he and his entire family had waited vainly around all afternoon in the garden at Berkhamsted, in the hope of seeing Louis Blériot make the first flight from London to Manchester.

Greene always maintained that 'childhood is the bank balance of the writer'. 'The creative writer perceives his world once and for all in childhood and adolescence', he wrote in *The Lost Childhood*, published in 1951, the same year as *The End of the Affair*, 'and his whole career is an effort to illustrate his private world in terms of the great public world we all share.' Our choice of reading as adults mirrors our desire to see our own features 'reflected flatteringly back' – as in a love affair. One of Greene's favourite books was *Night Flight* by Antoine de Saint-Exupéry, a French air-mail courier pilot to North Africa in the Second World War and the author of the bestselling children's book, *The Little Prince*. And one of Greene's most vivid early memories was of reading *The Pirate Aeroplane* by Captain Gilson, a colour illustrated *Boy's Own* story of a 'villainous Yankee pirate with an aeroplane like a box kite and bombs the size of tennis balls', at least six times.

In 1946, private flying was undertaken on a very different scale to what it is today, when every computer mogul, playboy or sports star has a refurbished Lear jet with all the leather trimmings and a satellite phone. After the war, it was a Lucellan luxury. In fact, the War Office had only removed the ban on civil flying on 1 January 1946. Marshall's aerodrome in Cambridge was one of the leading small airports in the country. Its chief flying instructor, ex-RAF squadron leader Leslie Worsdell, had been the first pilot in England to fly with a new civil licence, shortly after 9am on 1 January 1946, using a Tiger Moth that had been stored in an old farm barn not far from Thriplow. Cambridge Airport had been founded before the war by David Marshall and his son Arthur (later Sir), Harold Abrahams' 100-yard-sprint arch-rival on the Cambridge Blue team (beating him on several occasions), and a member of the legendary (*Chariots of Fire*) British track team at the 1929 Paris Olympics. The airport's official opening by the Secretary of State for Air in October 1938 – at the height of the Munich crisis – included the first public display of the Spitfire. After the war, new flying clubs were only allowed sixty-hours-per-month fuel rations for 'taxi and charter aircraft', whilst private owners were allowed to fly only four hours a month. Harry and Catherine Walston were among the wealthiest of Marshall's first private clients; years later, as Lord Walston, Harry gave the address at Sir Arthur's wife's memorial service.

A Marshall's advertising pamphlet ('Travel By Air!') from 1946 gives specimen charges for 'chartering' private aircraft at 6d. per passenger mile – 'Cambridge–Paris–Cambridge £13.13.4.' – and boasted: 'Qualified Radio Operator Carried in Aircraft. Race Meetings a Speciality'. As soon as Catherine's phone booking from Thriplow was taken by the on-duty clerk in the controller's ground-floor office, preparations were begun to wheel a four- or five-seater Proctor V from No. 1 Hangar out into the fading light of a wintry afternoon.

Meanwhile, the Walstons' driver (for many years Porter, an Irishman with dark hair and heavy-set features), prepared the car that was to take the Greenes and Mrs Walston to the airport. The Walston fleet over the years included a black Mercedes, Jaguar sports cars, and Rolls-Royces of various colours and specifications; in particular, there was a black and yellow convertible Rolls with red leather trim interior in which the small Walston children used to be driven at speed to Sunday mass, sitting behind the headlights on the front mud-guards.

Thriplow Farm, just set back from a narrow country lane close to St George's Church, looks like a New England stud farm. Back in 1946, its wooden clapperboard slats were painted white, making it look like an experimental mistake that Frank Lloyd Wright might have dreamt up after staying the night in a Bavarian hunting lodge. A regular weekend guest during the mid-1940s was John Rothenstein (later Sir John), the young director of the Tate Gallery, who has described how Catherine's American background made a strong impression on visitors to Thriplow:

Life at . . . Thriplow was an engaging blend of the luxurious and the radically simplified. The family living quarters were constructed out of what in other circumstances would have been a hay-loft, the stables that housed a fine stud of Arab horses being situated underneath. The household was organised with an American style of intelligence to achieve a labour-saving efficiency appropriate to wartime whereby a large family of small children was housed at close quarters to their parents and yet with a skill that excluded the typically American sacrifice of the adult to the child. Much hard and concentrated work went into this amusing and smooth-running life, but it was lived with so much style and flair that the picture, as far as Catherine was concerned, was rather of a Marie-Antoinette in elegant jeans or (according to the season) jodhpurs.

Before they left, Graham Greene and his wife may have been asked to sign the Thriplow visitors' book. Had Greene flicked through the pages as he reached into his jacket for his Parker 51 pen, he may well have double-blinked. The guest-book included such names as George VI, Elizabeth II, Dwight Eisenhower, Bob Hope and Ingrid Bergman. But like the sliding panel in the dining room, this was another family joke. The names had been mischievously written in by John Rothenstein after staying there himself.

The route the Walston chauffeur would almost certainly have taken in 1946 – the road from Thriplow towards the old London road (A10) – passes within a few hundred yards of Newton Hall, the Walstons' vast neo-Queen Anne red-brick pile, into which they moved around Christmas 1950. Just as Greene spent many weekends at Thriplow in the late 1940s, so he would regularly be invited – or invite himself – to visit Newton Hall in the 1950s. The vast house witnessed some racy scenes, with midnight swimming-pool sexual scandals involving Catholic priests as well as Cabinet ministers. Certainly for the original champagne set of Labour politicians (Hugh Dalton and Dick Stokes, for example), along with various hanger-on Catholic intellectuals, Newton Hall had all the 'facilities' of Tory, right-wing Cliveden. Only Fleet Street didn't know about it.

In December 1946, Newton Hall was still occupied by the British army, who had commandeered it as a training camp. The army even went to the trouble of tearing down the wrought-iron entrance gates and pillars. Before the Labour government handed it back to the Walstons, it was used as a women's agricultural training college.

Had the Walstons' car had time to stop, they would have found rooms full of Edwardian furniture stowed away under dust sheets. Nissen huts were erected on the front lawn, used as dormitories and lecture rooms. The 'Long Room', where Lord and Lady Walston were to later entertain guests like the Shah of Persia, was locked up. Old Lady Walston, widow of Catherine's late father-in-law, Sir Charles Walston – who had been a fellow of King's College, Cambridge and Slade Professor of Fine Art – had been required to move out.

As the Walston chauffeur drove on up the lane towards the old London road, Greene's sense of excitement must have been increased by the proximity of Harston House – only a mile from Newton Hall – the walled off seventeenth-century Queen Anne country house of Greene's rich uncle, Sir William, who helped found the naval intelligence service. Harston was where Greene had been happy as a young boy in those Edwardian summers away from his father's school at Berkhamsted. It was there he dreamt of pirate aeroplanes, hid behind the 'potting shed', and witnessed violence in the form of tennis matches. As he states in the preface to *The End of the Affair*, Greene was obsessed by such coincidences; what a Catholic would call 'divine purpose'.

Later, he enjoyed the paradox of linking his Elysian childhood at Harston and his not-so-innocent sexual adventures with Catherine Walston in the fields just a mile down the road. The childhood memory of Harston provided the setting for the garden in *The Ministry of Fear*, his last thriller written before the war; and for his dark short story *Under the Garden*, in which a man dying of cancer returns to the old family home.

> The garden was of a rambling kind which should have belonged to childhood and only belonged to childish men. The apple trees were old apple trees and gave the effect of growing wild; they sprang unexpectedly up in the middle of a rose-bed, trespassed on a tennis-court, shaded the window of a little outside lavatory like a potting-shed which was used by the gardener . . . A high brick wall divided the flower-

garden from the kitchen-garden and the orchard, but flowers and fruit could not be imprisoned by a wall. Flowers broke among the artichokes and sprang up like flames under the trees. Beyond the orchard the garden faded gradually out into paddocks and a stream and a big untidy pond with an island the size of a billiard-table.

[*The Ministry of Fear*]

As a writer, Greene was obsessed with the random shrapnel of human experience that can never be extracted from the memory. In *The Heart of the Matter*, which he was writing in December 1946, Greene describes Wilson's first disinterested look at Scobie as one of those occasions a man never forgets: 'a small cicatrice had been made on the memory, a wound that would ache whenever certain things combined'.

Such a moment awaited Greene shortly after the Walston chauffeur dropped Catherine, Graham and Vivien at the Cambridge aerodrome on the Newmarket Road. They walked into the hallway of the Civil Building, the administrative head-quarters, with its oak balustrade staircase and dark-green leather easy armchairs, built in 1937 and now a listed building, unchanged from 1946. They were shown upstairs to the flying club lounge area, where they were offered tea or a drink.

During the war, the Royal Air Force Volunteer Flying School had trained over 600 pilots prior to the Battle of Britain, and over 20,000 pilots by the end of World War II. Many were instructed at Cambridge. They were interviewed and signed their papers in the club lounge (now the chairman's office of Marshall's Aerospace). In December 1946, Cambridge Airport still only had a very simple grass field airstrip.

A Marshall's pilot – there was a team of five, all ex-RAF – dressed in Biggles goggles and a jacket and tie, was called from the pilots' mess and walked across the glittering snow-covered airstrip, lit only by a few paraffin gas flares.

The distance between the controller's office, where the trio buttoned up their coats, and the tiny waiting aeroplane could not have been more than thirty yards. Greene huddled next to Catherine in the snow, and then, as they climbed into the plane, her wave of thick, dark hair brushed his face. It happened again during the flight.

One of the most prized letters of Catherine's was a hand-written poem from Greene entitled 'After Two Years', which describes the intense love of their first two years together. The second verse begins:

In a plane your hair was blown

Writing to Catherine a year after the flight, he remembered this moment. 'The act of creation is awfully odd and inexplicable like falling in love. A lock of hair touches one's eyes in a plane with East Anglia under snow and one is in love.'

Catherine and flying became inexorably linked in his mind; he wrote to her on many of his plane journeys, not to pass the time but because it was there, in the limitless sky, that she had become vivid to him. Writing to Catherine in 1948 from his desk at Eyre and Spottiswoode, about a business trip he was making to America, where they planned to rendezvous, Greene said: 'I long to see your seaplane coming down in Augusta.' From Salzburg in 1951, he wrote that 'I can smell your hair in a plane, and every plane I take I look for you in the seat alongside.' This love of planes formed an idea in Greene's mind. Writing to Catherine at Newton on 17 August 1955, following twenty-seven hours' flying, via Toronto, to visit his daughter Lucy in Canada, he added a post-script that he had an idea for a book of reminiscences called *100 Odd Airports*, based on a similar project their friend Norman Douglas had written about visiting cards.

Greene once referred to himself as 'God's spy'. Not, perhaps, an entry to include in one's passport under 'profession'. But as he was a man obsessed by crossing borders, human, psychological and geographical, airports were among the few places where he seemed to belong. The combination of airports and snow – he arrived in Vienna in a blizzard to write *The Third Man* in February 1948 – always triggered a sense of private elation. Airports were his means of escape from himself as well as from other people – with the exception of Catherine. With her, they symbolised the point of meeting, not 'The Point of Departure' (the original title of *The End of the Affair*).

On 2 September 1955, he wrote again from Vancouver, saying that he had started the new book, now called *110 Airports*. 'I'm afraid I'll have to leave out the most important', Greene wrote to Catherine, 'Cambridge and snow on the ground and hair across my nose.' Writing from Beaulieu in April 1949, he says, 'sometimes these last days I've felt the same sort of in-love feeling as after the plane ride to Oxford, as though I'd never had you and probably never would, but longed, longed, longed to hold hands at a movie.'

A year later the flight still obsessed him. 'I just can't believe that the plane trip Cambridge to Oxford, was not designed, any more than I believe that there's anything wrong in loving you using my body as well as my mind "With my body I thee worship",' wrote Greene to Catherine on Palm Sunday in 1950. His words imply the sanctity of marriage rather than the sinful state of adultery. On the preceding line, he quoted from the French theologian Jean-Pierre de Caussade:

> Nothing happens in this world, in our souls or outside them, without the design or permission of God: now we ought to submit ourselves no less to what God permits than to what he directly wills.

Greene was a Catholic fatalist. Lady Longford, who herself converted to Catholicism in 1946, remembers a particular conversation she had with Greene on this theme when he gave a lunch party at his flat in St James's Street; 'I was very pleased to find myself sitting by him.' Greene asked her whether she had read de Caussade. 'In the most impressive way he then proceeded to explain de Caussade's doctrine of "Submission to

Divine Providence". It was a case of accepting all the eventuali-
ties of life as God's will, in all circumstances.'

It was certainly something Greene believed in without com-
punction. 'It was part of his views, he didn't have to grope
towards what he believed and it was all there,' said Lady
Longford. 'It came to this: that the last word on life had been
given by de Caussade, a priest who had a whole lot of women
in . . . Switzerland or France; his job was advising them and he
had a great sort of court and the basis of what he taught was that
one must *accept* what God said and that was the beginning and
the end and you couldn't question it; and this is what he practised. He told me, he said, this was what he held onto.'
Nonetheless, if his affair with Catherine was something ordained
by God, then Greene was freed from any feelings of personal
guilt; it certainly relieved the mind, as his comment to Lady
Longford reveals: 'I can recommend it to you,' he said. 'You
will find that it will solve many problems.'

The steel propeller of a single-engine Proctor V is started by an
electric button close to the control dials. Planes were automati-
cally re-fuelled on landing, so the tiny Proctor would have been
immediately ready for take-off once the oil gauge indicated the
correct temperature. To fly towards Oxford, the pilot would
have set his 360-degree flying compass to 245 degrees, begun to
taxi out slowly onto the snowy grass, and then fired open the
throttle heading directly into the westerly East Anglia wind. In
1946, No. 1 Hangar had 'CAMBRIDGE' painted in huge black
letters across the roof as a landing sight device. The Civil
Building had been camoflauged during the war but had been re-
painted white in the summer of 1946.

'Greene and Walston would have been in the air very quickly,'
said Terry Holloway, Marshall's group support executive, through
his walkie-talkie pilot's head-set, just before we took off to follow
the exact Cambridge–Oxford flight-path that his company's old
Proctor V would have taken in 1946. 'The air would have been
crisp and cold – good visibility,' he added after we were in the air.

Within moments, the Hornby-like tracks of Cambridge railway station stretched beneath us. Just below, to the right, were the towering spires of King's College.

To our left, heading west towards Thriplow – Newton Hall is visible from several miles away – they would have seen the smoking chimneys of Fulbourn Hospital, the old Cambridge lunatic asylum. 'With snow, hedgerows stick out like solid lines,' added Holloway. 'The landscape turns a very brilliant white. Very intense colours, with glittering dark blue shadows falling behind farm buildings and trees. The fields really sparkle beautifully.'

According to Herbert Tappin, one of the Marshall pilots in 1946, inside the plane was 'quite comfortable, not cramped, like a motor car'. Passengers wore overcoats and seat-belts, and would have been able to talk clearly once they were flying at about 2,000 feet. The flight to Oxford took about forty-five minutes. Of the five ex-RAF pilots who were employed by Marshall's and could have been working before Christmas in 1946, three were still alive in 1999: Worsdell, Tappin and Tony Farrell. All still have their flight log books. None have a record of a flight to Kidlington. I can only assume the pilot must have been one of the two (Wallis and Hubbard) now dead.

Without radar, the flight was made by pilot visibility alone and it would have been nearly dark when the plane came in to land at about 4.30pm at Kidlington Airport.

As they climbed out of the plane, Greene told Vivien to walk on ahead. While her back was turned, Catherine, her hair swept back by the wind, kissed him on the lips. 'My heart stopped for everything', he later wrote to Catherine, 'one winter evening in a plane over the snowy fields.'

The tall figure of Greene walked slowly back in the gloaming light towards his wife, who was standing alone on the edge of the airfield. As he got closer, his flushed sense of joy became soured with a sense of personal failure regarding his marriage. Long doomed, he had to put an end to the misery. Crossing the snowy field, he walked into the old farm building to ring for a taxi.

The memory of first kissing Catherine Walston at Kidlington

Airport was to haunt him for years. Writing to Catherine from his cabin on board Alexander Korda's yacht, the *Elsewhere*, in the Aegean at 7.40am on 18 June 1951 after a bad night's sleep (*The End of the Affair* was about to be published), Greene associated their love with the 'wonderful, heavy ruins' at Mycenae that he had seen the day before. Seeing 'our chauffeur' – as he described the old Greek taxi driver – standing at the quay that *they* had once used, Greene experienced a powerful Proustian moment:

I've dreamed of you all night, dear heart. Vague, sad dreams. The cabin began being very big and homeless the first time I went into it, and I wish the type-writer wasn't there – it looks like a returned ring must look on a desk [. . .] We used the old chauffeur [. . .] and he had candles in his pocket to light Agamemnon's extraordinary beehive tomb, and he was very sweet [. . .] An odd thing happened after you left: I fell in love with you all over again. Rather like when you dropped me at Oxford out of the airplane. It feels fresh and exciting and sad like then.

In the taxi to Oxford in December 1946, Vivien said nothing. By five o'clock, they were back at 15 Beaumont Street.

2

a sense of reality

This is an inquiry into the creative debt that literature owes to adultery, as well as an investigation into one of the most remarkable secret literary love affairs this century, albeit an 'open secret' amongst Graham Greene and Catherine Walston's circle of friends. It is a story of deep betrayal, sexual obsession, secret vows, jealousy, hatred, tortured religiosity, confessional walkouts, guilt, despair, blasphemy and literary revenge.

Greene himself never expected love and happiness to exist together. His own view was that 'one can be unhappy and be in love'. Ultimately – like most illicit love affairs – this is a story of human failure. As the seventy-one-year-old grand man of English letters admitted over lunch with David Lewin in Antibes during the 1975 Cannes Film Festival: 'Looking back, I have written two or three good books [*The End of the Affair* was arguably one of them]. I have accomplished a little but failed a good deal.' Like a schoolmaster composing an end of life report, he added mournfully: 'Failed in human relations, which is much more important than writing.'

The biggest failure of his life was not to 'win' Catherine Walston. Between 1948 and 1950, the years in which he wrote *The End of the Affair*, Greene became obsessed with trying to persuade Catherine to leave her millionaire husband, the future Lord Walston. Their affair endured, through many dark storms, for at least thirteen years, maybe fifteen. One of the worst came after the publication of the novel in September 1951. Writing to Catherine from Malaysia in January 1952 – a ban on seeing each other had been imposed until April – Greene wrote: 'My dear, my dear, do you think we'll really ever get each other back? Well, it depends on you, and if you are not too tired to fight. Because there will be a fight . . . [with] Harry in April, you may be sure.'

Yet, despite being arguably the most critical creative influence of his life, Lady Walston was not named in a single newspaper obituary of Greene when he died in Switzerland in 1991; a contemporary comparison would be not having mentioned Sylvia Plath when Ted Hughes died in 1998. But, you might say, Catherine and Greene weren't married. However as I discovered in the course of my research in America, they did exchange secret marriage vows in St Augustine's Catholic Church (now Tesco's) in Tunbridge Wells around the time *The End of the Affair* was completed. On 23 September 1951 Greene wrote from London to Newton Hall referring explicitly to their 'strange' wedding Mass and saying she was now his only wife (despite being legally married to Vivien). Certainly, their secret vows affected Greene deeply. Writing to Catherine from his C6 Albany flat in London's Piccadilly a decade later in 1962, he told her: 'I feel I've made an awful mess of things. You remain the most important person in my life and you always will. I love you . . . I feel completely married to you – my only marriage . . .'; repeatedly he referred to himself in letters as 'your husband', and was to dream regularly about the gold ring he gave her (which I have seen).

Catherine, although not the only great love of Greene's life, was certainly the most volatile. After finishing a chapter of his autobiography in 1970, he wrote: 'I miss you too, darling. The best part of life was with you. What remains is a peaceful coda.' Her influence on Greene from 1947 to the early 1960s – during which time he wrote many of his masterpieces – was integral to his creative drive. However, when asked about his often highly complicated private life, Greene's automatic mental reaction was

to slide on the safety catch. If cornered by inquisitive journalists – to whom, he admitted, he often 'lied' to protect his
personal life – his standard evasive reply was: 'I am my books.'

Even when the interviewer was the beautiful young daughter
of an old friend, Yves Allain, a murdered French resistance
leader, he remained intensely guarded. *The Other Man:
Conversations with Graham Greene* by Marie-Françoise Allain was
reviewed by Auberon Waugh, himself an old family friend who
must have known of Greene's lengthy illicit affair with Lady
Walston. After reading its 197 pages, Waugh observed that at the
end of perhaps the longest literary lunch interview in
memory – the talks *à deux* with Marie-Françoise went on for
weeks in Antibes – readers of Greene's work were left with 'an
infuriatingly incomplete jigsaw where the author's personality
and emotional history are concerned . . . how hard it is to
form a judgement about anything if one is denied the full background.'

Q: Was Malaya one of your main preoccupations in 1951?
A: Not particularly. *Life* had sent me there. I took advantage
   of this to escape from certain private worries.
Q: What kind of worries?
A: I can't say. There are some things I can't talk about because
   they also concern other people.
Q: 1951 coincides with *The End of the Affair* . . .
A: More or less. Perhaps we can get back to the real ques-
   tions.

This book is a detective investigation that aims to provide the
'full background' to *The End of the Affair*. Yet however tempting
it may be to read the wrenching drama of Bendrix and Sarah's
illicit war-time affair as holding up a twin mirror to Greene's tormented *ménage à trois* with Walston and her husband, it is a naïve
over-simplification of Greene's art to assume that Sarah is
Catherine and Bendrix is Greene. Greene invented Sarah as a creative vehicle for transferring many of his experiences relating to a

range of women, certainly not just Catherine. For example, Sarah's cremation scene in *The End of the Affair* is 'borrowed' from Greene's attendance of Vivien's mother's funeral in Golders Green back in 1933. The novel's VE Day scene was drawn from his experience of VE Day in 1945 with Dorothy Glover. His very real 'private worries' were a painfully raw source, built up over many years, and transformed – through Greene's imagination – into some of the most powerful works of twentieth-century fiction.

It is instructive to examine the epigraph to *The Spy's Bedside Book*, an anthology of espionage and detective fiction edited by Greene, in which a quotation from Balzac illustrates the qualities he admired in the frustrating occupation of a spy. The same words can be applied to the trade of literary detective, investigating the secrets of the Greene–Walston affair:

> The trade of a spy is a very fine one, when the spy is working on his own account. Is it not in fact enjoying the excitements of a thief, while still remaining the character of an honest citizen? But a man who undertakes this trade must make up his mind to simmer with wrath, to fret with impatience, to stand about in the mud with his feet freezing, to be chilled or to be scorched, and to be deceived by false hopes. He must be ready, on the faith of a mere indication, to work up to an unknown goal: he must bear the disappointment of failing in his aim; he must be prepared to run, to be motionless, to remain for hours watching a window [. . .] The only excitement which can compare with it is that of the life of a gambler.

Greene's tactic of evasive silence on the subject of Catherine Walston was certainly effective. Indeed, in dozens of boxes of files, I found almost no mention of Catherine Walston in any newspaper article – and there are hundreds – on Greene before his death in 1991. Certainly, he didn't talk about her in interviews. Nor was Catherine mentioned by name (he refers to his 'mistress') in Greene's autobiography, *Ways of Escape*, published in

1980, two years after her early death, aged sixty-two. This memoir only contains a brief chapter on the background to *The End of the Affair*, cautiously stating that the novel 'described a lover who was so afraid that love would end one day that he tried to hasten the end and get the pain over. Yet there was no unhappy love affair to escape this time: I was happy in love.'

But one shouldn't take what Greene has to say about himself in his prefaces or private letters too seriously. In fact, at this time, Greene was often quite miserable. He once wrote admiringly that Henry James, in his prefaces, 'had a marvellous facility for covering up his tracks (can he be blamed if he had a reason?)'. The same applies to Greene, who certainly had his reasons.

In 1951, Eddy Sackville-West wrote a brilliant article for *The Month* – the Catholic rival to Cyril Connolly's *Horizon* – entitled 'The Electric Hare', one of the first pieces in which a friend who *knew* Greene commented on the connection between his life and art. Sackville-West compared Greene to Hazlitt, and suggested that his travel writing and autobiographical essays were exercises in self-evasion. 'Where his own personality and spiritual development is concerned, Graham Greene is like the electric hare whom the racing dogs are not *meant* to catch.'

Indeed, not long after appointing Norman Sherry as his official biographer in the 1970s, Greene wrote to him from Brighton asking for his word that he would not interview 'certain women he had known'. One reason why Greene may not have wanted Sherry interviewing 'other women' is that he was rightly worried about what they – as well as Catherine – would learn about each other. Greene was not only secretive, but also he assiduously compartmentalised his life, a sure sign of the serial adulterer.

Part of this book is an examination of why sexual deceit and personal betrayal were so much a part of Greene's nature (on receiving the Shakespeare Prize from the University of Hamburg he gave a lecture entitled 'The Virtue of Disloyalty'); and why these themes were essential, it seems, to his work as both a novelist and, during the war, a professional spy. But he was, of course, always unflinchingly loyal to one cause: his fictional art. To this end, I have viewed the years in which he wrote *The End of the Affair* as almost a test case of Cyril Connolly's opening line of *The Unquiet Grave*: 'The more books we read, the clearer it becomes that the true function of a writer is to produce a masterpiece and that no other is of any consequence.' Greene's life from 1946–50 certainly seems to bear out Faulkner's dictum on this subject: 'He will be completely ruthless if he is a good one.'

Perhaps the biggest problem faced by those on Greene's trail is in always believing what he wrote in even his most intimate letters. Did what he wrote to his 'other women' belie his love for Catherine? Of course, it could be argued that no intelligent woman would make the mistake of believing everything a professional writer, especially a novelist, writes down in a love letter, but it makes it extraordinarily awkward for any literary detective when they cannot trust even a subject's most intimate private correspondence.

In order to get at the truth of Greene's wrenching emotional history – of the importance of Walston to Greene's creativity in the late 1940s and early 1950s – I have talked to, or corresponded with, various 'other' women in his life – Vivien, his wife; Australian film-set designer Jocelyn Rickards, his mistress of the early 1950s; Swedish actress Anita Bjork, his great love of the mid-1950s; and Yvonne Cloetta, his mistress of over thirty years – about what he said of them in his letters to Catherine, and asked them to tell their side of the story.

This book is also inevitably a literary investigation into the 'act of creation' itself. I want to examine why powerful creative figures like Greene have found themselves so drawn towards 'dangerous women' (in Greene's case he saw Catherine as the embodiment of 'dangerous goodness'). And vice-versa. Catherine had a paradoxical and provocative nature, the essential ambiguity of which represented to Greene a powerful and mysterious sexual driving force whose mythological pull goes back to Homer, with a literary cast ranging from Delilah to Keats's

Belle Dame sans Merci (Catherine Walston was described by Malcolm Muggeridge as 'so *belle* but *sans merci*'). Catherine was the dark river that runs through much of the most anguished, and joyful, vistas of Greene's finest work; a dark, twisting, dominating – occasionally sado-masochistic – sexual force, up whose banks I set out to search for the creative source at the darkest heart of 'Greeneland' (a phrase that Greene, in his typically subversive way, professed to dislike).

But 'Greeneland' is indeed something of a misnomer. Neither Greene's fictional nor his private universe are rooted or nailed to any 'land', or the ground. In his imagination Greene identified Catherine with the 'other' world of the limitless sky, dreams, opium, whistling – a deep subterranean ocean of their own. He always linked her in his mind with the places of their love. Greene ended his letter of 15 January 1952 from Malaysia with a nostalgic evocation of 'their' places: 'Dear heart, have you found any stand-ins? I haven't "yet", and I'm still looking . . . I love you, Catherine, here as I loved you on Achill, Capri, Venice, Paris, Ravello, Limerick, New Jersey, Naples, London, Cambridge, Tackley – the world seems covered with foolships.'

In *The End of the Affair*, Bendrix says that 'so much' of a novelist's writing is done in the subconscious. 'War didn't trouble those deep sea-caves, but now there was something of infinitely greater importance to me than war – the end of love.' Fittingly, Greene completed *The End of the Affair* in August 1950 on board Alexander Korda's yacht, the *Elsewhere*, which was named after Shakespeare's defiant words of Coriolanus, who is hounded out of Rome to exile in 'a world elsewhere'.

This idea is crucially important to an understanding of the secret lovers' world that Greene and Catherine invented for themselves. We know this from a revealing letter (wrongly catalogued at Georgetown) Greene wrote to Catherine in June 1967 after coming perilously close to being killed when on a journalistic assignment during the Arab–Israeli Six Day War. 'I thought I had finished with the world,' a rattled and bruised Greene wrote to her afterwards. With a companion, he stepped out of the Dan Hotel in Tel Aviv to do some reporting, hoping to find an 'incident' to use as copy. Greene suddenly found himself lying face down on a sand dune, shrapnel flying above his head – for nearly three hours as they were caught in the middle of Israeli artillery 'mortar and machine gun fire'. The scene was a strange parallel to how, seventeen years before, he had described Bendrix waking up in a cloud of smoke and dust, lying under a door, after the Blitz bomb blast that destroyed his Clapham Common South bed-sit in *The End of the Affair*. The near-death experience – Greene was sixty-three – made him reflect on his life and what was most important to him.

> We were caught in a beastly position just behind the Israel artillery who didn't know we were there, so we were included in the barrage. I said Hail Marys and thought a lot! My companion got a chip out of his cheek. I only got a sore from leaning on my elbow and the hell of a sunburn. In the blitz one always had a drink but I had nothing but fizzy lemonade for two days. As you can imagine one thought a lot about one's life in between flattening for an explosion.
>
> And you are so much of my life. My darling, I know how upset I've been and I don't suppose you'll believe me when I say that you are the greatest love I can ever have – and it continues. It was a tormented love which made me more happy and sometimes more miserable than I'll ever be again. I have a real quiet love for 'Y' [his long-term French mistress Yvonne Cloetta] 'Peaceful as old age'. I don't want to do any more harm. I'm afraid now of our love – so often nothing and nobody could stand against it. But it stays there – Tunbridge Wells [referring to their secret marriage vows] is in my heart also. Only at 63 I haven't courage or strength – except for artillery bombardments! But you are part of my life and always will be. I was scared of Capri, but it was all right only because it was so different. I never try to reproduce our life. That belonged to you and me.

On the preceding day he had written:

My darling with you I found a strange beautiful underwater
world like Cousteau's and nothing can ever make me forget
it . . . I loved and admired the dark waters and the coloured
fish and I'll never forget that world but I wanted to see clearer
and couldn't: it was a contradiction and then I began to have
secrets too but I could never keep them for very long. You
wanted the clear water as much as I did but you didn't realise
I wanted it too. Now I'm too old for diving. I don't love the
clear stream more than your ambiguity and when I am bored
(that side of my melancholy which still remains) I always
remember that never for a moment have I ever been bored by
you; encaptured, excited, nervous, angry, tormented but
never bored because I lost myself in searching for you.

No wonder Greene was paid extravagantly well to write
movie scripts. But knowing exactly how much of this – and
dozens of other similar outpourings – to believe has been the
most difficult part of this investigation. Just as *The End of the Affair*
is an illicit love affair as seen through the eyes of that most unreliable of modern narrators, Maurice Bendrix, so I have come to
see Greene as simply the unreliable narrator of his own life – a
deliberately self-delusional voyager-on-the-edge. Indeed, this
book itself is an inquiry into the theme of unreliable narrative.

The Graham Greene Birthplace Trust Festival, an annual four-
day gathering of Greene scholars, admirers, fanatics and literary
tourists – with fleeting appearances by members of the Greene
family – is held in Greene's old home town of Berkhamsted,
around his birthday on 2 October. It's meant to be a friendly sort
of occasion: inexpensive wine is served after talks; old Penguin
editions of his novels, with the covers drawn by Paul Hogarth
(*The End of the Affair* shows a middle-aged man, who looks like
Alan Bates, staring into the void of a future, with a lipstick-red
rose protruding insolently from the corner), are laid out for sale

on a wooden trestle table at the back of the Berkhamsted School lecture theatre. The atmosphere is a cross between a provincial book fair and a David Lodge-style academic conference.

On my visit, however, the school fête meets book-hunt-heaven atmosphere was rudely interrupted at around 11.30am on the Saturday morning of what would have been Greene's ninety-sixth birthday. Dressed in dog-collar and clinical black suit, Father Leopoldo Duran, Greene's drinking companion, priestly confessor and the model for *Monsignor Quixote*, had been invited to address the assembled 'brethren', as *The Tablet* described his 150-strong congregation (die-hard Greene addicts had flown over from around the world). During his emotionally charged, but not always comprehensible speech, eighty-two-year-old Father Duran (author of *Graham Greene: Friend and Brother*) steered the subject onto his rival biographer Michael Shelden. The moment he spoke Shelden's name, the grey-haired Spanish priest began shaking with rage, his face clenched up – like his fist – with vitriolic anger.

'His was the most impudent book I have ever read,' Duran exclaimed, before smashing his fist down on the table with the sort of enraged thump that Victorian evangelists used to reserve for assaulting the pulpit in sermons on the devil. 'A disease seems to have taken hold of the empty heads of some people . . . and it is my obligation to defend my friend.'

Since I only met Greene once, and briefly at that, I feel under no such obligation. This book is not a defence of Greene (one hardly needs it when your books have sold over twenty million copies) but rather an attempt to restore a sense of balance to the study of one of this century's most important novelists during the most productive but emotionally violent period of his life.

'Every creative writer worth our consideration', Graham Greene once wrote, 'is a victim: a man given over to an obses-sion.' The extent to which my own search for the truth had turned into a personal obsession became evident after giving a talk at the Graham Greene festival about my experience of researching the Greene archives in America and the importance of drawing a line between Greene's life and art. I returned to my car, parked by the school, to find the rear window smashed and my briefcase and computer lap-top stolen. Now I knew just a little of how T.E. Lawrence must have felt when he left the original typed manuscript of *Seven Pillars of Wisdom* in a railway station waiting-room, never to see it again. In my briefcase were months of computer file research notes from various libraries in America, in addition to the entire transcripts of Greene's 1,200-odd letters to Walston. More important were the three hours of taped interviews in Antibes with Greene's French mistress of thirty years, Yvonne Cloetta, that I had just recorded.

Yvonne had refused to continue co-operating with Norman Sherry after she was so 'disgusted, to the point I had to go and vomit', by his second volume of biography (covering 1939–55), which repeatedly seemed to insist, or at least infer, as she told me, that Sarah Miles and Catherine Walston were almost the same person. There was also the additional insinuation that Catherine was the greatest love of Greene's life. Yvonne wrote saying that she would speak to me exclusively before the forthcoming Neil Jordan film of *The End of the Affair* to avoid any more tawdry tabloid speculation of the 'He Seemed A Sexual Monster Who Mocked His Faith' school (as a *Mail on Sunday* cover story headline pronounced in anticipation of the new film). She wanted to set the record straight, and tell me what Greene, over the course of thirty years, had told her about Catherine.

When I saw the smashed car window, I felt as if I had received news of a violent murder in my family. In a state of bewildered shock, I ran up and down the High Street punching the air in my distress. Finally I sat down on the wall by Berkhamsted School. My girlfriend attempted to comfort me. Distraught, we tried to look around a few local rubbish sites, graveyards, council estates. We ran down to the canal area, where we were told teenagers sniffed glue, until it was too dark to see anything. After reporting the theft to the police, we drove home to

Shropshire. And to think that I had laughed, only a few days before, when Yvonne Cloetta, drinking a Scotch at the Le Glacier bar in Antibes, had told me how Sherry had sobbed on her arm after showing Greene the proofs of the first volume of his official biography. Greene had flown at him for, amongst other things, his excessive use of the cloyingly sentimental early love letters to his wife, Vivien.

'I mean Graham was very, very tough on him,' Yvonne recalled, 'saying what he thought, and I remember he said to him, "You know what worries me is that I think that you are naive and that can be very dangerous," so I took poor Norman, he was crying on my shoulder, and he was saying, "I've worked so much on this . . .". I tried to soothe him by saying, "Look, you couldn't expect Graham to be happy with a book which talks about himself." He hated talking about himself, and I said that, "Tomorrow will be another day and he will feel better tomorrow." But Norman was absolutely stunned, and weeping, so I took him in my car back to his hotel.'

Thankfully, I was more fortunate than T.E. Lawrence. The Berkhamsted police rang me just before lunch the next day to say that a woman walking her dog near a disused railway embankment had found an odd collection of Greene books, notes and files scattered along a footpath late the previous night. 'It would appear, sir, that the thief looked into your briefcase, went through your files and decided the contents were not to his taste.'

'Any tapes?' I asked. There were two C-90 'Cloetta' Sony audio-tapes in existence, one of which had been recovered.

Two and a half hours later, I was back at the police station. The computer was missing – though most of the files had been backed up – and the policeman had drawn a map of where the scattered remains of my case had been found. 'A word of warning, sir, it is a very dangerous railway embankment, there's thick undergrowth and trains go through at over one hundred miles per hour. One slip and you are dead.' He added, 'Actually, I shouldn't allow you to go there, climbing onto a railway embankment is against the law.'

It was a wet, late autumn afternoon. The October sun shone dimly through the sombre, overcast clouds. Rugby posts had gone up on the local school fields. A thick ruffled carpet of damp, fire-orange leaves covered the badly lit pathway that ran alongside the commuter railway line. We used the full beam headlights of my car – the window still smashed and rough chunks of concrete lying on the back passenger seat – to act as a kind of search spotlight on the heavy scrub undergrowth. It was useless. My girlfriend found a few soggy credit card receipts from my trip to Austin, Texas, but no sign of any grey plastic Sony tape.

I remained obsessed. My girlfriend went back to London; I spent the night in a local bed and breakfast. The next morning, up at 7am, I drove to see the kind woman who had made the find – Greene's *Collected Short Stories*, a souvenir copy of the Brighton *Evening Argus*'s *Brighton Rock* film fiftieth-anniversary supplement, a dog-eared paperback of *The End of the Affair* (with its Penguin cover photograph of a bleak, desolate, misty Clapham Common torn off), and a bound, laminated file in which I had written all the details of Greene's Hermès 'Agenda' pocket-book appointment diaries from the 1950s to the 1970s, crucial in sleuthing down whom Greene was seeing, where and when. The woman had thought the accumulated mess odd, littered amidst the usual rubbish of disused old beer cans and condom packets by the side of the path; she gave me more directions and back I went to the railway line.

It had been raining. I began a one-man police-search-style recovery exercise, kneeling down in an attempt to sift through the forest of ivy-like creepers and undergrowth that stretched before me. The tape could have been anywhere on the railway embankment near Berkhamsted Common. Within a second of praying to St Anthony, however, I rather half-heartedly dug the toe of my shoe into the roots of a thick bush, and to my disbelief, there was the missing tape. At the time I did have to wonder, just as Bendrix does after Sarah's death and the miraculous cure of the atheist Smythe's strawberry birth-mark in *The End of the Affair*.

The voluminous love letters from Greene and Catherine's personal diaries, upon which this book is mainly based, were collected from Hoare's private bank at 37 Fleet Street in London by Nicholas Scheetz, Manuscript Librarian of Special Collections at Georgetown University. After being locked away for twelve years, Catherine's entire collection was acquired by its Lauinger Library shortly before Greene's death in 1991. The letters were originally kept by Catherine, locked in what she and Greene referred to as the 'Black Box', a metal trunk that she kept close to her type-writer in her private upstairs study overlooking the front lawn at Newton Hall. It seems remarkable that while several Greene biographies have appeared, there is no biography of Catherine Walston.

The lasting impact that Walston had on Greene's life and work is now indisputable. It was the wrenching drama of Greene's tortured, guilt-ridden affair with Walston that provided the basis for the moral and religious dilemmas faced by the major characters in many of his books, from *The Heart of the Matter* (1948) to *A Burnt-Out Case* (1961), including *The Quiet American* (1955), *Our Man in Havana* (1958), the screenplays of *The Fallen Idol* (1948) and *The Third Man* (1949) and his most successful plays, *The Living Room* (1953) and *The Complaisant Lover* (1959). After Greene's affair with Walston finally ended, his creativity never fully recovered. Neither did his Catholic faith.

By the end of the 1950s, Greene's passion for Walston – and for Swedish actress Anita Bjork – had reduced one of the most successful writers of the twentieth century to a creative husk. In addition, in 1959 his mother died. As an attempted cure for his black depression, he set off for a leper colony in a northern tributary of the Belgian Congo. Although he was to meet Yvonne Cloetta there – her Swiss husband worked for Unilever – his two-month journey into the Congo, which inspired Conrad's *Heart of Darkness*, had resulted in Greene's bleakest novel, *A*

Burnt-Out Case. Its subject is a once-famous Catholic architect and adulterer for whom nothing is worth living for any longer – in particular, women. At the time, Greene told friends it would be his last novel.

Greene finally pulled out of his creative depression, but it took him five years to produce another book. After Catherine finally began to fade from his life, he was no longer able to write what his friend Evelyn Waugh once referred to as his 'baptised novels', those written as if held down under the deep waters of life. Greene resorted to 'entertainments', or comedy.

Part of the answer to why the 1950s were Greene's most prolific period lies in the importance of adultery to literature and the relationship of sexual obsession to literary creativity, subjects that have received little serious literary study since the late Tony Tanner's admirable two-volume *Adultery in the Novel*. Tanner, a supervisor of mine at university, was a fellow of King's, Cambridge – a college with close family ties to the Walston family (Greene received his honorary Cambridge degree there in 1962). Is adultery good for literature? Tanner argued that adultery was not only the defining event of the great nineteenth-century bourgeois novel, from Flaubert's *Madame Bovary* to *Anna Karenina*, but provided the life-blood that saved the novel from narrative impotence. It broke the genre free of the idea of social limits. 'For the novelist it is often not really marriage that initiates and inspires his narrative', wrote Tanner, 'but adultery.'

As an acute literary critic, and a close reader of the English novel, Greene knew full well that adultery and narrative in a novel are inextricably bound; from *The Heart of the Matter* and *The End of the Affair* onwards, the subject of adultery becomes the life force of his fiction. One might speculate that, as far as his own life went, he saw adultery as a form of literary re-birth or salvation. It offered the hope of starting a new narrative; the next chapter in his life; his next book.

Greene's most important literary influence was the late Victorian fiction of Henry James and Joseph Conrad. When

Theatre Arts critic Richard McLaughlin met Greene for lunch in New York in 1949, he could never forget the way that Greene kept referring to James's *The Turn of the Screw*. 'He talked of the book with its palpable sense of evil until I began to shift uncomfortably in my chair.' Reading Tanner's book, I was struck by the Greene-like paradox that lies at the heart of the nineteenth-century novel; that adultery is at once a threat to society, yet, at the same time, it is through the act of adultery that the world of story and narrative is made to come alive. As Tanner suggests, in this great period, heroines who commit adultery 'find a devious way back to an experience of the sacred'. For so many heroines of literature, from Stendhal to Flaubert, adultery (at least temporarily) is their way back into a world of meaning once they feel the story of their life has begun to die.

This is arguably true of Sarah Miles in *The End of the Affair*, living with her dull civil servant husband at the bourgeois address, 14 North Side, Clapham Common. Adultery is the ultimate social and moral border crossing, pushing out the human boundaries and limits of experience in a way that Greene relished in both his fiction and life. Sarah has to physically cross Clapham Common to reach Bendrix's house. As Tanner puts it, adultery in the novel is 'a leap into limitlessness'. So, of course, is literature. Geoffrey Hill, the distinguished British poet and critic, calls his brilliant 'Essays on Literature and Ideas', *The Lords of Limit*, for this very reason. He takes his title from Auden: 'O Lords of Limit, training dark and light'.

When Bendrix talks about Sarah's 'leap into limitlessness' – with its suggestions of a death wish, the act of sex (Greene refers to it as the 'little death'), and the possibility of saintliness or eternal life – one starts to understand the complexity of Greene's private universe, and why 'Greeneland' is inaccurate. In reference to a paragraph by Proust that Greene had underlined, Christopher Hawtree once referred in the *Times Literary Supplement* to Greene's 'subterranean city'; 'of words', he should have added.

In *The End of the Affair*, Greene's very deliberate use of 'I' –

the first person possessive – is a narrative device that is itself a bid for possession of Catherine, an act of literary ownership. The whole book is seen through Bendrix's eyes. Once Sarah's story is dead in the novel, Greene found it almost impossible to continue with writing the book. It ends shortly after her death. Yet in reality, for years after their impassioned affair ended, Greene would sometimes write several letters a week to Catherine until her death in 1978. It seems that Greene found it easy enough to kill off Sarah in the novel, but impossible to write Catherine out of the narrative of his own life.

In fact, Greene's letters written to Catherine *after* they separated as lovers are arguably more revealing about their relationship than those written whilst they were lovers. It's almost as if Greene had become addicted to drawing on her creative influence in order to be able to write. Without her in his narrative – albeit the narrative of his imagination, through his letters – he felt creatively threatened. The deep spring of their love continued – in his letters he keeps returning to his memories of the years 1947 to 1950 – to provide him with inspiration, as if, having used up the resources of his childhood imagination, he had to find a new source of material.

A brief note about the secrecy of the relationship. Although the Greene–Walston affair was not widely known to the public until the *Sunday Times*' Geordie Grieg broke the story shortly after both Greene and Lord Walston's deaths in 1991, Greene himself had allowed glimpses of it to surface in published volumes of letters by such friends as Evelyn Waugh. Other evidence of the affair crops up in memoirs such as Richard Crossman's *Diaries*, when as a Cabinet minister he used to stay at Newton Hall. By 'secret', I also mean in the sense that both Greene and Catherine kept many aspects of their other liaisons from one another (indeed, that was a cause of the failure of their affair); Greene, as has been well documented, was addicted to secrecy.

In July 1994 a batch of letters from Catherine to her sister Bonte, dealing with a series of weekends of rows and bedroom confrontations at Newton Hall was sold at Sotheby's in London. These confirmed the crucial importance of Walston to Greene. A month later the Greene–Walston affair flared up into a furore between rival Sunday newspapers when the second volume of Norman Sherry's official biography was published at the same time as Michael Shelden's. Shelden infamously contended that Greene and Walston made a point of visiting foreign brothels, with Catherine dressed up as a man, in addition to reporting stories of sadomasochistic cigarette burns and their committing adultery behind every church altar in Italy they could manage.

Riveting; but was any of it actually true? The squabbling between the rival Greene biographers has long resembled a black farce. An infamous Waterstone's debate in Hampstead in the autumn of 1994 deteriorated into a public slanging match between Sherry and Shelden. The latter – a bearded American biographer who was forbidden from quoting from any of Greene's work – walked up to the podium chewing gum and declared: 'You can take my book out into the street and burn it if you don't like it.'

Many thousands of people – especially Greene's literary estate and his army of admirers – certainly felt like doing so. In the *New York Review of Books*, John Updike singled out Shelden's biography of Greene as marking 'some sort of sensationalist low point in literary biography'. Shelden went on to accuse Greene of being linked to the Brighton Trunk murder of 1936, as well as being anti-Semitic, a sadomasochistic blasphemer and allegedly a homosexual who used his secluded villa in Capri to seduce local boys. In fact, Shelden did unearth a warren of intriguing new material – such as Catherine Walston's sexual appetite for Catholic priests that Sherry either missed or preferred to ignore.

Whilst Sherry is the Tacitus of Greeneland, Shelden emerged as arguably its Suetonius. 'Ecstasy on the altar of adultery' ran the bold *Daily Telegraph* headline on 3 July 1994. Shelden, like the gossipy Roman biographer of *Lives of the Caesars*, began his

career with two well-received biographies. But just as the
one-time secretary to Emperor Hadrian suddenly found himself
divorced from his 'privileged sources' in AD 122, and no longer
allowed to use the imperial library, so Shelden was subjected to
much the same fate by the Greene estate, who denied him access
to 'restricted' unpublished papers.

Following the literary scandal of 1994, Catherine Walston was
stereotyped by the British media as an American *femme fatale*
stepping out in her Dior stilettos from the pages of *Les Liaisons
Dangereuses*. Meanwhile, *The End of the Affair* as a novel was
reduced to the level of human soap opera, seized upon by journalists (with the exception of Christopher Hawtree) as a bromide
of the truth about Greene's messy entanglement with Catherine
and her husband. This is insulting to Greene's art of narrative.
The secrets of Greene's 'private universe' were shared with
nobody – certainly not his readers. The drama of his darkly tortured and twisted affair with Walston helped to inspire some of
the most powerful fiction this century. But to confuse his life and
art is to fall into the most obvious and dull of Greeneian traps.
The truth is more interesting.

The advertised title of my talk at Berkhamsted was 'The Secret
Archives of Greeneland'. Trawling through the contents of the
trunk at Georgetown University had taken several weeks, during
which I was surrounded by glass cases displaying the covers of
C.S. Forester's own collection of first editions of his work (the
Hornblower TV mini-series had recently been showing in
America).

As I read through all seventy-two boxes of the
Greene–Walston letters, the dramatic saga of their personal war
(1946–78) appeared more epic than any Hornblower sea battle. I
read (deciphered is more accurate with Greene's scratchy, ant-like
hand-writing) letters scrawled frantically on the back of
American Airways or Air France in-flight paper; love notes written on the back of pizza menus in Capri, or on the back of
letters from his London bookseller; poems composed on scraps

of paper, with titles like 'To Catherine who asked for a piece of verse while she filled up the passport form, American Embassy. 5.35pm Dec 29 1949'. And endless letters headed: 15 Beaumont Street, 5 St James's Street, Thriplow Farm, Newton Hall, along with drawerfuls of hotel stationery swiped from the Hotel Hassler in Rome, the Sachus Hotel in Vienna, the Shelbourne in Dublin, the Excelsior in Naples, Europa in Venice, the Ritz in Paris, the Algonquin in New York, the Ritz-Carlton in Boston, not forgetting the crested stationery of William Randolph Hearst's Ocean House in Santa Monica, the *Queen Elizabeth* liner, and Sir Alexander Korda's luxury yacht, the *Elsewhere*.

But that was only one side of the story. Part of the difficulty of investigating the truth that lies behind the pages of *The End of the Affair* is that – as Greene told both Yvonne Cloetta and Norman Sherry – he burnt all Catherine's letters to him during the 1960s. Anybody hoping to restore a sense of balance to Greene's life and work is required to travel not only to Washington, but also to the University of Texas in Austin, where much of his personal and business correspondence from the 1950s is stored, along with his set of Hermès appointment book diaries; and also – most crucially – to the John J. Burns Library at Boston College, the nineteenth-century vaults of which hold a file marked 'Walston' in Greene's hand-writing.

This file contains the surviving private correspondence from the Walston family. It includes Lord Walston's letter in reply to Greene after Catherine's death ('I've thought a lot but still don't know what to say. Of course you caused pain . . .') as well as later letters concerning his reasons for turning down Greene's cash offer of £10,000 for Catherine's letters after her death. Her husband – they remained married for forty-two years – preferred to accept the $150,000 offered by Georgetown University. On 16 February 1990, as he put his papers in order, Greene wrote from Switzerland (he told friends he lived 'between blood transfusions and vitamin injections') to Lord Walston's solicitors about his instructions regarding his letters to Catherine. Paradoxically, after having been so closely guarded about his life with

Catherine, he now changed tack: 'I don't demand privacy as far as I am concerned, but Lord Walston might prefer privacy until his death.' A year later, both men were to die within weeks of each other.

The file also contains Greene's private correspondence with Catherine's second son, Oliver Walston, who acted, after his mother's death, as a literary go-between for Lord Walston and Greene, and the intriguing series of letters sent to Greene by James Walston, Catherine's 'fourth son'.

Also held at the Burns Library archives are stacks of boxes containing the random clutter of miscellaneous papers and files relating to Greene's private affairs in the late 1940s, 1950s and early 1960s. These include charming love notes from ballerina Margot Fonteyn – her giant loopy hand-writing at odds with her tiny body – for whom Greene very nearly left Catherine after apparently being given the 'green-light' when he met her in 1952 on the *Elsewhere*; letters to Greene from the likes of Nabokov, Noël Coward, Sir Alec Guinness, Henry Moore, John Le Carré, Tom Stoppard, Harold Pinter, Margaret Drabble (as with so many others, just writing a fan letter), Muriel Spark and Kim Philby; thank-you letters to Greene and Catherine, post-marked Italy, from Norman Douglas and Greene's old Oxford adversary Sir Harold Acton (after staying with Graham and Catherine in Capri); and hoards of letters (address: 114 Mount Street, the Mayfair address of London's Jesuit Farm Street church) from his priest friends Father Philip Caraman, editor of *The Month*, and the fiercely intellectual Father C.C. Martindale, whose advice Greene sought on theological questions for *The End of the Affair* (invariably with an added invitation to come over to his St James's Street flat for a Scotch).

But there is one letter – scrawled on A4 lined paper in an intelligent, free-flowing female hand – that stands out. It has no fancy letterhead, and is not written on four-star hotel onion-skin note paper. Stamped like some Papal bull with the red ink crest stamp of the John J. Burns Library, the hand-written address, in the top right corner, is 4 Garth Close, Rudry, Mid Glamorgan.

The date is 17 September 1976. It is from a twenty-five-year-old woman, Margaret Cambell, who had just returned from holiday in Italy where she and her husband had read aloud to each other an old Penguin paperback copy of *The End of the Affair*. She had been brought up a Catholic but stopped going to church at the age of seventeen because she didn't believe any more. She told Greene he was probably her 'favourite' author, having read *The Power and the Glory*, *The Heart of the Matter* and others, including his *Collected Short Stories*. Her letter confronted Greene with several very 'real questions' that various generations of readers of the novel have long wanted to ask; and that Greene managed to duck or swerve when quizzed by journalists or interviewers.

We finished reading it (*The End of the Affair*) ten days ago and it has haunted me ever since. The first thing I think of in the morning and the last thing I think of at night is this book. I don't know what to do to become free of it. I have cried every day since we read the last part of it . . . I say to myself time and time again, it is just a story, they weren't real people, but it makes no difference. I don't know why this is happening to me but it is making my life miserable and has caused a kind of rift between my husband and myself, because I cannot talk to him about it. After we finished the book, he was crying too and later we did talk about it indirectly – we talked about God and suffering. I said I couldn't believe that God would make people suffer and that I couldn't believe that God's rules are so inflexible and that right and wrong are so clearly defined by him. Surely God considers every aspect of a situation before deciding whether it is good or bad?

I have thought about God a lot since reading your book, and I feel certain now that there is a God and that God is the same no matter which faith you try and reach him through. I keep thinking about Sarah Miles and Maurice Bendrix and trying to follow different avenues – if only she had not coughed he would have kissed her . . . From your writing I understand you to be saying that God was there at every critical point, pushing them away from each other, and why, why, should he do it. Why should God want to make people so miserable? The reason I cannot discuss this with my husband is I don't think he would really understand why I have been so affected by this. Perhaps it is because I believe they really did exist. And that it is a true story.

I hope you will not think my writing to you impertinent but it was the only thing I could do that would be a positive action. I'm sure all writers want people to believe in their created characters but surely they don't intend for them to be brought to life as vividly and unendingly as Sarah Miles and Maurice Bendrix have for me. I find it so difficult to understand; it is not a case where I am identifying with them, either of them, because I wasn't even born when the events took place (although it was published in the year I was born 1951). I am very happily married to my husband and we love each other more than we did when we married five years ago. This is the first time something has troubled me deeply that I am unable to share with him. The only common factor is London. I was born there and lived there until four years ago, but surely this would not make me subconsciously identify with the character to any great extent.

This has made me think of you as a writer actually doing the job of writing. This book seems to me to be weighted down with unhappiness and suffering as if the actual words are only the surface of it and whole lives full of pain are behind it. That is why I think it must be a true record, or based on a record of real relationships. I am not asking you to tell me that you were one of the characters, or who was, but if you could tell me just whether or not it was real, I think it would help me a lot; at least then I would know my unhappiness has some basis, or I should know to look somewhere else for the reasons.

There is a faded carbon copy of Greene's typed reply. He was fastidiously polite about responding to correspondence from those genuinely interested in his work, and dictated his letters into a tape machine and sent the tapes to his sister Elizabeth (and later her daughter Amanda Saunders) in England to be typed.

Dear Mrs Cambell

I really am sorry that you have been so troubled by my book *The End of the Affair*. The characters are fictitious and so is the story, but naturally an author tries to make his characters seem alive – or rather they come alive to himself in the writing. I think perhaps some of the ideas worry you because the book is written entirely through the eyes of Bendrix. My object was to show a jealous and rather disagreeable character without a belief in God who becomes convinced against his will in the existence of a God whom he hates. This, however, I meant only to be a stage in his life and there's no reason to suppose that he sticks at this stage. Perhaps the book is rather different from my others – I wouldn't know that.

For a rather happier unhappy picture of love you might try *The Honorary Consul*. I do hope your letter has relieved your feeling. I do think you have a bit misunderstood the book.

But, again, was Greene telling the truth? By 1976, Catherine – now Lady Walston – had only two years to live, and had become a sad, alcoholic, wheelchair-bound shadow of the dazzling woman that Lady Diana Cooper used to simply refer to in her postcards to Greene as 'Beauty'. Cooper herself knew all about being turned into a fictional heroine. She was the close model for Mrs Stitch in her friend Evelyn Waugh's *Scoop* and in the *Sword of Honour* trilogy, in addition to being a very striking woman in her own right. Exactly twenty-five years before Mrs Cambell, as it happened, she had also read *The End of the Affair* in Italy 'aloud under olives and the hard shade of cypress'. 'I loved – adored y Saint. Thank you – give my love to your argosy of Talent . . . the benignant Medea' she wrote to Greene on a postcard from San Vigilio in August 1951.

Some answers to Mrs Cambell's questions can be found in the thick 'Walston' file held at Boston College, which contains the final batch of letters, some typed and some written in her still stylish (although shaky) hand, that Catherine sent to Greene before she died in 1978. Reading them, one can be certain of one thing. Greene was far more than just a 'stage' in her life; and likewise for him. In a 1993 *Times* article on the Greene archives, Christopher Hawtree quoted the last line of the final letter Catherine wrote to Greene on 18 July 1978: 'There has never been anyone in my life like you and thanks a lot.'

Greene's reply to Mrs Cambell is predictably paradoxical. An important irony about *The End of the Affair* is that whilst Greene's letters and poems to Catherine at the time are filled with references to the lives of 'living' saints – from St Thérèse of Lisieux to St Thomas the Apostle (and Padre Pio who, of course, wasn't dead) – in the novel itself it is not adulterous 'saint' Sarah who most 'seems alive' for the reader but the God-despising Bendrix, an atheist and connoisseur – like Hazlitt – of 'hate'.

When their affair really ended is a secret that Greene and Walston have taken to their graves. Their separation was not, I think, as black and white as has been supposed. Whilst editing the Evelyn Waugh letters, Mark Amory wrote to Greene querying the nature of his relationship with Catherine. In a private note sent back to Amory in 1978, Greene replied that he and Catherine were 'lovers for twelve years' and then remained friends until her death. This subsequently became the official version of the British media in 1994.

Writing in *The Spectator* in 1994, Catherine's son Oliver Walston, the distinguished BBC broadcaster and outspoken farmer (he lives at Thriplow today), replied to the 'cheapened and much distorted accounts' of his mother's marriage. 'Looking back', he wrote, 'it is plain that my mother's long and painful decline started at almost exactly the time that she and Greene parted in 1959.' Yet anybody who takes the trouble to decipher the Pepysian codes, ink scratches and initials of Greene's Hermès pocket-book diaries from the early 1960s will find it very hard to believe that their relationship was merely 'friendly' when they went on holiday to Capri, or when they met for 'drinks C', 'dinner C' or 'movie C' in London. I believe the date he gave Amory to be false; another lie, not to protect 'other people' so much, but to protect himself, or rather the start of his busy new affair with Yvonne Cloetta. What I suspect Greene really meant in his comment to Amory was that they ceased being faithful to one another as adulterers.

By 1999, Oliver Walston had changed his mind. 'There really was no conclusive end to the affair. It peaked after about thirteen years, but he went on visiting her after he met Yvonne.'

There is little question that *The End of the Affair* is 'rather different' from Greene's other books. For a start, its printed pages were the culmination of, as the *New Republic* critic observed, Greene's shift in focus from outer action to the 'inner world of passion and thought'. Privately, in letters to Catherine before, during, and whilst revising the manuscript, he always referred to the book as either his 'I' novel, 'her book', 'your book' or his 'Great Sex Novel'. He sent the manuscript to her for correction prior to publication. The love diaries he gave her for Christmas 1949 and 1950 were filled with a reef of literary references from his manuscript. Indeed, the novel was a form of badly needed literary therapy for Greene. At the time he wrote it, he knew the affair was doomed as she would not marry him.

But the crucial point is that the novel is not *about* Catherine; it is a book *to* her. Writing to her from Singapore on 1 December 1950 – back in England, Catherine had spent the morning interviewing a butler and his wife for Newton Hall – Greene ominously says that 'dear heart, this is the day of your move', and that he had 'gloomily' started revising the novel. A few hours later, he added a more cheerful post-script: 'I'm not nearly so gloomy about the book. I've reached p.87 and taken out quite a bit. Perhaps it won't be so bad after all.'

The day before, Greene had written to say that he was being gnawed at night by mosquitoes (though 'quieter' than those in

Capri, they 'bite a lot'). He had been given a long bolster in his bed which he was supposed to 'clasp like a woman and sweat into, but it doesn't feel a bit like you'. Although he knew he had lost her as a wife, he had been dreaming of her 'every' night. 'I carry you around like a sore. God bless you.'

The first letter that Greene wrote to Catherine at Newton Hall was from Kuala Lumpur on 5 December 1950. 'I realise I haven't got your phone number – like Bendrix,' he said. 'Don't leave me please like Sarah.' The day before he had written to say that the book was 'working out', thanks to suggestions made by Eddy Sackville-West. Sackville-West was a highly respected *New Statesman* literary and music critic who had converted to Catholicism himself in 1949. Greene had asked him to read the manuscript of *The End of the Affair* for his critical assessment before deciding whether to publish it. Sackville-West (Waugh described him as a 'pansy') had said he wasn't personally taken by it, though Greene should have the courage, like Victorians, to publish the book without caring about the effect on his literary reputation. Sackville-West also went over Greene's 1953 play *The Living Room*, (also dedicated to Catherine) which dealt with many of the same themes – sexual and religious guilt, manic jealousy, faith, hate, love – found in *The End of the Affair*.

Greene could see that Sackville-West had some valid points. He was going to rearrange the chronology of the journal, except for the first entry which would be different. 'I believe the book won't be too bad after this revision.' He asked her to ring his secretary, Mrs Young, and get her to send out a copy by mail. 'Dear heart, I want to dedicate it to you, seriously, what would be the best. "To C", "To Catherine Crompton" [her maiden name]. I wish I could put "with all my love".' In America, the dedication was 'To Catherine with love', although Greene nearly cabled Viking to pull it after Catherine's husband – aware that publication of the novel could be damaging to his political career – threatened to ban Greene from Newton Hall.

Apart from the dedication 'To C', one of the few other clues to Catherine Walston's existence is in the slim volume of love poems that Greene had privately printed in 1949, entitled *After Two Years*. Only twenty-five copies were made, most of which were lost when Greene moved house (two surviving copies remained in his Paris flat). For collectors, the search for the lost copies has become like the quest for the holy grail of 'Greeneland'; one sacred copy – probably worth at least £15,000 – is owned by a private collector abroad. It is the actual copy that was owned by Greene, and inscribed at length by Catherine. The dedication itself is a closely guarded secret (according to a reference in a letter Greene wrote to Catherine, it also includes some poetry from the Irish poet J.M. Synge, written in by her). When I asked the London book dealer who sold the book if he could contact the owner, he laughed. Were it to be published it would reduce the value of the book. So determined was Greene to remain reticent about the relationship whilst Catherine was alive that in 1969 he removed all reference to what he called the 'private' book from his *Who's Who* entry.

The plot of *The End of the Affair*, of course, revolves around a dogged London private investigator called Mr Parkis, who steals Sarah's personal diary; as a result Bendrix discovers that the reason his war-time mistress suddenly broke off their affair was not because of another lover; his only rival was God. I have been able to read and transcribe – but not photocopy – Catherine's diaries for 1949–51 when Greene was writing *The End of the Affair*. Based on this first-hand evidence, and Greene's not-always-to-be-believed letters, I have set out to be an 'agent of truth', in Conrad's phrase. Although Norman Sherry has quoted heavily from Greene's letters to Walston he has not – at least according to the comprehensive footnotes in the second volume of his official biography – drawn on Catherine's private diaries as a major source. This, frankly, seems incredible. Shelden appears to have taken down a few notes, but clearly didn't have time to read every diary entry very carefully. Having so gleefully made allegations about Greene and Walston 'committing adultery behind every high altar in Italy' – his source, Catherine's friend Diana Crutchley, told me she never meant what she said to be taken *literally* – it seems odd that he didn't bother to mention Catherine's diary entries relating to her visit with Greene to a lesbian nightclub in Paris, followed by her 'orgasm' in the presence of the virginal French saint, Thérèse of Lisieux.

Greene himself was an avid reader and collector of detective novels, a literary genre that he referred to as the modern 'fairy-tale'. The first book he ever read was an adventure of Dixon Brett, detective. He would also read Sherlock Holmes to the Walston children. He would thus have approved of the contents of the exhibition case at the entrance to the Harry Ransom Humanities Research Center, where some of Greene's personal papers are held. Instead of literary manuscripts, the glass case holds Conan Doyle's old golf clubs. The appeal of the Victorian detective novel, which Greene preferred, is that it imagines a purist world of absolute justice; one refreshingly far removed from the shifting grey and black shadows that Greene's own paradoxical and unsettling fiction inhabits. In *The End of the Affair*, we are given the God-hating believer, the adulterous saint, and the innocent and sentimental private detective ('a clown' in Waugh's words).

The private investigator Mr Parkis, Greene wrote, was his attempt to introduce a 'humorous' tone into the novel. The reviewer of the *Times Literary Supplement*, for one, was not persuaded ('an uninspired and rather humourless novel'). I disagree with his opinion, enjoying the extremities and absurdities of Greene's bleak and grim comic vision. Obsessive love – and hatred – is often funny in a Bergsonian sense. Certainly, Greene's own obsessive relationship with Catherine, with its violent pendulum swings of emotion, often came close to black melodrama.

The story of Catherine and Greene, needless to say, is certainly no 'fairy-tale' (although Greene did have a fixation on Catherine's 'red slippers'). If anything, it has the fatal, brooding sense of a later Henry James novel – a beautiful and sexually precocious young American from Rye, New York, marries a fabulously rich English suitor, the heir to a German-Jewish New

York fortune, not for love, but as her gold-stamped passport to a new life in Europe. Like Isabel Archer in *Portrait of a Lady*, when it is too late, Catherine finds herself faced with a tragic choice.

Rather tediously, Greene liked to romanticise failure. He claimed in his preface to *The End of the Affair*, that it was a 'greater success' with readers than with critics. But with a few notable exceptions, the novel was applauded on both sides of the Atlantic. The editors of *Time* do not boldly decorate their cover ('Adultery Can Lead to Sainthood', 29 October 1951) with an English novel that has been critically panned in London.

Evelyn Waugh likened it to *Brief Encounter*. As Waugh acutely observed, Bendrix is a 'distorted' narrator, 'whose real story is only beginning at the conclusion of the book, who is himself unaware of the fate [i.e. Bendrix's possible acceptance of God in his life] we can dimly forsee for him. *The End of the Affair* is an ironic title; the affair has not yet reached its climax when the record ceases.' In the Epilogue of *Brideshead Revisited*, published in 1945, that other rather 'disagreeable' and unreliable narrator, Captain Charles Ryder, takes half an hour off from his military duties and walks over to the old art nouveau family chapel with its beaten-copper lamp of 'deplorable design' burning above the altar. Unlike Bendrix, Ryder does take the leap into faith at the end of the 'fierce little human tragedy' in which he plays a part.

Margaret Cambell was certainly not alone in being 'affected' by *The End of the Affair*. Had Greene been alive in 1997, he would probably have been amused by a *New Yorker* profile of the American horror novelist Stephen King. The article described a challenge King made to his teenage son over a game of tennis at their house. The loser had to make a home-made taped reading of *The End of the Affair* to listen to in the car! And back in November 1951, under the heading 'Saint's Progress', Anthony West, writing in the *New Yorker*, called the novel 'electrifying' from the opening pages.

They have a quality that is immediately recognisable, the quality one becomes aware of as one hears the first few words of one of the plays of Ibsen's maturity. It informs one that what is to follow is to be an exhibition of an artist's complete control of content and technique . . . The book is undeniably a major work of art, and even those who cannot agree that their search for truth can be pursued in the neighbourhood of the miraculous and the supernatural will find in it rich aesthetic satisfactions.

Though a literary sophisticate of high credentials, West – like Mrs Cambell – felt overwhelmed by the truthful force with which the main characters were conceived. 'Their reality, and the reality of their situation, is astonishing,' he admitted. William Faulkner, with whom Greene was on the Nobel Prize shortlist in the early 1950s, famously described *The End of the Affair* as 'one of the most true and moving novels in anybody's language'. The novel silenced critics who had accused Greene of creating poorly delineated female characters. In the *Saturday Review*, the distinguished writer Anne Freemantle compared Greene's technique to that of Stendhal, in 'its minute neatness, its exquisitely tidy, fugal counterpoint, and its lyrical, mellow compassion'. She added, 'In Sarah, the slut who becomes a saint, Greene has created a girl to match Moll Flanders, and who, it seems to me, will weather literary history.'

Certainly, the literary cult of *The End of the Affair* continues today. Take the cover article by Roger Rosenblatt in *Esquire* in 1996 – 'In Praise of Dangerous Women'. Badness, Rosenblatt argued, has become so obvious it can hardly be considered dangerous any more. It has become a pose. A much more lethal cause of sexual obsession over a woman was if she possessed an antiminian quality of 'spiritual rightness'. 'I would have to say that in the hierarchy of dangerousness, far more dangerous than Bad Girls are genuinely Good Ones. There's a line in a Graham Greene novel in which a character remarks the ultimate seductiveness in a woman is goodness. That stopped me in my tracks.'

Then there was the November 1995 *Harper's & Queen* twenty-fifth anniversary birthday issue, with Elizabeth Hurley on the cover. The writer reported that when he interviewed her down the phone in her South Africa hotel room at 1.30am, she was propped up in bed in her silk pyjamas reading *The End of the Affair*. She rarely went 'anywhere for extended periods' without carrying her old Penguin copy in her suitcase. In it, the writer later learnt, certain passages of Sarah's journal had been heavily underlined in green biro.

In *Ways of Escape*, Greene recalled that Pope Pius XII had read *The End of the Affair* (it was an international bestseller). Afterwards, the Pope had a private word with Bishop Heenan, a friend of Greene. 'I think this man is in trouble. If he ever comes to you, you must help him.'

Needless to say, Greene never went to the bishop for help.

3

a sort of wife

My appointment to see Mrs Graham Greene at 11 o'clock on a Wednesday morning in early October had been made nearly a month before. On the phone, she sounded extremely lucid for ninety-five years of age. I only became nervous when she told me that she was nearly blind – her letters are read out to her by her lady companion, Margaret – and that she was just setting off for a two-week holiday to Estonia. 'It's a *challenge*,' she told me in her unwavering voice. Each morning I opened the paper uneasily, looking for news of any elderly British tourists in fatal accidents abroad.

Parking my car in the drive of Grove House, in the village of Iffley, just south of Oxford, I saw a large abandoned dolls' house covered in a plastic sheet under a tree in the overgrown garden. Indeed, the slightly worn-looking Victorian house itself looked like a giant dolls' house in need of repair. A museum-like plaque on the wall by the flaking turquoise-painted front door stated that Cardinal Newman's mother had once been resident here. Another, smaller sign read: 'Visitors from 1–4pm by prior appointment only'.

I rang the old bell. After a long wait, I heard the rattle of keys and several locks turning. As she led me past a glass case of lace-dressed dolls, and straight into the drawing-room, Mrs Greene's white hair stood out in contrast to her large-framed dark glasses.

'Graham always used to say that at 11 o'clock the only drink to serve is champagne,' she told me. Standing beside a vase of tall, white lilies on a coloured marble table was an ice-chilled bottle and two fluted glasses.

The room seemed to stand still in time. On one wall hung a painting of 'The Goldfish Bowl' by William Daniels, 1868. Underneath was a glass case of exotic stuffed hummingbirds, lit up by a set of Christmas-tree fairy lights. Also on the walls were Edwardian paintings of rosy-cheeked children. Mother-of-pearl boxes stood on the fireplace. A marble solitaire set was placed next to a Dickensian solicitor's clock. The effect was a Miss Havisham world preserved in Victorian aspic.

I had not been expecting the interview to be a champagne sort of occasion. It was with a certain apprehension that I had written to Vivien Greene asking to interview her about Greene's life in the late 1940s and early 1950s; and the turbulent emotional background between the writing of *The Heart of the Matter* and *The End of the Affair*. Being left by one's husband for another woman is never a happy subject to reflect on, but as I twisted the cork out of the bottle and poured two glasses, it occurred to me that Vivien Greene may have been waiting for fifty years to speak her mind about Catherine Walston.

'Revenge was good for the character: out of revenge grew forgiveness,' says Scobie in *The Heart of the Matter*, Greene's 1948 novel of colonial adultery in war-torn West Africa, mostly written as his marriage to Vivien was finally dying. 'Life being what it is, one dreams of revenge,' was a line that Greene liked to quote from the diaries of Gauguin. In the second volume of Norman Sherry's official biography, he relates how, standing on the platform at Tunbridge Wells railway station with Greene one morning, the novelist had a 'look of total dismay' on his face when he related to his biographer that he had heard that Vivien planned on writing a book about their marriage. He then began to sing in a 'melancholy' drawl from an old music hall number: 'Shovel the dust on the old man's coffin and take up your pen and write.' When I mentioned this anecdote to Vivien, she burst into laughter: 'That must have come from his own subconscious,' she said. 'I never thought, for a moment, of writing.' The only two books that Vivien has written herself have been on dolls' houses.

Mrs Greene didn't strike me as vindictive. But she was happy to talk. Much later that afternoon, at about 5.30pm, the drawing-room nearly dark, Vivien came to the end of the painful saga of what had happened between Greene, herself and Mrs Walston. 'That's how writers behave,' she said with remarkable equanimity considering what I had heard.

But was Vivien herself a reliable witness? In a letter to Catherine in 1953, Greene expressed his love as a form of fatal wound: 'I can't get you out of my heart, you've splintered inside it and surgeons are useless. They say one day I may die of the splinter, but it can't be removed.' But if what Vivien said *was* true, then Greene's heart was too hard for that splinter to pierce. Greene, by his own admission, acknowledged this side to him. After his mother, to whom he had been close, died in 1959, Greene told Catherine that he wished so many people hadn't written to him. Once something was 'over', he added, the human heart is unsentimental. 'People don't understand that he was really, basically, a very cold man,' Vivien said. 'There was a lot of sex and that sort of thing, but he could be cold in relation to other people.'

She gave the example of when, in 1947, Greene's secretary rang and told Vivien that she was being summoned to the Kensington Palace Hotel (as her memory recalled). Bed and breakfast had been booked and Graham was going to meet her there for dinner. 'So I went up. I didn't know what he was going to say or what he was going to do. I dressed for dinner and he never came. Seven; half past seven; eight; half past eight. It was really dismal in this hotel bedroom, being told you were going to be taken to dinner. And I think it was at nine that he turned up. And he said he had had dinner with Mrs Walston and that they had decided to go away together and he was "leaving me permanently". I was on the floor crying with my head on his knee. And he said – and this was so extraordinary – "But I'll always send my proofs for you to read before they are published". You know, forty years of being lonely. Left alone. You know, the whole prospect of horror – and him saying, "But I'll always send you my proofs for you to read".'

'He actually sent you *The End of the Affair*?' (Her first edition copy was inscribed 'To Vivien with love, September 1951'.)

'At the time it seemed to me heartless,' Vivien said. 'Awfully heartless. Oh, and afterwards,' she continued, 'that was also extraordinary. I was sent the hotel bill by Mrs Young. And, of course, I had no money.'

'Did you ever think of vengeance?' I asked.

An awkward silence fell upon the gloomily lit room.

'She wouldn't know what the word means,' proffered Margaret, sitting with Vivien's cat on her lap.

'I did say one very cruel thing as a response,' Vivien finally answered. 'I mean so much had been put on me. I had to fight back. One day I said to Graham, "Don't you *mind* that she sleeps with all these other people?" Well, she did! – the Labour MP who left her a large fortune, that Irish Jesuit and the English Dominican priest. Graham reddened right up to his forehead. And he said, "I have other women, why shouldn't she have other men?" And I thought, well, of course, if that satisfies you . . .

'I don't want to think about it again,' she added. 'My talents were for nest-building. And that was the last thing Graham wanted. If one had only realised.'

But Mrs Greene's version of events is, of course, only one side of the story. When, about a week later, I had Sunday lunch at the Parsonage Hotel in Oxford with her daughter Caroline (who changed her Christian name from 'Lucy'), she acknowledged that there was a rift between her parents that was out of character for Greene. He remained on very good terms with his other lovers and mistresses; his wife, however, was a different matter. Vivien's own view is that the way he treated her was inexorably linked to the guilt he felt. 'Frustration had a lot to do with it,' admitted Caroline. Exactly what type I didn't like to ask, although one can fairly surmise that it may have been to do with sexual frustration. According to Anthony Mockler's unauthorised account, against which Greene took legal action after copyright infringement in the *Sunday Telegraph* serialisation, Vivien and Graham's bedroom was divided by a curtain.

A story may have no beginning or end, as Bendrix says on the opening page of *The End of the Affair*, but the slow death of a marriage by desertion always has its inevitable dates carved into time. Or, rather, in Vivien's case, *scratched*.

Shortly after I sat down, Vivien Greene held out her hand to show me the diamond cluster ring with which she had engraved the words 'Christmas Day, 1958', alongside the initials 'G.G.', 'V.G.', and those of their two children, into a window in the drawing-room at Grove House. In the right-hand bay alcove, by the cracked marble chimney-piece, one can clearly see her razor-thin handiwork in a pane of glass looking out into the garden where visitors such as Cardinal Newman and Lewis Carroll used to sit having tea. The 1958 date – cut into the window as her husband's car drove away after Christmas lunch – marked the last time, until his death in 1991, that Greene was in the same room with his wife and two children.

But the last real Christmas Greene spent with his family was at 15 Beaumont Street in 1946, only a few days after the fateful plane flight from Cambridge across the snow-covered East Anglian countryside. In the window of the upstairs drawing-room are another set of initials carved with a diamond ring into the glass. But it was only after I had seen them myself, and then reminded Mrs Greene of them, that she could vaguely remember etching the window to mark, she thinks, a family visit by Greene just before he finally left her. 'I wanted to forget it all. It has been very difficult, you see, I told you I made a new life. I put everything behind me. So it's very painful making it real again. Because it was a dreadful time.'

A Handful of Dust was written in 1933 after Evelyn Waugh's first wife (also called Evelyn) ran off with an Etonian called John

Heygate. It was an event that was to leave deep scars on his fiction, as well as provide further evidence of how adultery can be bad for marriage but good for literature. Waugh's black novel is a brilliantly savage stripping down of the chaos lurking beneath the hard, chromium veneer of upper-class England, where adultery is regarded as a smart after-dinner party game. Harold Acton recalls Waugh in his *More Memoirs of an Aesthete*:

> Perhaps because I had met him at Oxford when we were both young if not unfledged, his writings struck me as an essential part of him, even the black humour and vein of cruelty, sharpened by the failure of his early marriage. *A Handful of Dust* was written in his blood.

The scars as well as his anti-Americanism are revealed when the whisky-drinking Mrs Rattery (the new mistress of Jock Grant-Menzies MP) arrives by private plane, landing like a bird of prey in a field beside Tony Last's Gothic mansion of Hetton. The moment is turned by Waugh into a nefarious symbol of capricious fortune:

> She was a little over thirty. She was American by origin, now totally denationalized, rich, without property or possessions, except those that would pack in five vast trunks . . . She arrived by air on Monday afternoon. It was the first time that a guest had come in this fashion and the household was appreciably excited. Under Jock's direction the boiler man and one of the gardeners pegged out a dust sheet in the park to mark a landing for her and lit a bonfire of damp leaves to show the direction of the wind . . . She climbed out of the cockpit, stretched, unbuttoned the flaps of her leather helmet, and came to meet them. 'Forty-two minutes,' she said, 'not bad at all with the wind against me.'

Greene was clearly impressed at being flown back to Oxford after lunch by Mrs Walston. Indeed, he sent an immediate telegram to Thriplow on 20 December 1946, thanking Catherine for the 'wonderful present'. She also received a home-made Christmas card, obviously made by Vivien (depicting a female hand with bright-pink varnished fingernails holding up a blue spangled star) but signed only from 'your Godfather' Graham Greene.

Godfather? Greene and Catherine were indeed introduced in highly unusual circumstances. As Vivien recalled to me, what was especially unnerving about Catherine's 'snatch', as she put it, was that it was she who had brought about their introduction. One morning at Beaumont Street in September 1946, Vivien received a call from a young American woman who had recently decided to convert to Rome. 'She [Mrs Walston] rang me up and said I'm so impressed [presumably she was referring to Greene's novels *Brighton Rock* and *The Power and the Glory*], your husband was really the cause of my becoming a Catholic, I'd like him to be my Godfather. Will you ask him? I said, "Yes, certainly". And I rang Graham (in London) and passed it on. And he laughed and said, "Buy her some flowers to give her". He was sort of off-hand. That was early days. That she was becoming a Catholic made *no* difference, because within three weeks of meeting they were sleeping together.'

The phone call may have come as a surprise to Vivien, but Greene and Catherine must have quickly established that they had various mutual friends, notably John Rothenstein, director of the Tate Gallery, and his wife Elizabeth. Indeed, according to the Rothensteins' daughter Lucy, her parents were the ones who made the introduction: 'Catherine met Graham through them and I think the family were a little upset, but you don't know what is going to happen when you introduce two of your friends.'

During the war, the Tate had evacuated their best paintings to Sudeley Castle in Gloucestershire, a short drive from Oxford, where the Rothensteins had been lent a flat. Their daughter Lucy was also a friend of the Greenes' eldest daughter Lucy at St

Clothill's Convent in Lechlade; indeed (according to Vivien) the reason why Lucy Greene changed her name to 'Caroline' was because of a girlish squabble over the use of the name at school. Both girls were fanatically keen riders; summer holidays were spent at local gymkhanas. During the war, the Rothensteins became close friends of the Walstons.

John Rothenstein's diaries – which he used whilst writing his first volume of memoirs, *Brave Day, Hideous Night* – are held in the archives of the Tate Gallery. Rothenstein relates his first vivid impression of meeting Catherine Walston in May 1944 at the house of Winston Churchill's nephew, John Spencer-Churchill. The director of the Tate had been asked to 'inspect' a set of drawings that the Prime Minister's nephew had made of the evacuation from Dunkirk. He was politely enquiring whether the Prime Minister himself had much time for painting when his attention was suddenly 'distracted from my host's reply by the proximity of a young woman of unusual beauty: sympathising with my distraction he introduced me to Catherine Walston'.

Shortly afterwards, Rothenstein went to dinner at the Walstons' Hays Mews flat in Mayfair. Just after dinner there was an air-raid. The bombs did not interrupt Catherine's intense conversation, although one did later destroy the Rothensteins' house at Primrose Hill. When Catherine's husband Harry Walston learnt that Rothenstein and his family were homeless, he remarked: 'What I can't understand is why you don't come and live with us.'

When the Walstons moved into a flat at 6 St James's Street, above the hat shop of Lock & Co., John Rothenstein took up their offer and lived with them between 1944 and 1949. (In 1948, through Catherine's influence with the smart law firm of Drivers, Jonas & Co. that controlled the private leases, Greene himself moved in next door to 5 St James's Street. Remarkably, Harry Walston did not seem to mind, nor when he followed them to C6 Albany in the mid-1950s.)

Although Greene's own conversion to Catholicism had been

on 'intellectual' grounds – it was only later, on the trip to
Mexico that produced *The Lawless Roads*, that he found himself
becoming personally involved in his faith – Catherine's initial
interest seems to have been more emotional than strictly theological. As John Rothenstein put it bluntly, 'the range of
Catherine's reading was exceedingly narrow'.

Beginning with Tolstoy (he was shocked that she had not
even read *Anna Karenina*), the high-brow Rothenstein gave her
a reading list that she diligently 'read and re-read'; he tutored her
informally, opening her intelligent but undeveloped critical
imagination to the worlds of art, literature and religion. 'Her
reading and the ensuing discussions so stirred her imagination',
he wrote in his memoirs, that she ended up assembling a 'fine
library'.

When I asked Lucy Rothenstein (later Lady Dynevor) if it
would be accurate to say that her father appointed himself
Catherine's 'tutor', she replied: 'Yes, there was very much that
kind of relationship.'

Rothenstein drew up his reading list in 1945, at exactly the
same time as Greene's novel *The Power and the Glory* was published, so it is possible that Greene featured on it. Within a year,
England's most acclaimed novelist had taken over from the director of the Tate and appointed himself Mrs Walston's literary and
religious supervisor. (Vivien Greene told me: 'I know Graham
and Mrs Walston would sit up in bed reading theology together.')
Not a bad set of personal tutors for somebody who had apparently dropped out of Barnard College in New York.
Rothenstein has left a detailed account of Catherine's religious
education, which began in total ignorance. (Her husband Harry
was Jewish, but non-practising, having been educated as a
Protestant at Eton and Cambridge.)

> When I first came to know them [the Walstons] their intel-
> lectual attitude towards religion was of immense tolerance;
> they could have disapproved of no one on account of his
> beliefs. But Christianity, or even any concept of God, was a

phenomenon remote from their personal or imaginative experience and they were no more concerned with it than they were with Buddhism. Catherine occasionally accompanied me to Mass, in the same spirit as one might go sight-seeing to strange places well away from the beaten track. On the first such occasion, in Newman's chapel at the National University of Ireland, when the bell rang for elevation and I whispered, 'Better kneel now,' she irritably asked, 'Why should I?'. 'You kneel,' I said; 'I'll explain later.' I might as well have related a myth about a god from Olympus. On another occasion she asked whether there were any differences between Catholicism and Protestantism, and received my explanation as though it were in principle a legal quibble. Towards the end of 1945, and more markedly the beginning of 1946, however, signs became more frequent that Catherine was increasingly attracted to Catholicism, and in the course of a visit to us in February she told us of her wish to be received into the Church.

John Rothenstein also recalls his first meeting with Graham (and presumably Vivien) Greene on Easter Day 1945, at a party given by the Jesuit priest Father Martin D'Arcy, Master of Campion Hall in Oxford, on the evening of Lucy Rothenstein's first Holy Communion. D'Arcy had received such bright young intellectuals as Evelyn Waugh into the Catholic Church. Greene, however, never saw eye-to-eye with his snobbery; he preferred to drink Scotch in London with Father C.C. Martindale and Philip Caraman SJ (whom he later came to 'hate' for trying to break up his affair with Catherine), at the Farm Street Jesuit church in Mayfair.

Catherine was herself received into the Catholic Church, not by the fashionable intellectual D'Arcy but by a young Jesuit at Campion Hall called Father Vincent Turner, a close friend of John Rothenstein. Lucy Rothenstein recalls Turner coming over to their house at Garsington to help with 'some heavy work' – brick-laying, garden-digging, and so on – to get away from his 'intellectual pursuits' as an undergraduate at Oxford.

I asked Vivien if she thought that Mrs Walston was after her husband from the very start.

'Yes. I think she was.'

But Greene's life was complicated enough by September 1946. Preoccupied with his publishing work in London, and his seven-year relationship with his mistress Dorothy Glover, he gave little thought to the prospect of an affair with his new 'god-daughter', herself married with small children. The very first letter Greene wrote to Catherine was sent by the late afternoon post on 25 September, hand-written on Eyre and Spottiswoode stationery. Almost a fortnight *after* she had been received into the Church by Vincent Turner, Greene wrote to apologise for his delay in sending his congratulations and for not giving her a present. He laid the blame on his secretary for (so he claimed) failing to wire a telegram as instructed.

The letter, however, was wrongly addressed to Mrs Walston at Keel, Achill Island, in Ireland's Co. Mayo. Greene's apparent indifference to his new god-daughter prompted her to write a note from Achill addressed 'Dear Godfather', which had the desired effect of getting Greene to write back immediately saying that he admired her 'brave decision' to become a Catholic, adding, rather oddly, considering that he had converted in 1926 in order to marry Vivien, that he had converted *before* he had any responsibilities or ties of his own. Greene often quoted Conrad's line: 'He who forms a tie is lost.' 'How lovely the west of Ireland sounds,' he wrote. 'Do come and tell us about it in Oxford when you get back.'

On the day of Catherine's reception into the Catholic Church – 12 September 1946 – it had been Vivien who repre-sented her husband at the tiny Gothic church (attributed to Pugin) at Dorchester-on-Thames, about fifteen miles south of Oxford. In *Brideshead Revisited*, published the year before in 1945, Dorchester-on-Thames was the setting in which Antoine Blanche took Charles Ryder to an expensive dinner at The

George Hotel to pass on some dark gossip about Sebastian's 'murky' Catholic family.

The important day began with a fine morning drive with the Rothensteins in the early September sunshine to Vincent Turner's ordination as a Catholic priest at Heythrop Park, not far from Oxford ('a luminously clear and deeply impressive ceremony', wrote John Rothenstein). Their group included the Rothensteins, their daughter Lucy, who, although aged only ten, was to be godmother, and Catherine's close friend Robert (Bobby) Speaight, an ardent and rather pompous Catholic and a well-known stage actor and writer, who had starred in T.S. Eliot's *Murder in the Cathedral*.

Afterwards they drove back to the Rothensteins' own parish in Dorchester, where Catherine was received as a Catholic by the newly ordained Vincent Turner. 'After these many years I can see her face, radiant with happiness, shining out, as it were, in the darkness of the little church,' wrote John Rothenstein.

An intriguing black and white photo exists of Vivien Greene, dressed in a tweed suit, standing behind the smiling and chicly dressed Mrs Walston, just after the ceremony. John Rothenstein, in a dark grey flannel suit, and Vincent Turner, with his gleaming new white dog collar, are both wearing glasses and looking directly ahead. Vivien's eyes are not focused on the camera, however. Her head and hat are tilted to the right, her eyes directly angled towards Catherine's face. Already Vivien looked oddly concerned, as if she had some intuition that Catherine had an ulterior motive for making Greene her godfather.

The following morning, back in Oxford, everyone assembled again for Vincent Turner's first mass at Campion Hall, followed by a champagne breakfast party on the college lawn. Catherine finally caused an excited stir when she left after breakfast with Bobbie Speaight in her chartered private aeroplane, which later circled low over the Rothensteins' as a 'gesture of farewell' before flying on to London or Cambridge. 'It was rather a lovely occasion,' remembers Lucy Rothenstein.

As the plane swooped overhead after the christening, Vivien

Greene recalled one of the priests saying, 'If she crashes, she'll go straight to heaven.'

'We were THRILLED by the flight,' wrote Vivien Greene to Catherine Walston in her thank-you letter after their own plane ride back from Cambridge. 'It was a marvellous "present" – Graham arrived before 5pm!' The next day another gift from Catherine was already on its way. Elizabeth Rothenstein called Vivien to say that Mrs Walston was giving her a plump, fresh Thriplow turkey for Christmas. According to Lucy Rothenstein, 'It wasn't anything out of the ordinary' to receive a turkey from Thriplow, because 'we used to get one . . . the Walstons raised turkeys anyway, but they also raised a certain number to give to friends at Christmas time.'

Vivien was speechless with rage. Indeed, the fate of the bird may provide a critical clue as to exactly when Greene and Walston started their affair. Writing to Catherine on 21 December 1946, Vivien couldn't actually bring herself to write the word 'turkey'; instead she drew a picture of a fat, trussed bird, adding that it 'at present swings despondently in our larder! . . . My breath was simply taken away when Elizabeth rang with the good news.' She went on to describe her role as home-maker: 'Please forgive the delay – the children broke up the next day and I have been as busy as you may imagine one who has a 5 storey house and no domestic!' Actually, this wasn't strictly true. Vivien told me that she had a woman 'help' who would sometimes ride in from twelve miles away on a bicycle. She ends her letter with details of her careful preparations for Christmas, as if to remind Catherine that she was now a Catholic and that her 'godfather' had a family: 'our "crib" was ready on Sunday and we decorate the tree this afternoon: I ice the cake tonight, for we have The Tea on the Eve and light the Tree then too.'

The 'crib' was by the window of the downstairs dining-room; bizarrely, a local madman used to stand outside the window singing carols to himself each year the crib went up. Today, the dining-room is used as an office by the vicar of St Mary

Magdalen, an expert on the Greek and Russian Orthodox Church who lives in the house. Books with titles such as *Sex and Theology*, and dozens of multi-lingual bibles bulge out of his study bookcase, and one can still see the serving alcove where the Christmas lunch would have been hoisted up on a dumb-waiter from the kitchen below. Downstairs in the basement kitchen, its walls hung with reproduction Greek icons, the 'larder' remains unchanged since 1946; only instead of being stocked with powdered eggs, spam, Heinz tomato soup and rations from Grimbley Hughes grocery store in the Cornmarket, where Vivien had to queue for bread, it now has Sainsbury's cereal and pasta. As I turned the stiff wooden and steel handle of the dumb-waiter, the vicar told me that he still uses it for Sunday lunch.

But did the Greene family really enjoy a stuffed turkey from Thriplow Farm for Christmas 1946? Writing – again – to Catherine on Boxing Day, Greene said that his children gorged on the turkey until limp. But, as Vivien told me fifty-three years later, she never cooked Catherine's turkey. 'I thought it was most insulting. *Most* insulting. To take a person's husband and sleep with him. And send a turkey. I gave it at once to the local nuns.'

I said that I hadn't realised the affair had started by Christmas.

'Oh yes, I think it had. I think it started directly after she got an introduction to him through me. She was very predatory.'

I wanted to get this point right. To clarify Vivien's memory, I read out the letter she had sent Catherine on 21 December 1946.

'Are you quite sure you didn't have the turkey?'

'Oh, we didn't have it,' Vivien replied. 'That was the *letter*. It [the turkey] arrived that day and I put it in the larder. But I gave it to the nuns. It was a rare thing. Of course they had a big farm and everything, but to get anything to eat was quite an accomplishment.'

When I asked Greene's daughter Caroline (Lucy) if she could remember 'gorging' until limp on a Christmas turkey in 1946, she said she could not. Besides, she said, her mother always cooked goose. Caroline's most vivid memory of that Christmas was of her father bringing back a brand new biro from London. 'I remember him showing me the newest pen and it was absolutely fantastic because it dried . . . and it didn't smudge . . . It was an absolutely incredible magic pen that didn't have ink as we knew it.'

So it seems possible that Greene may have fibbed about the 'lovely' turkey in his Boxing Day letter, so as not to offend his wealthy god-daughter, and also because he badly wanted an excuse to write asking for a lunch date in the New Year. He wanted to hear about a trip she was planning to Poland, Conrad's birthplace.

Greene told Norman Sherry that he first met Catherine for a drink one evening (in late 1946), perhaps being introduced through Bobby Speaight. The drink went well. They quickly got onto the subject of Greene watching nude models pose on the stage of the Windmill Theatre. Not long afterwards, before Christmas, Catherine invited her novelist 'godfather' and his wife up to Thriplow for lunch.

There is certainly a small possibility that the affair *may* have begun just after Christmas, though before 25 December seems very unlikely, despite Vivien Greene's suggestion. By the end of 1946, Greene was certainly not living at Beaumont Street during the week. Whilst working at the Bedford Street offices of Eyre and Spottiswoode, where he was bringing in authors such as François Mauriac, Wyndham Lewis and Ford Madox Ford, he shared Dorothy Glover's top-floor flat in Bloomsbury at 18 Gordon Square, a short walk from his office.

But he can't have spent all his time in London shopping for biros or drinking with Dorothy. If Catherine had been in London, Greene may have seen her again surreptitiously on his return after Boxing Day. Whatever the case, he couldn't wait to get back to his Bedford Street office to receive Catherine's call about lunch; quite possibly – like Bendrix and Sarah – at Rules in Covent Garden.

Laid out in 1822 on the site of Beaumont Palace – a royal residence built by Henry I – Graham Greene's Regency terrace house at 15 Beaumont Street could not have been a more marked contrast to the modern concrete apartment building of Residence des Fleurs, with its dirty orange canopy flapping over a noisy fourth-floor balcony, where Greene made his one-bedroom quarters in Antibes after leaving England in the 1960s. 'I'm in that ugly block, by the mariner' is how Greene described his Antibes flat in the 1970s after lunching with his friend V.S. Pritchett. As Greene got older, he built up his sense of home, like Scobie, 'by a process of reduction'. His holiday-let-style apartment comprised of a small living-room with a kitchen table for a desk, a bamboo sofa and his books.

But with Vivien in the 1940s, first at 14 North Side, Clapham Common – Sarah's address in *The End of the Affair* – and then in Oxford at Beaumont Street, Greene lived rather differently. Writing of the smart row of ashlar-faced pale yellow Cotswolds-stone houses on Beaumont Street, Nicholas Pevesner called the street the 'finest' address in Oxford. The semi-pillared front of No. 15, is about sixty yards across the street from the Ashmolean Museum, and less than a hundred yards from the front steps of the Randolph Hotel. Henry James once spent the night in the Greene house in 1897.

Bad memories. For years, whenever Vivien walked past the Randolph, she was reminded of the pavement outside the hotel – just by the Oxford Playhouse – where she first felt humiliated by the obvious irregularity in her husband's relations with his god-daughter. She and Graham had been walking down Beaumont Street when they saw – by chance, it seems – Catherine Walston and her close friend Lady Barbara Rothschild, the estranged wife of Lord Jacob Rothschild, across by the Ashmolean.

Vivien recalls: 'Graham said, "There's Catherine. Let's join them." And I said, "I don't see why." But they crossed over to us.'

Catherine looked a 'dazzling sight', wearing a beautifully cut plain apricot cashmere coat with a huge topaz brooch on the shoulder.

'They were extremely rude,' Vivien told me. 'Barbara was

saying to Catherine, "Are you going to wear your rocks?" There was going to be a big party. Very smart, grand party in a day or two [to which Vivien hadn't been invited]. "Are you going to wear your rocks?" This meant nothing to me. And they were talking, three of them were talking and laughing, and I just stood there. They didn't include me at all. I could almost identify the slab of pavement now. I just stood there quite silently. They were all talking about this wonderful party. Of course, afterwards I realised "rocks" meant diamonds. She always had beautiful diamond necklaces. "Are you going to wear your rocks?" "Oh yes," she said.'

The date of this meeting is important. Norman Sherry states that it 'must have been in late 1946'. But, unless she knew their affair had already started, at that time there is no reason why Vivien should have made a point of not wanting to cross the street to speak to them; or why Catherine, as Greene's god-daughter, would have been quite so rude. If Sherry's dating *is* correct, then the meeting provides a possible clue that the affair may have begun before the New Year.

Vivien cannot remember when this meeting occurred, only that she seemed to think it was 'some time when Mauriac was coming for a degree'. That would have made it May 1947, however, and Sherry may simply have misdated the event. By the spring of 1947, with their impassioned affair well underway, Vivien's reluctance to cross the street to say a polite 'hello' to her husband's new lover would have been quite understandable.

Another detail that may be incorrect (or perhaps over-romanticised) in the official biography about the start of the affair concerns the crucial flight across the frozen Cambridgeshire countryside. When the tiny airplane landed at Kidlington, Sherry wrote, 'He walked alone in the darkness and rain to where Vivien and his children waited.' But when, during lunch, I asked Caroline about this flight – something a thirteen-year-old would surely remember – she was certain that she never flew with her parents to Kidlington. Nor did she ever go to Thriplow. Her first flight was in 1947 to Switzerland on a family holiday. Moreover,

Sherry adds that as Greene walked away from the plane, thinking of Catherine, 'he felt an extraordinary happiness'. A note sources this quote as coming from a letter to Catherine dated 30 September 1947, in which he recalls how love first came to him when a lock of Catherine's hair touched his face in the plane.

Greene actually wrote two letters to Catherine on 30 September, a Tuesday. The first, written from his desk at Eyre and Spottiswoode, was a note sending her a form that had to be signed before some travel tickets could be sent to Thriplow; it ended with an amused post-script definition of the 'New Rich': he had been 'solicited' the night before by a prostitute kerb crawling in her own car! The second, written excitedly at 11pm, after a solitary dinner and a drink in the Café Royal reading the *The Aran Islands*, described how, whilst going to relieve himself at a public lavatory in Brick Street on his way to bed, he had suddenly been struck with inspiration for the plot of *The Third Man*. But there is no mention, in either of the letters, of 'extraordinary happiness' as he walked through the 'darkness' to his wife and children at Kidlington airport.

Another piece that doesn't fit came to light shortly before Terry Holloway and I reconstructed the original flight path to Oxford from Cambridge.

Rummaging through his bottom desk drawer in the same 1938 controller's office that Greene, Catherine and Vivien would have passed by before boarding their Proctor V aircraft, Holloway pulled out his flying guide to daylight times in England. He raised his eyebrows when I related how Greene had looked at his watch at five minutes to three and Catherine had said she would fly with them and also fly *back*.

According to his guide, in late December it would be almost dark in Oxford by 4.30pm. The pilot had no radar and flew by sight and intruments. With a grass airstrip covered in snow, and the only landing lights being crude paraffin flares, Leslie Worsdell, Marshall's chief pilot in 1946, now eighty-three, told me that Catherine may not have been able to fly back to Cambridge that night.

It is not impossible that Catherine stayed with Barbara Rothschild at Tackley, only a few miles from Kidlington. Barbara was to play a very important supporting role in her friend's affair with Greene. In January 1946, having separated from Lord Rothschild, she had bought the 'Little Manor' at Tackley, a pretty village near Woodstock. Her new boyfriend was Rex Warner, a classicist, novelist and poet. The fine Cotswolds-stone William and Mary house, built in 1690, was to become one of Greene and Catherine's most favoured places to conduct their illicit affair in the late 1940s. After it was in full swing, Greene's letters to Catherine often ask: 'Couldn't we have a really long Tackley weekend?' Although a comfortable size, the house only had two guest bedrooms; the best one, where Greene and Walston probably stayed, has a giant double bed, its own bathroom and looks out across the front lawn.

When I went to see it, I learnt an odd fact as the current owner spread out the old deeds of conveyance in his drawing-room on a bright autumn Sunday morning. Lady Rothschild had paid £10,000 for the former Old Rectory in Tackley. The first thing she had done on moving in was to upgrade her address to the 'Little Manor'. 'It's odd because it's not a large house,' said the present owner's wife. 'Sounded grander, I suppose.'

If Lady Rothschild felt so socially insecure around her diamond-wearing friends like Catherine Walston, then it is hardly any wonder that Vivien Greene – with her utility furniture, meagre allowance and ration book – felt so completely out of her depth. It is clear that Greene was impressed with Catherine's wealth. Indeed, novelist Piers Paul Read believes that part of Greene's sexual attraction to Walston was the freedom that such luxuries as having a private 'taxi' plane account with Marshall's could buy. He had known about Greene's affair with Catherine as a boy from his art critic father Herbert, an old friend of Greene's who wrote film reviews for *Night and Day*. Discussing what he termed the Greene–Walston relationship's 'cult of sin' in 1994, Piers Paul Read commented: 'It is clear that what passes for sexual love is sometimes no more than the expression of dubious subconscious desires. Greene was not rich at the time, and what attracted him to Catherine Walston seems to have been as much her husband's money as her slim body or lively mind.'

There was a typical Greene paradox here; on the one hand he seemed to place little value on 'possessions' – living in his simple Antibes flat, giving away his original manuscripts, encouraging his friends and lovers to sell their letters, and donating his royalties to such causes as Trappist monks and Nicaraguan guerillas – yet on the other he was financially ambitious in his literary and film deals, with a reputation as a tough negotiator. This goes back to Greene's days as an undergraduate, when he defended himself from a brutal critical attack by Harold Acton, who accused his poetry style of belonging to the 'middle ground'. Greene's response was that the 'reviewers have succeeded in making the poetry of the Centre party sell, I must confess that I find a strong pleasure in the making of money'. At Eyre and Spottiswoode he would spend half the morning on the phone to his stockbroker. In his letters to Catherine – often written at his desk – he was always trying to impress her with vague details of how much money he was making. Once he had money, Greene would regularly complain jokingly to Catherine that he wished he wasn't so 'successful & rich'.

Vivien's memory of her visit to Sunday lunch at Thriplow is of a 'very smart nurse' (called Twinkle), the prize-winning Walston herd of Jersey cows, and some Arab horses. 'It had a feeling of great richness – money everywhere. And not only that but resources. I think Graham was impressed by riches because I remember he was very struck when the film man, Korda, gave him a gold tooth pick. It was only a tooth pick. But he was quite impressed by it.'

In *The Heart of the Matter*, written at this time, Scobie looks at his poetry-loving wife Louise as 'fifteen wasted years'. Vivien, it is true, was fond of poetry. Through her mother she had published a volume of poems in the 1920s. But then so did Greene.

At the University of Texas there is a large black book in which Greene has hand-written all the love poems he wrote to Vivien, each with little notes attached, some of which appear in *Babbling April*. The quality of the verse is mainly very adolescent and sentimental; in fact, his mildly sneering tone at 'literary' Louise's poetry reading and her 'library' nights could be seen as a form of authorial self-loathing. One purpose of his 'book-hunting' expeditions around the country with his brother Hugh was to track down any old copies of *Babbling April* and destroy them. It wasn't until 1983 that he felt secure enough to publish his second volume, *A Quick Look Behind*; the Author's Note states: 'Having no claim to be a poet, I am confining these verses written over a half century to a very limited number of readers who may have a personal interest in the writer. Perhaps it will amuse them to speculate for what reason, on certain occasions, he was driven to abandon his natural medium of prose & jot down these footnotes in verse.'

But Catherine was the muse of his best poetry. In *A Quick Look Behind*, the section marked '1950s' contains the poem, 'I Do Not Believe'. Sherry believes it was originally written about his love for Catherine, but not published until five years after her death.

> *I can only believe in love that strikes suddenly*
> *out of a clear sky;*
> *I do not believe in the slow germination of friendship*
> *or one that asks 'why?'*
>
> *Because our love came savagely, suddenly,*
> *like an act of war,*
> *I cannot conceive a love that rises gently*
> *and subsides without a scar*

Towards the end of his life, Greene became a benefactor of the Arvon Poetry Foundation, after receiving a fan letter from Poet Laureate Ted Hughes, who declared himself a great admirer of his novels (admittedly he was hoping for a cheque). When Scobie packs up Louise's books in Freetown in *The Heart of the Matter*, he carefully wipes down her copy of the *Oxford Verse*. Just after the war, Vivien had hopes of turning 15 Beaumont Street into an Oxford poetry salon; on her first poetry evening, Elizabeth Jennings, Dylan Thomas and David Cecil read their poems in the drawing-room. 'It was a very cold night and the room was most inadequately heated,' said Vivien, referring to the coal shortage at the time.

It has been assumed that the guilty conflict felt by Scobie, torn between his mistress and his wife, reflected Greene's state of mind about Dorothy and Vivien before Catherine. Greene once wrote that Scobie was based only on what lay in his subconscious. To probe this I quoted to Mrs Greene the scene of misery between Scobie and Louise before he leaves her, that Sherry states 'may reveal the probable form of arguments between Greene and Vivien'.

> Louise said, 'I've known it for years. You don't love me.' She spoke with calm. He knew that calm – it meant they had reached the quiet centre of the storm: always in this region at that time they began to speak the truth at each other.

'That's not out of life,' protested Vivien, although she admits she did use 'Ticki' as a nickname for Greene and he disliked it. 'He's a *writer* and you have to accept that a writer has his own life and things that he has written are much more real to him than the person who's living there with him.'

Despite Vivien's efforts at Christmas 1946 – putting a home-made crib in the dining-room window and a tree decorated with aluminium stars made from silver milk-bottle lids ('there weren't such things as ornaments', she told me) in the drawing-room – the Greene marriage was already in serious trouble before Mrs Walston entered Greene's life.

Greene had met Vivien in 1925 as an undergraduate from Balliol. She was working at Blackwell's and wrote to him complaining of his use of the word 'worship' in reference to the Virgin Mary in an article he had written for the *Oxford Outlook* on why the modern world had become too obsessed by sex. He sent her hundreds of love letters, which she kept in shoe-boxes, but they are for the most part so tediously repetitive that after reading through some 200 at Texas I had to give up: 'My miracle worker . . . you've given trees shade, and the flowers scent, and the sun a gold it never had before,' he gushes.

One in particular must have sounded a warning bell: as proof of just how much he loved her, he revealed the truth about their first meeting for tea. If he thought her 'pretty' he wrote, 'I'd suggest myself in love with you. Just as a change from Oxford.' No wonder Greene cringed when confronted by them in the proofs of Sherry's biography. Caroline, Greene's daughter, told me that she too had seen Greene make Sherry cry after it emerged that Sherry wanted to name various chapter titles after the women in his life (whom Sherry refers to as the 'Big Five'). 'Graham doesn't really get het up you know, if he is angry it's a rather cold anger and rather scary,' said Caroline, 'but he was really furious about that and Sherry started to cry; it was absolutely ridiculous, saying, "I'll give it up, I won't write any more."'

For her part, Vivien Greene told me she had not read Sherry's 783-page first volume that deals with her marriage as she had been in an Oxford nursing hospital when she received her copy. 'I had broken my hip and the book was just too heavy for me to hold.' Her lady companion tried reading some extracts, but also had to give up.

'It is much too big to sit and read aloud,' Margaret added. 'It was just impossible.'

'I think a great deal is lost if they don't know how his wife lived, or how he treated her,' added Vivien. 'I don't mind. I'm not resentful. I do think, looking back, that very few people could have lived as I've lived. I had two children. I never said anything to them to put their minds against him.'

Certainly, Caroline views the breakdown of her parents' marriage with equanimity. 'My mother has a one-sided view. I don't say she's completely wrong, but she's not completely right either; there is, as you say, another side to it.'

By 1946, it was clear the couple had profoundly different natures. For a start they had such different tastes. Vivien began collecting dolls' houses in 1945 (in 1990 *The Times* described her as the world's leading doll expert); Greene couldn't bear his wife's obsession with mother-of-pearl, Edwardian embroidery and Regency furniture. He once wrote a curt letter saying that he couldn't write a word on a Regency desk. As Caroline said, 'They were both very young.' Vivien consoles herself today by acknowledging that it was simply not in Greene's nature to be faithful. He would have gone off with other women whoever he married.

Yet Greene's affair with Mrs Walston wasn't just another mid-life crisis. By the time Catherine entered his life in 1946, Greene was more than ready to plunge into the dark, exciting waters of an affair with a beautiful thirty-year-old American, who also happened to be his Catholic godchild.

Did Vivien get the feeling Catherine Walston was different from other women in his life?

'He had so *many*,' she said, adding that she had started writing a list of his mistresses on the letter I had sent her. 'At the same time he was living with Dorothy Glover [in London], he had a regular mistress [a prostitute called Annette] who was in New Bond Street. He had given her his telephone number, which outraged me more than anything. She rang up. I knew straight away from her voice what she was.'

Whilst living in a thatched cottage at Chipping Campden with no electricity, and later – following the sale of the film rights of *Stamboul Train* for £1,700 – in the top floor flat at 6 Woodstock Close in Oxford, Vivien knew that his visits to London were often of a surreptitious nature. After going to Vivien's mother's funeral, for example, he found time to visit a favoured prostitute, a reference he later attempted to remove from his journal. Greene was certainly doing plenty of prowling around. 'It was hard on me,' Vivien said. 'And I felt very lonely.

I assumed that was what happened in all sorts of marriages. If you marry an artist or painter or musician, they are not like an ordinary person. They have their work, which means more to them than any general human attachment.'

Yet Greene was still clearly very much attached to Dorothy Glover. I asked Vivien what he saw in her. 'How shall I say this?' his wife replied. 'He and Hugh [Greene's brother] were very close. Very great friends. They would go to Paris together, and go book-hunting together. And they called her "Doll Tear Sheet" and I think they shared her. She was somebody who had no beauty. She was older than Graham. I don't know why but she may have had some sort of sexual attraction . . .' Dorothy was already in her late thirties when she met Greene in 1938 or 1939.

Vivien met her just once, at Greene's Albany flat in the mid-1950s. She had taken Francis to the Victoria and Albert Museum, coming up to London on the bus from Oxford. Before going back, Vivien had gone to his Piccadilly flat to see if he was around (they had been separated for years). After knocking on the door, Greene emerged to say he had someone coming for dinner. A few moments later, Glover tramped up the stairs and bumped into Vivien. 'She was very startled,' recalled Vivien. 'She said something very odd to me which was that, "I was just passing and needed to telephone my furrier". She was a short, stocky woman, not attractive at all.' During the Blitz, Malcolm Muggeridge, in his collected diaries *Like It Was*, remembers Greene saying to him that 'he had to have a row with someone or other because rows were almost a physical necessity to him'. When I mentioned the Muggeridge anecdote to Vivien she said that Greene rarely used to have physical rows with her. If he was angry, it would be directed in barbed comments or a cold silence. 'I think one of the charms of Dorothy Glover was that she made rows. She fought. She screamed. She shouted. I remember Graham showing me his hand where she had stubbed out her cigarette.'

'Wasn't that Walston?'

'No. It was Dorothy [it was both to be exact]. She was very noisy in character. Violent. He was rather proud of it, you see. My mistake was always to be quiet or gentle. Giving way. He would have liked it much better if I'd screamed, kicked, fought and so on. He had this really quite bad burn on his hand. And he obviously enjoyed it.'

There is a strange photograph of Dorothy Glover in a tug-of-war competition with Harry Walston. Her appeal seems to have been that masculinity which Greene always liked in his women, as well as her liking for drink, and they also shared a passion for collecting Victorian detective fiction. They met after Greene rented a work studio in Bloomsbury's Mecklenburgh Square where she lived with her mother.

By 1946, Vivien claimed to have had no idea about the realities of Greene's life. He never told her how much he earned, or any details of the lucrative film and foreign rights deals he was pulling off. For years her allowance was just £102 per month. 'That was twenty-five pounds per week. The other day I saw my old bank slips, ten pounds, ten pounds, ten pounds, for weeks, months, years. Ten pounds was spending money for food; the rest was telephone, rates, gas, electricity and a little for wages, as I had somebody once a week. I only found just a few years ago that at the time he had his books translated into nineteen languages.'

But didn't she read newspapers? The *Observer* profile of Greene in 1949 remarked that 'his success has been enormous. The sale of his last novel, *The Heart of the Matter*, has already exceeded 100,000 copies in this country alone.' It was this level of success that had allowed Greene to pay the high asking price of £10,000 for Grove House in 1947, despite its being nearly derelict. Its previous occupants were Chinese war refugees. (Greene certainly wasn't cheap when it came to buying his family houses.)

'I mean I had *nothing* when I came here except two utility beds and a table and no money at all. At the time, the big old country houses were being sold off for nothing. That . . .' she said, pointing to the ripped pale-green chaise longue to my right '. . . came from Blenheim, twelve pounds.'

Had she no idea about Greene's finances?

'No. One day, in Beaumont Street, he said, "We haven't got enough coat hangers," and he went off and bought six handsome padded coat hangers, and I thought that's a rich man, he must be rich to be able to just buy six beautiful padded coat hangers.'

I had to wonder, was this merely an embittered wife? Greene, I knew, had an exceptionally generous side to him. He treated his ex-lovers and mistresses well; he gave large amounts of money to strangers. Friends like Malcolm Muggeridge used to complain that he was a 'sinner manqué'. In his 1948 diary, Muggeridge relates how he always used to say to Greene that 'the great quest of his life has not been virtue but sin', and that his quest had been entirely fruitless. 'In the Blitz we used to spend a good many evenings together, and I remember the longing he had for a bomb to fall on him, but of course it didn't, and I told him it wouldn't.'

But Ibsen scholar Michael Meyer, who met Greene in 1944, holds a strong personal view as to why his old friend was so 'profoundly uncharitable' towards his wife. 'People are often mean in some respects and ludicrously generous in others. That quite often goes together. Graham was like that. Anybody who made him feel guilty was an enemy. It was as if they betrayed him. He had this *huge* sense of Roman Catholic guilt. But what he did to Vivien was really pretty awful. He blamed his bad conscience on her. Vivien was the mill-stone around his neck. I think he would have been very happy if Vivien had died. I think he would have flagellated himself for wishing it but he really wanted her to die.' Indeed, in September 1947, Greene had a dream that Vivien did die, which he wrote about to Catherine. In the letter he said that he couldn't pray for her to live, so he simply prayed that she wouldn't suffer pain.

But Vivien had been mortally hurt already. Just before the war, when Greene was a film critic (later literary editor) of *The Spectator* he had moved his family to the fine Queen Anne house at 14 North Side, Clapham Common. No. 14 had once been owned by Zachary Macauley, father of the famous nineteenth-century historian.

It was the first house that Greene had ever bought, and with a heavy mortgage, but even then he acted without consulting his wife. 'He took it without my knowing,' remembers Vivien. 'When I arrived he was quite pleased; it was a nice eighteenth-century house.'

In every way imaginable it was the opposite of Maurice Bendrix's rented one-bedroom bedsit on the wrong side of Clapham Common. The four-storey house had a big glass dome in the grand stone hallway. It was beautifully panelled thoughout, chiefly in pale grey. To guests like Anthony Powell and Ian Fleming, Greene's smart home must have made him appear the model of London literary success. Mrs Greene also had a housekeeper, Mrs Millard, who liked to read Balzac and who, Vivien remembers, could cook 'in four languages'. There was an impressive dining-room. At the back was a large garden.

A short ten-minute walk across the common was the Two Windmills pub, the model for the Pontefract Arms in *The End of the Affair*, and the place where Bendrix and Henry go for their drink after they encounter each other on the Common on a wet night in January. In 1938, there was an amusing account in *London Magazine* of Julian Maclaren Ross's lunch visit to the house. The twenty-five-year-old Oxford graduate and part-time travelling vacuum-cleaner salesman was adapting *A Gun For Sale* for a BBC radio play, and recalled walking across the Common with Greene and then carrying back two heavy jugs of beer for them to drink at lunch.

The Two Windmills – now The Windmill – on the south side of the Common near where Bendrix lived, is still very much open today (it is now also a semi-luxury hotel). Its old wooden-floor saloon bar, and its 'lounge' bar converted from an old eighteenth-century stable block, appear unchanged since the 1940s. Hanging up by the bar are various advertisements for post-war hangover 'medicines', that one can imagine Greene having experimented with. Unlike in *The End of the Affair*, the lavatories do not have bawdy graffiti scrawled on the walls.

But the Clapham Common Speaker's Corner – where Bendrix used to hear the atheist Smythe explaining the cold beauty of a Godless world – has been long since abandoned. At the spot where Smythe's sister used to pick up her brother's dropped cards, you will find only a lonely duck pond. A local council sign, partly vandalised and half covered with the poster of a pop star, says the corner is 'For Public Use Sunrise to Sunset'. The owner of the café next to it, however, told me he hadn't ever seen anybody make a speech in thirty years.

Greene's house was destroyed by a direct German 'flying' bomb hit in 1941. If you look closely at the brick of No. 14, North Side today – when I visited its basement flat was for sale for £220,000 – you can see the black scorch marks of the fire that destroyed all the Greene family furniture and possessions from fifteen years of marriage. During the war, with Vivien and the children evacuated to Oxford, Greene had stayed on in London, living with Dorothy Glover, with whom he worked as a fire warden at No. 25 Shelter off Tottenham Court Road. Several entries in Greene's 'Blitz Journal' contain similarities to Sarah's journal in *The End of the Affair*.

During the Great Blitz of Wednesday, April 16, for example, Greene had been drinking with Glover at the Horseshoe (a hotel bar that still exists off Tottenham Court Road). After the air-raid sirens started wailing at 9pm they managed to have some dinner at Czardas in Dean Street. The restaurant 'shook' when the bombs began to drop. As they headed back to Dorothy's flat, Greene wished he had his steel helmet. After changing and grabbing his helmet, he accompanied Glover on fire duty. As they stood at the corner of Tottenham Court Road and Alfred Place, a 'huge detonation' exploded nearby and nearly killed them. Greene and Glover only had time 'to get on their "haunches"' as they were showered with glass from a shop window. 'Looking back', he wrote, 'it is the squalor of the night, the purgatorial throng of men and women in dirty torn pyjamas with little blood splashes standing in doorways, which remains. These were disquieting because they supplied images for what one day would probably happen to oneself.'

In *The End of the Affair*, after a bomb hits his house, Bendrix finds himself in his dressing gown under a blown-off door, missing a few teeth and covered in blood. Meanwhile, his mistress, Sarah Miles, has made a personal pact with God that if Maurice lives she will break off their affair. Bendrix's experience was far from unusual. In his Blitz diary, Greene relates how a young priest he knew of was called to a demolished pub where the landlord and his family were half-buried under rubble. The priest managed to get under a billiard table to speak to them. 'A voice above his head suddenly asked, "Who's that?" and the priest heard himself saying: "I am a Catholic priest and I am under the billiard table hearing confessions". "Stay where you are a moment, Father", the voice said, "and hear mine too."' Like Greene, he was a 'rescue worker'.

Greene's nature thrived on guilt and paradox. He was too intelligent to see the world in black and white, good and evil, right and wrong. In his second letter to Catherine, after apologising for not writing and for getting the address of her Achill cottage wrong, he added, 'What would a novelist do without a sense of guilt?' In Greene's case, he may never have made it out of *The Times* subs room, where he worked in his early twenties.

It wasn't just *The End of the Affair* that was inspired by the Blitz. Greene later published a macabre short story called *The Destructors*, about a gang of vandals who set about finishing off a 'beautiful house' that has been hit by a bomb by gutting it with 'nails, chisels, screwdrivers, anything that was sharp and penetrating'. After the story was published there was a flood of letters from outraged readers, which were kept for years in a special file.

The story baffled many of Greene's friends, except for Muggeridge. In January 1949, after *The Heart of the Matter* had been published, Muggeridge noted in his diary what he remembered Greene had said about his return to his Clapham Common house after it had been destroyed by the German bomb. After arriving and finding it all roped off, he told Muggeridge that he actually felt relief because the mortgage represented a large financial burden. But when he told Vivien, he said, he was 'rebuked' for letting the children know what had happened.

Greene couldn't understand this. But Muggeridge did. He recorded in his diary that he didn't think it was 'unreasonable' at all, because Vivien felt that the destruction of their house was 'an outward and visible manifestation of the destruction of their marriage, and that Graham's satisfaction at the destruction of the house was not really because it released him from a financial burden, but because he saw in it the promise of being released of a moral one. And I said [to Greene] that everything that happened had to correspond with what was, and that's why life is at once so fascinating and terrible.'

'When I read that,' Vivien said, 'I thought that's quite true.'

the unquiet american

On the brilliant blue-skied morning of John Rothenstein's first visit to Thriplow in the April of 1945, he invited Catherine Walston to go for a walk in the East Anglian countryside. They had only gone a few dozen yards from the Walstons' white, wooden-slat farmhouse when his twenty-nine-year-old hostess abruptly turned back. She told Rothenstein that she never walked anywhere 'gratuitously'. (Wearing her favourite chocolate-brown cashmere coat, she would disappear off for walks after lunch across the fields with Graham Greene – but that was for quite another form of exercise.)

From her earliest days growing up in the 1920s in Rye, New York, Catherine had always been of bold and independent spirit. And she was always noticed. But a love affair begins with a person's nature, not their actions. Greene always believed that the human character was forged in childhood, or at least up to the age of about seventeen; in Catherine's case, her appetite for libertine adventurism, along with her reckless energy and striking beauty, were apparent from an early age. When she came to England, having married Harry Walston after the briefest of holiday romances in the mountains of New Hampshire, she had been more than happy to drop out of Barnard College, the all-girls private college that was part of Columbia University (a visit to Barnard College in New York on a hot August morning revealed no archive records relating to Catherine's academic achievements). She had already learnt the most important lesson: her natural sexual charisma brought power over men.

There is no question that her looks were exceptional. Lady Longford, a close friend of Catherine's (she is her youngest 'son' James Walston's godmother), told me that she was one of the few women she had ever known in her life (she is now ninety-six, and has been a leading society figure since the 1920s) who she just enjoyed '*looking* at', as if she was a *quattrocento* painting come to life. 'Being a rather visual person, I liked being with her; she was very, very beautiful. She wasn't at all dictatorial in an academic way.'

Catherine and Elizabeth Longford both had children at Ampleforth (the Walston children were sent to Ampleforth, Eton, and Downside). Pointing to the terrace by the Longford lawn in Sussex, where they had sat together, she remembered asking her why, whenever her children came back from school, she then sent them off abroad. There was a long pause, before Catherine – then Lady Walston – answered in her American drawl: 'For the *lang*-uages, of course.'

But Lady Longford wasn't thoroughly convinced. She believed the truth was that Catherine liked doing her own thing. 'I mean she liked to lay down the law, but as a fellow woman these were just opinions and she gave the impression her opinions were as good as anybody else's. She wasn't a great one for quoting other people. She was full of opinions, she was very opinionated with me. She may have been different with men and let them talk. But I liked it. She puzzled me so much and I was interested. She had a wonderful white skin and this reddish golden hair and like most Americans beautiful limbs, arms and ankles.'

Lady Longford wasn't the only person who enjoyed looking at her. After Anne Fleming, wife of Ian Fleming, met her in Capri, when Graham and Catherine joined her for coffee and green chartreuse after a lunch with Gracie Fields, Anne reported back to Waugh:

It was very nice to have a good stare at Mrs Walston . . . She seized my battered straw hat and declared it a most enviable possession, she tried it on at various angles and prinked and preened, and then displayed the same idiotic enthusiasm for Ian's old walking stick and pranced about with the uninteresting object expressing a violent desire for it. I suggested a swop for her frock at which she started violently undoing the bodice – she's a very maddening woman.

Anne had got it into her head that Catherine was called Mrs Ralston, which makes her sound like the capricious Mrs Rattery of *A Handful of Dust*. On another occasion, Anne called her 'Mrs Wolfstein' – a bizarre Freudian slip, although she was certainly not the first woman to see Mrs Walston as a highly dangerous predator – back-stage in Noël Coward's dressing room following his play *The Apple Cart*. She reported back to her friend Lady Diana Cooper, who also knew them both: 'Mrs Wolfstein has an enviable gift for flattery and praised the length and straightness of Noël's legs – apparently only comparable in beauty to Greene's shanks – there was nothing for me to do but relapse into morose silence'.

Anne Fleming had first met Catherine with Evelyn Waugh when she had been Lady Anne Rothermere. Not used to being upstaged by a beautiful American woman who would show up to dinner with Graham Greene hanging off one arm of her mink coat and her socialist millionaire husband on the other, Anne was – like Elizabeth Longford – intrigued by her. The perfect chance to get properly acquainted came in March 1953 when she heard that Greene and his mistress were staying at the Tower Isle Hotel in Jamaica, the island where Ian Fleming had his Goldeneye villa. Anne wrote to Evelyn Waugh:

I bombarded them with invitations but was unable to smoke them out though I finally extracted an invitation to cocktails, as I put on my best frock and accompanied by Ian, went in search of Number One Bungalow; it took us some time to find it as it was several unchaperoned miles from the hotel, a perfect place for lovers, two bed, two bath, one patio private beach and swimming pool. Mrs R. was dressed as a French porter but it did little to disguise her charms . . . I am now more interested in Mr Greene's character. Is he living in sin? Is he tortured? He remained remote from all, totally polite and holding the cocktail shaker as a kind of defensive weapon – please explain to me.

★

Catherine was always known as 'Bobs'. She was born in Rye in 1916. Her father was David Crompton, an Englishman who worked as a successful stockbroker in New York (Greene names the priest in *The End of the Affair* Father Crompton). Little is known of David's relationship with his three daughters, Catherine, Bonte and Belinda. The central tragedy of his life was that the year before Catherine was born, his older brother, along with his six children, were on board the Cunard luxury liner *Lusitania* when it was struck on the afternoon of 7 May 1915, by two torpedoes fired from a German U-Boat in the icy waters of the Atlantic off the coast of Ireland as it returned to Liverpool from New York. Around 1,200 passengers drowned, including 124 Americans (who had been warned by German authorities not to travel on the ship as it was carrying war supplies), making it a disaster on a par with the sinking of the *Titanic*. To compound the sense of family loss, David Crompton's cousin, Sir George Booth, had been head of the Cunard shipping line.

One does not have to be a psychoanalyst to work out the effect that this grief may have had on Crompton's daughters. The English Edwardian reserve almost certainly caused David to withdraw into his club shell. This may partly help explain why Catherine had such an appetite, or psychological need, for intimate male company throughout her life. As Brian Wormald, a former Anglican priest and fellow of Peterhouse, Cambridge, and one of her intimate friends in the 1950s, bluntly put it to me,

'I think she could be called a nymphomaniac; but that's not special . . . I think she regarded seducing people as rather fun.'

'What was her technique?' I asked.

'Talk, talk, talk, talk, talk, talk and drink, drink, drink, drink, drink,' Wormald said. 'I think she was having relationships with many other people, as well as me. And she warned me early on, she asked me if I was jealous and I said, "no."' He added, 'She was a profoundly interesting person. She was enigmatic, which all interesting people are.'

Being strikingly beautiful always helps if one is to embark on a personal odyssey of sexual adventurism. I think it's fair to say that Catherine was never prudish in her choice of lovers, although she especially liked men who were cleverer than her, who could teach her something, and whose own opinion she respected. One interesting aspect of reading through her diaries for 1949 and the early 1950s is that her entries are curiously lacking in emotional imagination. Yet Catherine certainly had an excellent aesthetic and critical taste. Greene encouraged her to write, and – like the lovers of many famous writers – she tried very seriously to write a novel several times; indeed, she was writing one simultaneously with Greene as he worked on *The End of the Affair*. But her diary records her frustration, as she was repeatedly disappointed by the results. She simply did not have the imagination. Her talents were better channelled into close friendships with artists, and, thanks to her husband Harry's cheque-book, collecting the sculptures of Henry Moore (with whom she was rumoured to have had an affair) instead.

Her father certainly maintained a reticent profile. In the middle of a very hot August, it took me two days of ferreting around Rye, searching through the civil, birth and death records, visiting the Episcopelian church, tramping around old cemeteries, until I managed to find a single public record of David Crompton. On the top shelf of a back storeroom in Square House, the tiny Purchase Street headquarters of the Rye Historical Society, I found a heavy green fine-leather volume entitled *Fifty Years of Apawamis 1890–1940*. In the back was an index of members of the Apawamis Club, Rye's most exclusive WASP golf and country club: 'Crompton, D.H. Elected 1918'.

I began reading chapter nine, 'The Recoil', dealing with the 'halcyon days' of the club in the 1920s: 'Money was the test and it seemed an easily obtainable commodity, as judged by the overnight birth of fantastic fortunes.' There was a long waiting list at the club. 'The recoil from the horror, the misery and the strain of the war was natural but there went with it attendant evils. Interwoven with the resurgence of happiness was the skein of a loosened moral, an implied liberalism in habits and customs, which affected all kinds, but more definitely those of the younger generation.'

I had visited the club that morning hoping for some help in tracking down an address for David Crompton. The Apawamis Club had a large file in the local library. 'The history of the town of Rye', began one clipping from 1955, 'is bound inextricably with that of the club and has been since 1890.'

Today the clubhouse is a vast stone house, with a phalanx of gleaming black Ford Explorer jeeps and BMWs parked outside. Inside is a finely carpeted drawing-room, the usual nineteenth-century Graeco-Roman urn reproduction prints, lemon-yellow wallpapered walls with a white cornice, a bare marble chimney-piece and a bunch of Mexican staff gabbling on the terrace, eating take-away food. I tried to explain to the secretary seated behind the desk that I was writing about the English novelist Graham Greene and *The End of the Affair* and was hoping . . . her already expressionless eyes glazed over.

Taking matters into my own hands, I walked upstairs and knocked on the general manager's office door. I was met by a mustachioed middle-aged Hispanic businessman in a dark blue suit who asked me what I wanted.

'I was hoping to look in your archives for any information you might have about a David Crompton . . .'

Before I had a chance to finish, the conversation was terminated.

'Our policy is not to give out any information about club members. Sorry.'

'But he must have been dead for about . . . [I had to guess] . . . forty years.'

'Sorry.'

Once I had established there *was* a reference to David Crompton, Phyllis Dillon, director of the Rye Historical Society, sprang into action. Within the hour, she and a colleague had found Catherine Walston's home address from a 1918 Rye street directory. 'David Crompton Esq., 1 Hidden Springs Lane' (before this he had lived at Dogwood Lane, with no street number).

Fifteen minutes later I had parked outside the black iron gates and was walking up the drive, past some old stables that had been turned into a garage (complete with basketball hoop) and some rhododendron bushes. Judging by the number of copies of the *New York Times* scattered on the doorstep, the owners weren't there. I took a snoop. The white clapboard house – just like Thriplow Farm – was large with black-painted shutters. Walking up the wooden steps of the porch, I peeked through the window by the black front door. There was a black and white marble hallway, a crimson carpet, chintzy white wallpaper with roses on it, and a copy of *Wine Spectator* on a table in the formal sitting-room; an old family portrait hung above the fireplace.

Catherine was clearly brought up in a very charming and sizeable colonial-style house (originally known as Jib Farm), with a large garden, only a few minutes' walk from Rye railway station. In the summer of 1928, when Catherine was twelve, an announcement was made in the local paper that 'soon Rye would have 172 trains to and from New York every day' (the commuter ticket was just over twenty-five cents). Just before the Cromptons moved in, 1 Hidden Springs Lane was the original clubhouse of the Apawamis Golf Course. The garden in which Catherine used to play as a child and teenager was, in fact, part of the ninth 'dirt' green of the old Rye Golf Course. The fairways had been cut by a flock of sheep. Inside the house, one can still see the original lockers used by the first club members.

When Catherine arrived in England, aged nineteen, she shocked her new husband's mother, Lady Walston, by performing a set of cartwheels on the lawn at a garden party given to introduce her to the Walstons' smart friends. Lady Walston was the widow of the distinguished Cambridge archaeologist and classical scholar Sir Charles Walston. The Walston (originally Walstein) family were of German-Jewish origin and – like the Rothschilds – had made a fortune in finance before the Great War; Catherine's great friend Lady Rothschild had married Jacob Rothschild in 1933. At the turn of the century, when many English feudal estates were being broken up, the Walstons had bought up around 2,000 acres (later increased to around 2,500 acres) on the Pemberton family estate around Newton and Thriplow in Cambridgeshire. (Francis Pemberton, whose monument is in the Newton parish church, is credited as one of the first war correspondents, working for *The Times* in the Crimea.) In 1909, Sir Charles commissioned the architect F. Foster to enlarge Newton Hall, turning it into a vast neo-Queen Anne pile with twenty-eight bedrooms. Sir Charles died when Harry was quite young, and as his only son Harry Walston was very well off indeed. But to say, as has been often stated, that Catherine married one of the richest men in England overstates the case.

Catherine seems to have inherited her devil-may-care, exhibitionist cartwheeling streak from her amateur actress mother, Lillian MacDonald Sheridan. If one digs up the old theatre programmes of the 'Community Players' (later known as 'The Barnacles'), founded in 1925, and Rye's leading dramatic society, the name 'Lillian Crompton' features prominently in the cast lists. The Cromptons had an English nanny, Frances McFall (buried near the Walston estate in Thriplow), who doubtless took the Crompton children along to watch performances in the Tredenoch Theatre, a converted old barn. As the chapter on 'The Twenties' in *Fifty Years of Rye, 1904–1954*, by Marcia

Dalphin, enthuses breathlessly: 'These amateurs were properly ambitious and presented such really grown-up fare as Shaw's *Man of Destiny*.' Other plays included *The Monkey's Paw* and *Great Catherine*, the latter would have held an obvious appeal.

Throughout her affair with Greene, Catherine would often return to America to stay with her mother. They remained close and Greene did his utmost to exert his influence on her – as he did with her siblings – to help him persuade Catherine to leave Harry. But, like Catherine, she enjoyed close proximity to the Walstons' wealth.

In May 1956, Evelyn Waugh stayed at Newton Hall when Catherine's mother was there and he recorded his impression of her American family. Waugh had just been staying at a run-down old country pile near Harrogate where he noted there were 'no pictures worth glancing at' and pronounced the food as 'adequate' and the wine 'not copious'. 'We found a family gathering, Catherine's horrible American mother, a horrible socialist brother, a son and his tutor, late naval Protestant chaplain. Harry provided good wine which I spilt. Their house (Newton) was a great contrast to Marchmont; Bohemian, profuse, full of objects of beauty and interest.' Waugh's son Auberon remembers visiting Newton as being a reward for getting a scholarship to Downside. His only recollection was that Catherine was an 'attractive woman' with a curious exotic parrot (which Greene gave her), and that Harry Walston struck him as 'an unsatisfactory imitation' of his father, sitting in the vast 'Long Room' (as the Newton drawing-room was called) 'with a cigar too big for him.'

By the 1920s, Rye had become, to paraphrase Tom Wolfe, an irresistible destination for wealthy New York commuters – and WASP residents like the Rockefellers – who insisted on being where things were *happening*. Although the locals were fiercely proud of the connection with their 'mighty ancestors' (as Miss Dalphin put it) in their spiritual birthplace of Rye back in England, Catherine's experiences as a headstrong teenager in the booming 1920s were far removed from any Roedean or

Rye-St-Anthony schoolgirl's; or from Greene's own stiff-collared Edwardian childhood in the fairly dull market-town of Berkhamsted for that matter.

Reading *A Sort of Life*, I had always assumed that Greene's idea of the 'green baize door' was used metaphorically. Only when I went on a tour of Berkhamsted School with a former housemaster did I realise that this private Berlin Wall that so haunted him was not merely an imagined symbol for the world of innocence versus experience, and the division of loyalties he felt as both a school pupil and the headmaster's son. Caught between the two, he said he felt like a spy. In the school's high-ceilinged, dark oak-panelled Dean's Hall, the portrait of Greene's father, Charles Greene, painted in 1926, captures him in his mortar board, doing his best to look stern in a *Tom Brown's Schooldays* sort of way. Through a large door on the right of the school hall, we were lead into a low-ceilinged tunnel. Greene's father's study (where boys were caned) used to be on the left, whilst at the top of the staircase to the right was Greene's out-of-term time-bedroom. (On the way up, I should add, the entire tour party, including several highly respected academic professors, and myself, lined up to inspect the old wooden-seated lavatory that Greene had used as a child.) As the door leading from the Dean's Hall closed behind us, I saw that it was covered in thick green baize, exactly as Greene had described. 'It's *never* been changed,' declared the old housemaster.

For Catherine, there were no such shadowy divisions between family and school; no gloomy passages and tunnels that felt like mental Checkpoint Charlies. Life in Rye during the 1920s – especially in the summer – was like a permanent Brighton bank-holiday weekend. There were new yacht clubs, beach clubs, riding clubs, lecture clubs, a garden club, music festivals; the first 'talking movie' theatre opened in 1928. Like Daisy Buchanan in *The Great Gatsby*, Catherine was brought up in a world of easy money, extravagant parties, and fun, fun, fun. In the 1920s and 1930s, Rye was famous for its 'Bathing Beauty Contests'; whether Catherine was allowed to enter is not known – if she wanted to do something, she usually would – but outraged locals often complained about the sight of teenage girls changing into swimming costumes in the backs of cars. Sherry relates one incident in which Catherine's maths teacher had told the class not to pull a light cord whilst sitting in the bathtub as one could be electrocuted; Bobs deliberately 'made the experiment and survived'.

As a boy, Greene's idea of excitement had been to tramp about in the ferns and heather of Berkhamsted Common pretending he was Rider Haggard on a dangerous mission. When he bored of that he resorted to inventing danger. It's been well established that Greene was guilty of an over-active imagination, 'colouring in' his claim of playing Russian Roulette as a boy on the Common. He admitted as much to V.S. Pritchett in an interview in the 1970s, after his friend had confronted him with a version of events that he had written in 1946 for the American *Saturday Book*: 'The revolver was a small genteel object with six chambers like a tiny egg stand, and there was a cardboard box of bullets. It has only recently occurred to me that they may have been blanks.'

But Catherine had the real thing on her doorstep. The day following Labour Day, 1927, an army of well over 1,000 workers invaded the town and began construction of the Playland family amusement park at Rye Beach, a vast 280-acre pleasure park, designed by the award-winning art deco architectural firm of Walker and Gillette. It featured some of the most terrifying rides ever.

Costing Westchester County $600,000, Playland was the first totally planned amusement park in America and the prototype of America's Disneyland theme park culture. At the park's historic opening on 26 May 1928, over 400 uniformed staff greeted the thousands who flocked to try such rides as the Tilt-a-Whirl, Aeroplane Swing, Whip, Derby, Noah's Ark, Dodgem Scooter; and to have tea in the Japanese Tea House; to walk in the picnic groves; to sit in the Café des Colonnades, modelled on a Paris sidewalk café; to visit the Dance Palace, Boat House and the Fun House. So popular were the frightening rides that a steamship service was added that brought thousands more visitors every day from New York.

Catherine was twelve when Playland opened its black iron gates. The park was to dominate the culture and economy of the town when Catherine was a teenager (as cars entered the gates, they passed a sign: 'Undressing in Cars, Against The Law. $5 Fine'). There is no doubt that Catherine spent plenty of time – and money – at the park. Her older sister Bonte was 'scared stiff' of the dangerous rides, but not Catherine. I had been puzzled as to why Catherine was always known as 'Bobs'. When I went to visit Playland, I found a plausible answer after I was given an old brochure with a potted 'History of Playland'. Before the park opened in 1928, Frank Darling had hired Fred A. Church, one of America's top amusement ride engineers, to build the most dare-devil ride in America. It was 3,600 feet long and, from the black and white photo, it towered above the park on wooden stilts, like a giant coiled python. It was called the Aeroplane Coaster, named in honour of Lindbergh's flight of 1927, and it was also known as 'Bobs', being of a similar design to the 'Bobs'-style coaster at Chicago River Park. Certainly, it would have fitted Catherine's daring character to be named after a 3,600-foot helter-skelter ride described as the 'greatest wringer and most violent ride ever'.

Flicking through the 'photo documentary' of the early attractions in the park, it was easy to see why being dragged out for a walk in the Cambridgeshire countryside might not have been Catherine's idea of fun. A photograph taken in 1932 – she would have been sixteen – shows crowds of people in hats and skirts watching a dangerous-looking open-air circus high-wire trapeze act. The 'Bike Diver' shows a photo of a maniac in just a pair of swimming trunks, diving through the air towards a tiny round swimming pool after riding a bicycle down a giant sixty-foot-high ski-jump-style chute apparatus. 'Hopefully the diver will hit the pool,' says the caption.

His fate is unknown, but this spectacle of a semi-naked man plunging headfirst towards the Playland tarmac provides a fitting image in helping to understand part of the reason why Catherine accepted Harry Walston's marriage proposal, made over the phone after only having known each other for three days; namely, the stock-market crash of 1929, followed by a bleak economic depression. Suddenly, playtime was over in Rye. Her teen pleasure palace now threatened to become a suffocating cage.

Catherine met Harry Walston on a skiing holiday in Pack Monadeck, New Hampshire, when he was studying Bacterial Science for a year at Harvard. One of them was injured on the first day so they both stayed behind whilst the others skiied. By the Monday she was engaged. Although neither Catherine nor Harry were religious in any way – Bobs had once pinched some communion glasses from a Catholic church as a dare – they were married in the Unitarian church at Wilton, where David Crompton had a farm. After driving there, about three hours north of Boston, I realised why Catherine was so keen to escape. The old mill town is pretty but so nondescript and sleepy that even today it doesn't have a single motel or anywhere open to eat after about 8pm.

On the day of their 1935 marriage, Catherine went for a walk with her elder sister Bonte.

'I am not in love with Harry,' said Catherine.

'But, Bobs, you cannot marry a man that you're not in love with.'

'Oh, I like Harry. He's very nice, and I can't stand life here.'

On 27 September 1935, another marriage took place, this time at Marylebone Registry Office, London, which was also to prove significant to Catherine. Her grandmother, Sarah Sheridan, had worked for many years as a nanny/confidante for the wealthy Elon Hooker family of New York. At a Sunday lunch party in June 1933, Helen Hooker, the twenty-eight-year-old daughter of the founder of Hooker Electrochemical Company, was introduced to the romantic figure of Ernie O'Malley, a thirty-four-year-old Irish poet-soldier, a leader of the 1916 Irish rebellion (in which he was captured and badly wounded) and a former general in the IRA. When Helen Hooker planned to travel to Ireland and marry Ernie (without her father's permission or knowledge), Sarah Sheridan was called upon by Helen Hooker's mother to go to Dublin and vet the suitability of the O'Malley family for a marriage into New York high society. Sarah Sheridan reported that the O'Malleys – who could pass themselves off as Irish Republican aristocrats, with their house at Burrishoole, close to Achill Island on the west coast of Ireland – were socially acceptable and she was a witness to the brief service. Because of the high-society connections of the Hooker family, there was a mention in the *New York Times* and *New York Herald*. Both papers also noted that Helen's younger sister, Blanchette, was married to John Rockefeller III.

When Catherine wrote to Greene from Ireland as 'Dear Godfather', just after her reception into the Catholic Church in September 1946, what she did not mention was that she was actually with Ernie O'Malley, with whom she was almost certainly having an affair, at her rented cottage in Achill. Moreover, although Catherine told Vivien Greene that the reason she wanted to convert was because of Greene's books, that was not the whole story. It had been Ernie O'Malley's influence, if anybody's, that first pushed her towards Catholicism.

This information was confirmed by Professor Richard English, author of the acclaimed biography *Ernie O'Malley: A Life*. He sent me an extract from a letter written by Catherine to Ernie O'Malley on 14 October 1946 – one month after her 'reception' breakfast on the lawn of Campion Hall – in which she refers to a conversation about her Catholic faith with Kevin O'Malley (Ernie's brother). In the letter, she said they talked of Ernie's Catholicism, the quality of his 'belief' and religious 'understanding' and how he had taught her 'so much' of what she now knew as a Catholic. 'This is most interesting in relation to O'Malley's influence over Catherine's religious outlook,' English wrote, 'and I do think it does alter the general assumption about Greene's influence here.'

There is certainly enough evidence in Catherine's own journals

and letters to assume that she and Ernie were probably lovers –
and possibly continued to be so after Walston began her affair with
Greene. Catherine first met Ernie O'Malley in America and they
met again in Galway in 1941. Catherine and Harry stayed at
Burrishoole shortly after they were married and extended an
open invitation to Ernie (and his son Cormac) to stay with them
in London or Cambridgeshire (Catherine was later to 'adopt'
Greene's friend Norman Douglas in a similar fashion). Ernie spent
the March and April of 1946 with the Walstons at Thriplow,
where he met such artists as John Piper. 'It's clear that the
Walstons, essentially Catherine, adopted Ernie during the later
years of his life,' says English. 'He repeatedly struck people as cap-
tivating, charismatic, compelling. The classic bohemian
revolutionary, he could tell unique tales of IRA shootings,
injuries, imprisonment, hunger striking, and so on, so artistic
people were frequently struck by the gritty drama of his life.'

Part of Catherine's intoxication with Ernie was that in addition to being an Irish Republican tough guy, he could also 'talk
painting, sculpture and literature'. Catherine introduced Ernie to
John Rothenstein, whom O'Malley then introduced to Jack
Yeats in Ireland (a painter also admired by Greene). O'Malley
tried – without much success – to get Rothenstein to promote
Irish painters at the Tate.

In the late spring of 1946, Ernie had Catherine to stay at
Burrishoole, along with her friend Barbara Rothschild. By that
time Ernie's marriage to Helen was in ruins. Helen, who had
previously befriended Catherine, had become deeply jealous of
her. Both marriages, the O'Malleys' and the Walstons', which
had taken place in the same year, were foundering for the same
reason. Writing to a friend in March 1947, Ernie O'Malley said,
'I have had some trouble with Helen for some years due to what
might be called incompatability.' When a batch of letters from
Catherine written to her sister Bonte were sold at Sotheby's in
1994, *The Times* quoted her as saying of her marriage: 'Sex
almost never comes into Harry's life nor does it hardly ever
come into his mind or imagination.'

Years later she confided to Bonte that she 'never' thought her marriage to Harry was real and that, if she found somebody else she liked more, she would leave her husband. Indeed, a close confidante of Catherine told me that the marriage began to fail – especially in the bedroom – within months of their 1935 wedding. After just one year Catherine confronted Harry and asked for a divorce. His reply was: 'But you simply *can't*.' Instead, he offered her an 'arrangement' regarding other lovers. Although Catherine was to have many (Harry had a fair number himself), she never did leave him. Partly, of course, it was his money. But there is no doubt that they had a close, almost brother–sister relationship. In a letter written to Catherine in December 1949, Greene laments: 'Oh, if only you'd married a man you disliked.' Earlier that year, he had congratulated her on what he called the 'staggering success of marriage': 'Harry has been really, really happy, and that's your achievement,' he wrote.

Sleeping arrangements were always a mystery to friends who stayed with the Walstons. What struck Lady Longford was how Catherine always went out of her way to give the impression that she was a good wife to Harry. 'She told me quite early on in our friendship [they first knew each other in the 1940s] that she and Harry always *believed* in the double bed. They always slept in a double bed because, she explained, they had all the children down in the morning and they all got into bed. And she was very pleased with that, it genuinely meant a great deal to her that she had created this warm family, physically, morally and mentally.' To Longford, the 'duality' of Catherine's life seemed distinctly odd, bordering on self-delusion. 'It did astound me, for I knew very well she was having an affair with Graham, and she really went out of her way to tell all of us that she had a very close real relationship with Harry.'

According to Richard English, who had access to all Catherine's correspondence with Ernie O'Malley (now in the possession of Cormac O'Malley, a New York lawyer), Catherine and Ernie spent much of the summer of 1946 together in Ireland, returning to London at the end of October (when Greene first wrote to her). Both Ernie and John Rothenstein, it seems, must have been staying at the Walstons' house at 6 St James's Street; according to English, he stayed there until the end of December 1946, around the time Greene slipped off to have his first drink with Catherine.

What is interesting about the letter Catherine wrote to Ernie on 14 October 1946, is that she stressed that 'your relationship with me is unique in my life' (English quotes this in his biography). These are almost exactly the same words Catherine would soon be saying to Greene. She, like Greene, appeared to believe it was possible to love two or more people at the same time. In his beautiful American Catholic god-daughter, Greene had met his match.

onion sandwiches

In his preface to *The End of the Affair*, Greene wrote that 'the story which now began to itch at my mind was of a man who was to be driven and overwhelmed by the accumulation of natural coincidences, until he feared that, with one more, the excuse of coincidence would break'. During the writing of this book, I often suffered from this exact same predilection. As the weeks and months passed, the number of odd coincidences – or flukes, like finding my Yvonne Cloetta tape in the bushes of the Berkhamsted railway embankment – began to stack up like a loaded deck of blackjack cards.

Early in the New Year in 1999, I took my girlfriend to see Sir Peter Hall's production of Peter Shaffer's *Amadeus* at London's Old Vic. I was back in London for Christmas having reached a crossroads in both my life and career. After working in America for eight years, I had turned into that most tired of clichés: a burnt-out journalist. My would-be big 'LA novel' remained unwritten: twenty-six cardboard boxes of notes and research lay abandoned on the floor of my office. Aged thirty-two, I had reached the (inevitable) border point in any writer's career when he begins to understand what Greene meant when he wrote: 'Success for a writer is always temporary, success is only delayed failure.'

But failure is a trap-door subject for Greene. 'The sense of unhappiness is so much easier to convey than that of happiness.

In misery we seem aware of our own existence, even though it may be in the form of a monstrous egotism,' says Bendrix in *The End of the Affair*. But one only had to look around the packed Westminster Cathedral on the occasion of his Memorial Mass in 1991 to realise that, as Marie-Françoise Allain put it to him, Greene himself certainly failed at failure.

This very subject came up on my second evening in Washington in July 1999, where I was researching the 1,200 letters in Catherine's Black Box at Georgetown University. At a book launch party, I found myself sitting under the stars on a muggy summer's night in a strange garden off Embassy Row, drinking a Washington society hostess out of Scotch, along with Christopher Hitchens. He had a lot to say about Greene, a fellow travelling left-wing Balliol intellectual and crypto-communist; and even more when we moved on at midnight to a badly lit basement dive that he knew. The talk turned to literary success, and failure. Hitchens told me it had taken *years* of living and working in Washington before anybody called him up to ask him to write on a subject because they wanted to know what *he* had to say (he doesn't have that difficulty today).

What Hitchens had outlined was the essential borderland of any journalist career: crossing the literary territory between reporting (even first-hand reporting) and writing. I think it was Norman Mailer who said the secret of good journalism was knowing when to get out. When I returned to England for Christmas in 1998, I was feeling as if I was slowly sinking into the San Fernando Valley quick mud. My career needed a fresh narrative, a new plot turn.

Hailing a cab outside the Old Vic after *Amadeus*, I gave the driver the address of a restaurant in Soho. It was a grey, wet January night, and raining hard. After crossing Waterloo Bridge, we found ourselves stuck in a gridlock in the swarm of red tail-lights along the Strand. With the traffic jolting forward only a few yards at a time, I told the taxi driver to let us out in the hope that we could find any restaurant still open. It was now past 11 o'clock. Crossing the Strand, we headed up the nearest dark alleyway. Ahead, through the heavy fog of rain, I could see a dim red light – looking like a strip club or a brothel – with a uniformed man standing under an umbrella. Glancing up at the Fifties-style glowing neon sign, I saw it said 'Rules'. For one deranged moment, I found myself jumping out into the rain and dancing a crazed flamenco in the street. I had assumed Rules restaurant had been either bombed or closed down years ago.

Despite it being a miserable night in January, the restaurant was packed. Remembering that Bendrix and Sarah preferred a 'couch' table, we sat down in a crimson velvet booth near the back stairs. Two Germans sat opposite. Outside, the rain streamed down the window. The menu, it was obvious, hadn't changed much; the steak and onions (excellent) was now priced at £17.95.

Reading through Greene's Hermès pocket-books and his letters to Catherine, references to Rules are scattered like forgotten birthday cards found at the back of a dressing-room drawer. There was only one difference from when Greene and Walston used to be regulars: now, each table has a rather naff glossy brochure with the restaurant's history since 1799. One does not go to a restaurant for a social history lesson. Yet Greene and Walston form part of that history; the upstairs restaurant – where the couple liked to sit in a corner – has since been turned into a series of private rooms, including the 'Greene Room'.

Looking round at the walls hung with 'Spy' prints, I imagined Mr Parkis, lurking in the corner, sipping his cocktail, as he tried to keep his eye on Bendrix and Sarah. I had given my girlfriend a copy of *The End of the Affair* shortly after we met. She had used a monologue of Sarah's to audition for her place at the Oxford School of Drama. I can still clearly remember the emotionally fraught lines she chose, when Sarah despairs at not being able to reach Bendrix on the phone after she has ended their affair:

I want men to admire me, but that's a trick you learn at school – a movement of the eyes, a tone of voice, a touch of the hand on the shoulder or the head. If they think you admire them, they will admire you because of your good taste, and when they admire you, you have an illusion for a moment that there's something to admire. All my life I've tried to live in that illusion – a soothing drug that allows me to forget that I'm a bitch and a fake. But what are you supposed to love then in the bitch and the fake? Where do you find that immortal soul they talked about? Where do you see this lovely thing – in me, of all people? I can understand you find it in Henry – my Henry, I mean. He's gentle and good and patient. You can find it in Maurice who thinks he hates, and loves, loves all the time. Even his enemies. But in this bitch and a fake where do you find anything to love?

Tell me that, God, and I'll set about robbing you of it for ever.

Halfway through dinner, after I returned from having a peek upstairs at the Greene Room – empty, with a few gilt plastic chairs around a long table – I turned to my girlfriend. I had an idea; what became the first idea for this investigation. If Rules was still around, I said, what other old relics of the Greene–Walston love affair remained?

One aspect of the first dinner at Rules between Bendrix and Sarah was taken straight from real life: the use of the word 'onions' as a private code-word for sex. This was because Harry Walston loathed the smell of garlic, which was changed to 'onions' in the novel. On 25 March 1947, Greene sent Catherine a one-line postcard from Amsterdam: 'I love onion sandwiches.'

By March, the affair was well under way. So much so, indeed, that Greene and Catherine had dreamt up a means whereby they could see each other on a very convenient basis. Greene would simply buy a house near Thriplow (15 Beaumont Street was rented from St John's College); at any rate 'house hunting' in Cambridgeshire provided an excellent excuse to get away from visiting his family in Oxford at the weekend.

Vivien knew what was going on. But she didn't seem to

know how to react. Her first line of defence was what today
would be called a major case of 'denial'. To Vivien's mind, she
saw it as keeping up the appearance of a happy family life. She
had a habit of dating her letters by Catholic feasts rather than
giving the actual date. On Candlemas Eve 1947 – 1 February –
Vivien wrote to Catherine about her help with the house
hunting: 'It is extremely angelic of you to set things going.'

By the end of January Catherine had already lined up two
very desirable period houses that Greene could afford. One was
referred to as the 'Tudor' house; the other – 'which sounds deli-
cious,' wrote Vivien to Catherine – was a Queen Anne house
with an Elizabethan brick back, in Linton, about ten miles from
Cambridge. As best as she could, without sounding pathetic and
without it getting back to her husband that she was on to them,
Vivien tried to explain her objections to her rival:

> The only difficulty is, it sounds rather 'fenced in' – I mean
> about the garden. I am not at all mobile, for I can't drive a car
> nor even ride a bicycle (through sheer incompetence, not
> because I don't love to go up to London or go about).
> Therefore, wherever I am, I have to really settle in, if it's in the
> country that means room for rabbit hutches (for the children
> of course) and somewhere to sit in a garden someone else
> works in. It's much, much nicer being in a village of course –
> think of all the happenings that one wouldn't miss for any-
> thing . . . I have to realise that Graham will have to spend
> quite a lot of time in London for quite a bit, so no Lady of
> Shalott existence for me.

The letter continues with some hand drawings of Vivien's
preferred style of table, chair, sofa and mirror (to this day,
she prefers anything that is inlaid mother-of-pearl), and a brave
attempt to explain her reluctance to move to Linton because of
a clash of aesthetic sensibility between the 'ingelnooks and
diamond paned windows' and her love of Victorian furniture. 'I
hope I don't sound cautious . . . because I really am grateful and

pleased.' She ends with a reference to Catherine's cottage in Achill, where she was soon to be heading off again: 'I can't *quite* visualise you on the earth floor in Ireland! It sounds as if it might be cold in February, but I think there must be the softest white lambskin rugs on it – and probably piles of books and some flowers?' She pointedly signed off, 'With love from both of us'.

St Valentine's Day, 14 February 1947, was not a good day for Vivien. Her son Francis had scarlet fever and had been rushed to 'isolation hospital' with a temperature of 105 degrees. As a result, she herself was in 'quarantine' and not allowed to see anybody, or even use the local library, for fear of contagion. But she reassuringly added to Catherine in a letter that she was not trying to poison her, as 'this letter isn't a "carrier"'. She wanted to let Catherine know that – how wonderful! – they were now going to be near neighbours. Greene had just rung to inform her that he had bought the Queen's House and made it over (presumably for tax reasons) into her name. 'I'm longing to see it,' said Vivien, 'but please don't decide to go away to California or Ireland before WE move in!'

'What did you think when Graham said he had bought you this house at Linton?' I asked Vivien.

'Without consulting me *at all*. Well, I think he was soon sorry because he realised the Queen's House was so close to her and that it would be impossible for me not to realise more.'

'He was being naive?'

'Very.'

'Did you ever see the house?'

'He took me there. There was a front which was Georgian. The back was very poky. It was awful.'

Neither Greene nor his wife spent a single night at the Queen's House. Quickly realising his mistake – having Vivien on their doorstep was the last thing they wanted – Greene instructed the house to be sold immediately.

In *The End of the Affair*, one of the 'trivial details' that Bendrix remembers about taking Sarah to the cheap hotel in Arbuckle

Avenue, near Paddington Station, is that it was cold and they didn't have any shillings for the gas meter. This detail may have had some basis in reality. January 1947 was freezing. The beginning of the year brought arctic-like north-easterly winds from Siberia to England. The final chilling of Greene's heart towards Vivien (and, to a lesser extent, towards Dorothy) coincided with what became known for years as the 'big freeze of '47', when England endured the coldest winter for over a century.

It lasted from late January, when the first deep snow fell, until March, when the floods were so bad it seemed like whole glaciers had melted. Early on, Big Ben stopped; its cogs simply froze up. As in the cemetery scene in the *The Third Man*, road-digging drills were required to break open the frozen earth to bury the dead. The ground became as hard as iron. As a *Reader's Digest* year-book account records, Britain was 'crippled' in January by the arctic snow-storm that caused ten-foot drifts across the Cambridgeshire countryside, a fuel crisis, gale force winds, and coal boats bound for London to become trapped in the ice in the northern sea-ports. Three hundred major roads in Britain were blocked off or impassable.

All this must have been rather convenient for Greene and his new soft-skinned American mistress. Nobody could travel anywhere. It was like the Blitz again. On 7 February, Emmanuel Shinwell, the Labour minister of fuel and power, declared a national emergency. Vivien Greene, like millions of other house-wives, was not allowed to use electricity between 9am and midday, and from 2pm to 4pm. On her own in Beaumont Street with her utility bed, four chairs, a table, her dolls, and Boots thermometer, the house was shrouded in darkness. There was hardly enough light – without candles – to read during the day. As her scarlet fever 'quarantine' prohibited her from using the library, she told Catherine, in her Valentine Day letter, that she was buying 'lots of new books'. She had just got a 'charming book' on the early Victorian Toy Theatre called *Juvenile Drama*. 'Everything was very hard,' recalled Vivien. 'I was alone. I knew I was alone. I knew for the next forty years I would be alone. Sort of general exhaustion from living. Very hard with two children.'

The Thames froze over. One weekend, though, Greene did manage to make it back to Oxford. His daughter Caroline recalls: 'He came down and I think my mother wasn't feeling well probably; there was this tension anyway.' Caroline remembers being taken by her father, along with her brother Francis, to watch the skating on Port Meadow pond. Her memory is vivid because as they slid about on the ice, it cracked, and they both fell into the sub-zero water. 'We only went to our waists but I remember being rushed home, soaking wet and of course cold, and my father absolutely running us from Port Meadow to Beaumont Street.' When they reached home they were given hot baths and changed into warm clothes.

The other clear memory Caroline has of this time at Beaumont Street is of an artist friend of her father's painting her bedroom wall with an erotic mural of a female figure. 'It's the most extraordinary thing to put in a child's bedroom; it's female, rather large in the thigh, and kind of lying in a sort of *posture*.' As a young convent girl, she didn't know what to make of it all. Nor, for that matter, did she know what to think about her father's increasingly long absences. She told me she thought it was normal. 'In that respect a lot of my friends had fathers who were in the forces and didn't see them for months on end because they were away fighting; and you know, I just sort of took it as for granted that I didn't have a father who was right there, because he was in West Africa, he was in London and so on. He came and visited, one saw him a little bit.' Later, she said, it wasn't a coincidence that she always wanted to be a boarder. Subconsciously, she admits, she didn't want to have to face what was happening at home.

April, indeed, was to be the cruellest month. On the afternoon of 28 April, returning to Beaumont Street with Francis after seeing some relations in Bath, a city that Greene loved, Vivien was surprised to find her husband and Catherine waiting on the doorstep. They had just returned from Achill Island, her husband explained, and Catherine was *exhausted*; she couldn't face driving home tonight. Would it be all right if she stayed the night?

Vivien let them in and went upstairs to make up the third floor spare room. 'I was sort of stunned that he should bring his mistress to my house,' said Vivien. 'Dreadful. Such an insult. Do you see what I mean? He was cold. He didn't imagine what it was like for a wife with his son to accept his mistress, make her bed, get some food for her. With Francis there there was nothing I could say.'

The next morning, 29 April, happened to be the feast day of St Catherine of Siena. Vivien mentioned to Catherine that it was her 'name-day'. 'Blackfriars is just around the corner. I'm going to mass,' Vivien recalls saying. 'And she said, "I'll come too." And she was beside me having holy communion. Shocked me very much. It horrified me, coming from Achill. Just the two of us. What could I *say*?'

I asked Vivien what her relations with Catherine had been like prior to this.

'Off-hand. Nothing. She was nothing. I knew she was a mistress. There was no reason for me to know her or have anything to do with her.'

Yet the rivalry between them was complicated. Whilst Vivien had every reason to be very upset, she had known about his other mistress, Dorothy Glover, for years. Catherine was clearly different. I found Mrs Greene perfectly charming, candid and remarkably unbitter considering what had happened – until I touched a few very sensitive nerves and she, or Margaret, interrupted. Inevitably, there is still pain there.

On the evening of 6 May 1947, before tackling 'van-loads' of washing up in the sink, and just a week after Catherine had stayed at Beaumont Street, Vivien wrote to Thriplow: 'I feel sad I didn't have much of a talk with you – if I was silent it was only because I was wondering if I had marked Lucy's hairbrush and where on *earth* she had put her bedroom slippers: the first day at school is usually hellish, but this one was delightful because you and Graham were there.' Vivien was more intellectual than Catherine and, with claws sharpened, she must have been writing with a nib dipped in vitriol. She then complimented Catherine on her timing. 'The middle days of the week are perfect, which was clever of you.'

The letter is one of the last Vivien wrote to her rival (or at least the last Catherine kept); as before, she dropped heavily the fact that the Greenes were a *Catholic* household. Elizabeth Rothenstein had just been to lunch, and afterwards they went to collect Father Corbishley (a friend of Vivien and Greene's and a highly respected Jesuit at Campion Hall) for a drive out to a 'tumbledown little antique shop'. Elizabeth's daughter, Lucy Rothenstein, believes that her parents were 'alarmed' by what they saw and heard as they had helped introduce Greene and Mrs Walston. 'My mother was very conventional and thought "my goodness *what* is going on!"'

What was even more extraordinary, perhaps, is that Vivien was writing to Catherine at all. One could possibly understand it if she was writing out of uncontrollable anger but rather – on the trip to the Cotswolds jumble shop – she describes in detail how Elizabeth nearly bought 'an enormous, very nice frilly Edwardian-looking pillowcase and I bought a very delapidated mother-of-pearl box', which she was going to sandpaper, and paint, and clean the embroidery, and sew spangles on. She also bought, for 7/6, a 'quite ordinary servants-bedroom looking glass on a stand . . .'

Catherine lived on a different scale completely. When she herself moved in as the chatelaine of Newton Hall, the huge gilt mirror hanging in her bedroom formerly belonged to a grand suite of Victorian inlaid and decorated papier-mâché furniture, reputedly made for the Great Exhibition of 1851.

On Catherine's visit to Oxford there had been talk of going on a retreat. One can't imagine anything more improbable than Vivien and Catherine kneeling down and praying together for a few days, but the idea appears to have been Catherine's. 'I want very much to come to the Retreat,' Vivien said, the only snag being that Greene and others were 'urging' for an honorary degree at Oxford for the French Catholic novelist François Mauriac whom Greene had brought to Eyre and Spottiswoode: 'I shall have to give a party for a very large number of people indeed – 60 or 100 – a great deal as *I have no domestic!*' Vivien wrote to Catherine.

But if she was trying to make Catherine feel guilty, Vivien almost certainly failed. Mrs Walston lived in another world. The Walstons believed in full employment. At Newton Hall they had a chauffeur, butler, ultra-smart nanny, cook and a team of gardeners, in addition to an army of estate workers; Catherine had her own personal maid. When Evelyn Waugh sent a note to Newton Hall saying that he was coming to Cambridge, and could he stay, Catherine replied by telegram: 'MUST WARN YOU I HAVE 150 DINING THAT NIGHT.' Waugh cabled back: 'WHO? HOW? WHY? PARTICULARLY, HOW?'

Greene's own explanation of his insensitivity towards his wife by bringing his mistress to her house is quite odd. In what appears to be an interview with Greene – there is no acknowledging footnote – Norman Sherry quotes the official explanation as being: 'We had already been to confession before that night . . . & had no intention of starting again. It was over & we didn't exchange a word of love or affection that night – she wouldn't have stayed over then if she had not been on the point of collapse.'

Yet this would seem to be at odds with what Greene always maintained about that first trip to Achill with Catherine, when their love affair really became serious. He was to experience a 'peace' there that he repeatedly tried to resurrect.

However, believing that an affair *seems* buried in the confessional has been the Catholic way of adultery for centuries. It is highly unlikely that you would fly from Dublin or Shannon Airport to Heath Row – as it was then known – drive straight to confession at Farm Street in Mayfair, and then up to Oxford, if your destination was Cambridge or London's St James's Street. If

your love affair was really 'dead and buried', it makes no sense.
Surely only a couple in love would behave like that. Indeed, on
30 April, the very next day, Greene sent Catherine a telegram:
'WOULD LOVE MANAGE SOUTHAMPTON IF YOU ARE INCLINED I WILL
PHONE THIS AFTERNOOn.'

Whether they made the original rendezvous for 'onion sandwiches' is unknown. But I don't think we should assume that
Greene wanted to be cruel to his wife. The truth is that by the
end of April 1947, he must have talked about the serious problems of their marriage with Vivien. Perhaps he just wanted to
clear the air, or, more likely, wanted Vivien and Catherine to be
friends. It sounds odd, but Vivien had actually wanted to be
friends with Greene's 'other' mistresses. When Anita Bjork came
to Grove House in the 1970s, they embraced each other and
cried. Greene also invited Anita to lunch in Paris with Yvonne
Cloetta.

Greene spent the weekend of 6 May in London and was missing Catherine badly. 'Mass wasn't the same at all,' he wrote of the
12 o'clock service he attended, having a drink afterwards at the
Salisbury pub in St Martin's Lane. Greene was again near Rules;
in *The End of the Affair*, after Sarah's first fumbling kiss with
Bendrix, she sits down and cries in an old 'Roman church'.
Greene was becoming infatuated with Catherine: 'I just missed
you all the time and felt guilty & depressed & restless. A bit of a
row blew up before I left – she said I had changed so much in
Ireland, but she [presumably this is Dorothy] still believes that it's
simply that I've come under the influence of a pious convert! . . .
She is taking the line this new Catholicism of mine won't last but
that she'll play it as long as I will.'

The night before he had dreamt of Catherine. 'You had been
with me virily [?] saying "I like your sexy smell" – of course I
had a sexy smell! It had been one of those nights.' The next
morning his depression had cleared; he felt 'blissfully happy'.
And wrote another 1,000 words (of *The Heart of the Matter*). He
added in pencil, scrawling the words in much larger writing: 'O,
how I want the peace of Achill and you darling. I hate every-

thing here. I'll be lunching Rules 1.30pm tomorrow & in office from 2.15. Do come or ring.'

Before he left for Ireland, he sent Catherine his first typed letter because it contained some 'important points' and 'I know you can't read my writing'. The main one was to invite her and her husband Harry to the important party he was giving for François Mauriac at Beaumont Street at 9pm on Wednesday 28 May. Another concerned the 'case of Ernie O'Malley', who was visiting London in his capacity as poetry editor of the Dublin literary magazine, *The Bell*.

Greene, it can be fairly assumed, had little idea of exactly why Catherine was going out of her way to get him to use his considerable literary influence to help the Irishman. He enclosed a 'whole batch of introductions' to his A-list literary friends and contacts in London, and 'I hope he will find them useful'.

On 14 May, Greene was in a dejected state about 'complications' over the selling of the Queen's House at Linton and a previously arranged holiday to Ireland that he had promised Dorothy, whom he invariably refers to in his letters to Catherine as 'My Girl' or 'the girlfriend' (Vivien is always 'Vivien'; Catherine's name appears in many forms in the early letters: 'Cafrin', 'Cafryn', 'Darling Cafryn', but mostly, 'Cafryn dear'). The moment he arrived in Dublin with Dorothy on 16 May, he felt depressed and bored. 'This is a very second rate Ireland,' he complained. After trying to cheer himself up with lunch at Jammet's – the best French restaurant in Dublin – he fled the city. 'I felt rather sick with wanting to put the clock back or forward.' He didn't help himself by wearing the cream Achill knitted sweater that Catherine had given him back in April. He went out and bought himself a tweed suit, but it was no good. 'My God, how bored I am,' he wrote. Not even work or 'hot whisky' could cure him. He was nearing the end of *The Heart of the Matter* and wanted 'to finish the book properly'. But he couldn't write. He felt trapped. Before pulling out the leaf of foolscap pages he always wrote on, he had to drop Catherine a love note. Two days later, on a post-card of 'Ireland's Eye,

Howth', he scrawled: 'complete absence here of onion sandwiches'.

The Mauriac party at Beaumont Street is a sensitive nerve-
point with Vivien, an event that still upsets her over fifty-two
years later. In addition to celebrating Mauriac's honorary degree,
the event was a sort of pre-publishing party for his new novel, *The
Unknown Sea* (*Les Chemins de la Mer*), due to be published by Eyre
and Spottiswoode in 1948. The novel dealt with a theme that
Greene knew only too well; as the original Penguin edition put
it, the novel was impressive 'for its suggestion of the turbulent
depths that lie below the conventional surface of French life'. It
revolves around the web of complicated relationships that a
wealthy bourgeois lawyer from Bordeaux finds himself caught up
in. Like Scobie, he ends up failing and committing suicide.
Greene must have re-read the last line to the brief prologue to
The Unknown Sea, with an all too knowing glint of self-recogni-
tion: 'That is the moment when they must choose their path.
Either they must take the final plunge, or they must retrace their
steps . . .'

Greene had no intention of going back to Vivien. He wanted
Catherine as his new wife; and he wanted a new life.

The party that Greene was giving was to be reciprocated in
the January of 1948 in Brussels, when he had been invited to do
a lecture 'double-act' with Mauriac on the portentous theme of
'The Future of Christianity in Civilisation'. So Greene wanted it
to go smoothly. Vivien didn't mention the Mauriac party to me
until 6pm, after she had shown me the crayon marks on her
drawing-room door, where she has marked the height of Queen
Elizabeth II and the height – about five inches beneath – of
Queen Victoria. Sitting back down on the sofa, where the
remains of the tea stood on a silver tray, she said quietly: 'It was
a dismal occasion. I might as well get rid of it now, and I won't
refer to it again.'

In 1947, the Institut Français in Oxford happened to be in
Beaumont Street. Greene went to considerable efforts to invite
his smart London friends from his days as literary editor of *The*

Spectator. He would provide the drinks; Vivien was expected to prepare some snacks and canapés (Greene brought some chocolate from London). 'I was in despair,' says Vivien. 'This was just after the war and you only had two ounces of butter a week.' After enlisting the help of Trinity College kitchens, she 'did what I could. I did my best. Drinks were all right. You could buy drinks, all right. But food was impossible.'

Guests were asked to arrive at 9pm. There was soon a heaving throng of literati in the upstairs drawing-room. John Rothenstein was there, the novelist Rosamond Lehmann, Mauriac, various colleagues from Eyre and Spottiswoode, Catherine and Harry Walston, Barbara Rothschild, Rex Warner, Maurice Bowra, David Cecil, Father D'Arcy and Vincent Turner SJ. John Rothenstein later wrote that Vivien walked around like a lost soul, and that she appeared to be more interested in her dolls' houses than in any of the guests. 'Well, that was because I didn't *know* any of them,' said Vivien, her voice full of emotion. 'Graham didn't introduce me to anybody.' However, quite a few of those at Catherine's reception breakfast at Campion Hall must have been there.

Vivien was perhaps slightly out of her depth but that had never been a problem before. One such occasion was the Christmas party for J.P. Priestley that she had attended with Greene at Heinemann before the war, when they were in love. As she bustled about at the party in 1947, trying to look as if she was occupied, most of her anxiety came from catching sight of Greene and Catherine sitting in a little patio at the back of the small garden in Oxford that had been used as a children's sandpit. 'It was a fine night,' she added. 'The French windows were open, and he simply sat there with her.'

Eventually, after being ignored all night, she went up to her husband, who was talking and laughing with Mrs Walston.

'Could you *please* come and help with the drinks? We need some more bottles opened,' Vivien said.

'I'm not the butler,' Greene replied, before turning back to Catherine.

Greene's comment does seem cruel; if he wasn't the 'butler' then he had at least said he would be in charge of the drinks. Clearly Greene did find being responsible for Vivien's happiness – as well as Dorothy's and Catherine's – a burden. They were mismatched. But the hurt that Vivien felt was real. There is a letter in the Greene papers at the Bodleian Library that Vivien wrote to John Rothenstein, saying how 'utterly miserable' she felt by the suggestion that she was only interested in her dolls' houses. He said he would correct the record in any later edition.

In June 1948 – just over a year later – Greene wrote a frank letter to his wife, explaining why his paradoxical, guilt-ridden, tormented relationship with Catherine was so essential to his work. 'The fact has to be faced my dear is that by my nature, my selfishness, even in some degree by my profession, I shall always & with anyone have been a bad husband. Unfortunately the disease is also one's material. Cure the disease and I doubt whether a writer would remain.'

Greene's relationship with Walston was partly used as a testing ground in which to explore some of the themes of *The End of the Affair*; the idea of hate as a springboard for love and sin as the seed of virtue and salvation. Greene took it further, writing pornographic short stories to Catherine. In Catherine's personal papers at Georgetown one such work just survives, having been ripped to pieces and then put together again like a jigsaw. It is about a man who decides to put his hand up the skirt of the woman sitting next to him in a cinema; she does not object. Whether this was the reason Greene was always so keen to watch movies with Catherine is unknown (25 September 1962: 'Can we go and see *Lolita* together?'), but it certainly allowed him (at least in his imagination) to examine sin as an unholy paradox, or as Kenneth Tynan put it after interviewing Greene in 1953, 'sin the pleasure-giver, sin the pain-inflictor'.

In Greene's case, the pain he must have caused Vivien is hard to fathom. So many people told me the very opposite, that he had a broadly sympathetic, generous nature. I had read through much of Greene's private correspondence and had come across countless examples. I also had another source of proof – a letter sent to me by Greene in September 1987, following my brief meeting with him in Antibes a few weeks before I started at Cambridge. I was on holiday in the South of France and, having read a piece about Greene's favourite restaurant being Chez Felix au Port in Antibes, I managed to persuade a friend of mine to try it out. It was a crowded Saturday afternoon. Not long after we sat down by the walls of the old port, the stooping figure of Greene, aged eighty-three, suddenly appeared in the doorway. My jaw dropped as my teenage literary idol (as Martin Amis has said, we have been reading Graham Greene all our lives) sank his lanky frame on to the seat next to mine. I can vividly recall his hooded, slightly puffy eyes with bloodshot rims. We sat talking – he complained about the lack of any good bookshops in Antibes – before his mistress, Yvonne Cloetta, finally arrived.

I refused to leave the restaurant until Greene did, so I kept ordering more courses, and more wine. A few days later I returned to the restaurant to find it closed and the port deserted; the season had finished. I left a package, in the care of a cleaning lady, addressed to Graham Greene, c/o Felix au Port, containing a new book I had brought with me on holiday to read (some pages were smeared with Ambre Solaire sun-tan oil): *The New Confessions* by William Boyd. Before sealing up the Jiffy bag, I stuffed in one of my own short stories (about an adulterous summer holiday affair that leads to a violent murder) that I had recently written.

About a fortnight later, on my return to England, I found a typed letter from Greene on his cream notepaper (La Residence des Fleurs, Avenue Pasteur, Antibes). He liked my story 'very much', adding it 'certainly grips the reader' and advising me on how to get it published. 'You will find no difficulty in publishing a collection of these if your novel is a success.' Ah, yes. Greene was now officially God.

But, as I was also aware, he may just have been showing kindness to a young fan seeking literary advice. It wasn't until I read the first volume of Norman Sherry's biography that I realised he really did have a generous nature. In my covering letter I had briefly mentioned that my great-uncle, Wilson Harris MP, had been editor of *The Spectator* when Greene was film critic and later literary editor before the war. What I didn't know was that they had a mutually shared pathological loathing of each other. As Geoffrey Wheatcroft recalled, on the 150th anniversary of *The Spectator*, Greene presented Harris with a gift to mark the occasion: a 'rubber [condom] stuffed with smarties'. On another occasion, when Harris was secretly hoping to be called by the Prime Minister to be offered a job in the government, Greene orchestrated a series of prank calls to *The Spectator*'s offices telling Harris's secretary to 'hold the line' for Number 10. 'Wilson disliked me very much,' Greene told Sherry. 'He objected to the poems I published . . . he took books away from my office to read at weekends and I noticed they were always called *Married Love*, or some such title.'

In fact, in my brief covering letter I unwittingly managed to drag up another personal connection with someone Greene particularly despised – Norman Douglas's biographer Richard Aldington. Greene didn't refer to Harris in his letter to me (although in *The Heart of the Matter* he calls two stuck-up public school bore characters Wilson and Harris) and couldn't have been more generous.

The day after the Mauriac party Greene and Vivien had a serious talk. She was thoroughly fed up with him, and knew how to make him feel guilty. Writing to Catherine from Oxford, he claimed, not entirely convincingly, that he felt suicidal; he was about to investigate his life insurance policy. 'Oh hell! darling. Achill looks like being the only good thing in 1947.' He felt like a cornered rat ('rat', he added, being the correct word). Vivien had agreed to let him have four days' holiday with Catherine in return for clamping his wrists and spending all future weekends at Oxford. 'Am I happy? The answer is definitely negative. I loved seeing you on Tuesday especially, but what the hell is the use? I rather hoped I wouldn't love seeing you. I can't live permanently in handcuffs, so I suppose either the handcuffs will go again, or I shall.'

But Catherine probably knew him well enough by now not to worry about such glum moods. He almost enjoyed such manic-depressive riffs. 'One would laugh if this was a book,' he wrote in the same letter. 'I ought to write funny books. Life is really too horribly funny, but unless one's an outsider looking on, it's all such a bore.'

It is ironic that Catherine should have joked to Greene, the internationally acclaimed novelist, that he had a lot to learn about writing to his mistress. Greene enjoyed such jestful role reversal. He had a subversive romantic streak, and in his heart, although he certainly liked 'experience' in a woman, he remained an idealist; occasionally even a sentimental one. 'Cafrin, I am in love with you. I love you & miss you. Is this how one starts a love letter? I don't know. You're quite right: I don't know how to write one.' But he was learning fast, firing off letters by the day, sometimes several times a day (he would leave the envelope open, for example, and finish it after a Rules lunch).

Their first serious tiff was to come a few days later, in the first week of June. Apparently Bobbie Speaight had been spreading gossip in London about Catherine and Greene being an item. They had already discussed the subject of 'secrecy' and decided there was no point in trying to be neurotically clandestine. Harry didn't seem to mind so long as Greene didn't create an embarrassing scene and jeopordise his would-be political career.

Harry had stood as the Liberal MP for Huntingdon in 1945, but failed to win the seat in the landslide Labour victory. Despite being a multi-millionaire, he had no problem defecting to Labour (he stood unsuccessfully as a Labour MP four times). Harry's political instincts were chameleon, to say the least. Father

Thomas Gilby, the Dominican priest with whom Catherine was involved in the late 1950s and early 1960s – he almost replaced Greene – remarked of him, 'He's a floater. Whatever happens – Communism or anything – he'll float'. Harry had apparently toyed with the idea of first standing as a Conservative. He ended up as a fat-cat millionaire Labour party benefactor in the 1950s, and was made Lord Walston in 1961.

Greene may have secretly encouraged, or at least enjoyed, the London literary salon gossip, so long as it didn't end up in the newspapers. He was proud of having such a glamorous, rich, American mistress, and might have seen society gossip as a possible means of bringing the increasingly strained situation between himself, Dorothy and Vivien to a head.

By June 1947, his head was fogged up and he couldn't decide what to do about the slow pulling-back of the rat-trap spring. He tried to play the 'let's be very adult' card. Better to 'walk out' on each other before things became too serious, he wrote to Catherine, because 'after all you made no promise of secrecy' after he had rashly told her that he was in love with her. 'My dear, it was good while it lasted & I wish it could have lasted a little longer. I shall miss Achill & Thriplow & St James's Street & Rules but in another month or two I'd have missed these twice as much.' He wasn't going to post the letter until the next day as he might change his mind. He didn't. 'What a bloody waste it all is.'

Greene immersed himself in work to divert his mind from Catherine. She returned his keys (for which house is unclear; Greene had no London flat of his own, and was still living with Dorothy in Gordon Square, and one can't imagine he had given her a set for Beaumont Street). He tied himself up with meetings with director Carol Reed and producer Alexander Korda, discussing the film adaptation of his story, *The Basement Room*. It was released in 1948 as *The Fallen Idol*, starring Ralph Richardson, Greene's own one-time idol with whom he was later to fall out. But not even the film rights cheque for £3,000 could raise his wretched and 'dreary' spirits. He still refused to believe that Catherine loved him, putting it down to self-deception on her behalf.

Greene had a habit of writing letters that were exercises in personal therapy. He would write fast; the more truthful he became, the more illegible his writing. The only solution, he scrawled, was 'to tell the whole truth' to Vivien. After taking this 'action', he would report back to Catherine on 'the end of the affair', for her interest. Here, the phrase that became the title – after much deliberation with Catherine – of his 1951 novel about the failed adulterous affair between Bendrix and Sarah, is used by Greene in the context of the final failure of his marriage. There is a whiff of romanticised self-pity about this first drawing-room drama attempt to break off with Catherine. He began to sound like a scrap of Terence Rattigan dialogue, rescued from his Brighton waste-paper bin. 'Well, my darling,' Greene wrote, 'you may as well have these letters. I think they are quite sensible. I expect this is the end. If it is you've given me the best morphine I've ever had. Thank you. Thank God, anyway that there's somebody I can't hurt.'

Just in case Catherine actually made the mistake of believing every word Greene wrote, he added as a post-script on the back of the envelope: 'Many happy returns to Oliver' (her ten-year-old-son). A strange way, one might think, to sign off on a failed affair.

The black clouds soon passed over Beaumont Street. On 11 June 1947, Catherine received a telegram at St James's Street: 'BOOK FINISHED THANK GOD LOTS OF LOVE GRAHAM.'

Not long afterwards, Catherine set off back to Achill. She was seeing Ernie again.

This is just a note to pursue you as quickly as possible to Achill & to remind you of three things – that I'm still terribly in love with you. That I miss you (your voice saying 'good morning Graham' at tea-time) & that I want you. I want to be filling up your turf bucket for you and writing next-door working . . . & I want to help you make bread. I am thirsty for orange juice at 3 in the morning. I want to see you in your pyjama top nursing the wood of the fire. Now I pin a lot of hope on India. It might be a way of being with you for 3 months and by God I'd get into your skin before the time was over. I kiss you, my dear, here – here – and there.

Graham

P.S. Have I written a love letter?

★

The summer of 1947 was as memorably hot as the frozen winter had been cold. Greene was in love; but he also felt on the rack. His guilt over Vivien he could cope with. Just. Dorothy was another matter. Although Greene and Catherine had privately agreed not to 'disguise' their relationship, they were careful not to go too far. When Greene was invited down to Brighton in July 1947 to the set of the Boultings Brothers' production of *Brighton Rock*, based on his acclaimed novel of 1938, his rather dumpy looking female companion was introduced to the director and crew as Dorothy Craigie. That was the pseudonym Dorothy Glover used as the illustrator of the dust jackets of children's books.

Unlike with Vivien, he seemed to be generous with her. When they wrote *The Little Fire Engine* (1950), which Dorothy had illustrated, Greene's agent Laurence Pollinger was mildly surprised, to say the least, when his top client informed him that he wanted all royalties to be made into the bank account of a Miss Craigie. Greene even went so far as to try to slip out of a lucrative three-book-option film contract with MGM by offering them *The Little Fire Engine* as a possible 'cartoon' film project. The studio had paid him a handsome retainer and were expecting a thriller treatment in the style of *The Third Man*. When Greene tried to off-load a *Thomas the Tank Engine*-style children's book, MGM's lawyers were not amused.

The hotel used by Greene for weekends in Brighton with both Dorothy and Catherine was the Albion, on the sea-front, by the end of the pier. Greene would go there when he was 'blocked'. Writing to Catherine in 1969 – their affair long over – Greene remained nostalgic for their days together there. 'They are ruining the town with sky-scraper flats, most of the machines on the pier don't work & the whole place is going to seed . . . except for the Cricketers [pub] and the Star and Garter, (and they are pulling that down) . . .'

Joining a coach tour, advertised in the *London Review of Books*, of Graham Greene's 'Brighton Rock', I found the same fate (or at least a major face-lift) awaited the Albion. The building had been gutted in a fire; the walls were boarded up; the sea-facing balcony suite where Greene used to write has been replaced with giant chipboard windows and scaffolding. Another relic to be sold off, refurbished, pulled down, smashed by an iron ball swinging from a crane. Opposite was a phone box, its walls plastered with prostitute business cards. Grey sea-gulls flew indifferently overhead.

During 1947, the production offices of *Brighton Rock* were also on the sea-front at the Grand. This is probably where Greene would have taken Dorothy. As he introduced her to the crew, an unfortunate piece of bad luck occurred. Dorothy and Greene had been forced to move from their flat in Mecklenburgh Square in Bloomsbury during the Blitz, when it turned out that the female warden in charge of the local air-raid shelter was the wife of Wilson Harris. My great aunt was a prim and starchy woman who would have been appalled to learn that Greene, who had a wife and children in Oxford, was secretly living with his London mistress. This time, it turned out that one of the make-up artists working on *Brighton Rock* had previously worked at the cheap hotel near Paddington Station where Greene first took Dorothy. She immediately recognised her and began to spread gossip around the set that Dorothy was Greene's illicit lover. Again they were forced to leave in a hurry before they became the object of a scandal.

It was a sure sign that all was not well between Dorothy and Greene in 1947 when he moved his suitcase out of Glover's flat at Gordon Square and stayed in temporary digs at the Authors' Club off Whitehall Court. Through Evelyn Waugh, Greene later became a member of White's, a few door's down from his flat in St James's Street, but resigned as he never went there. He once said that he liked the Authors' Club, as it was the sort of club where members had ripped out pages from *Who's Who*. In *The End of the Affair* it is clearly the model for the 'seedy' establishment, with paintings of Conan Doyle and Stanley Weyman hanging on the wall, where Bendrix invites Henry Miles to a 'hideous' lunch (ordering a Vienna steak, 'somehow he managed to ram the pink soggy mixture down') to inform him that he has hired Mr Parkis, a private detective, to keep Henry's wife, Sarah, under surveillance. Henry had confided in Bendrix a few weeks before that he was worried that Sarah may have been having an affair. That had been on the 'black wet January night' in 1946 at the Pontefract Arms on Clapham Common.

'I have always felt at home in the club because there is so little likelihood of running into a fellow writer,' says Bendrix. One can only speculate as to why Greene moved into the Author's Club in the summer of 1947; certainly his new passion for Mrs Walston had soured relations between himself and Dorothy, a relationship that had been kicking along for over seven years. And the flat at 18 Gordon Square was fairly cramped. Dorothy rented it cheaply during the war because it was on the top floor, and an obvious bomb hazard.

Just before 6pm on a Wednesday in late September, I pressed the buzzer of the top-floor flat to try and have a look round. The square is a short walk from Euston Station, No. 18 being one of a row of houses converted into various departments of the London University. A heap of rubbish, broken eggs and cardboard boxes in black plastic bags stood in the doorway.

A middle-aged woman's voice answered.

Could I see the flat? I explained the reason for my interest.

'I never let Graham Greene in, you know,' she said. 'I was in the bath, you see. It was about ten years ago . . . it wasn't long after that he died.'

'Sorry?'

Listening through the bashed-up old intercom, she said that Greene himself had pressed the buzzer of the flat back in the 1980s (she couldn't be exactly certain of the date – on a Sunday afternoon in the autumn, she thought).

Looking out of her top-floor window, she saw a tall, stooping, elderly man in glasses standing on the doorstep in an old Burberry-style raincoat (Greene usually bought them from Aquascutum in Regent Street, but switched to Burberry's, next-door, after Aquascutum refused to take a personal cheque from him without a card). Standing naked in her hallway, she told Greene that she was 'busy'. He thanked her anyway, and walked away.

Greene often revisited the haunts and scenes of his earlier life in order to recharge his memory's creative batteries. That, in his late seventies or eighties, he was meandering on his own around Bloomsbury and Tottenham Court Road, gives an indication of how important Dorothy Glover was to Greene. He once told Vivien that she was one of the great loves of his life. When she died in the early 1970s, he wrote to Catherine to say that he was devastated. Indeed, prior to her death he had gone out of his way to ask Catherine to help her out.

Thankfully, when I pressed the Gordon Square buzzer, the middle-aged tenant was fully clothed. She let me in. As I walked up the stairs, it struck me as a deep shame that she had been in the bath when Greene called. Had he walked up the first flight of stairs, he would surely have laughed to see the sign on the door: 'Department of Scandinavian Studies', along with a tourist poster of Stockholm. Stockholm was to play a major part in Greene's life in the mid- to late 1950s when he was seriously involved with the Swedish actress Anita Bjork, a relationship that was to cause the president of the Nobel Prize committee to remark, allegedly, that Greene would get the Nobel Prize for literature 'over my dead body'.

The flat was now rented out – free – to the maintenance manager of the London University properties around Gordon

Square. There was a small sitting-room, with a large TV set switched on, a computer game library in the kitchen/office, a pile of washing up in the sink; upstairs were two small attic bedrooms and a storage-room full of junk. It seemed odd to think that it was in this flat – somewhere in an old cupboard – that Dorothy used to hide Greene's trousers after sex so that he couldn't leave; the same happens to Scobie in *The Heart of the Matter*. The small attic bedroom was where Dorothy burnt Greene's hand with her cigarettes.

Back in Oxford on the last weekend of June 1946, Greene agreed to subject himself to being dragged off on a visit to Badminton House, home of the Duke of Beaufort, for a 'Georgian Group' tour. Flies invaded their country picnic. Greene was irritable and bored. 'One needs to be in love to enjoy that sort of thing,' he wrote to Catherine. 'I am beginning to positively hate beautiful houses and beautiful furniture.' Thinking alone to himself on the way back to Oxford, he felt determined to get a few days' 'happiness'. With the novel done, he resolved to pursue Catherine to Ireland; pursue her, and work on his *Fallen Idol* film script. 'Cafryn, dear', he wrote that night, 'I want to kiss you, touch you, make love to you – & simply sit in a car, be driven by you.' He also mentioned that he had been sorting through his drawers and happened to come across the first letter that she had ever sent him from Achill starting, 'Dear Godfather' and ending, 'yours sincerely, Catherine Walston'. Why had he kept it? Greene pondered. 'These are mysteries.'

In addition to being paid handsomely, working for Alexander Korda had other benefits. When all flights and ferries to Dublin were, apparently, sold out, Greene managed to get Korda to swing two seats on an American Overseas plane to Shannon airport (doubtless he assured him the 'peace' of Ireland would be helpful with the writing of the script). Korda arranged to send a car to Eyre and Spottiswoode at 2.45pm sharp and Greene should be in Shannon at 5.30pm. 'Will I really see you there?' wrote Greene in the undergraduate-in-love manner he used to write obsessively to Vivien in the 1920s. 'Where shall we spend the night? In sleeping bags on a turf field – or in Galway city? I won't care a damn. But *do* be there.'

Officially – presumably what Greene had told Vivien and Dorothy – he was away in Holland doing publicity. He began to cross off the days, and was now so obsessed with Catherine that he claimed he could only read poetry when he knew he was shortly going to see her. 'Now I'm going to see you again, I take poetry down again and it throws its stones at me, to make me ache for you,' he wrote.

Pulling out a volume from his shelf at Beaumont Street, he quoted:

> *Long roads and strong ditches*
> *And here's to nice girls*
> *And to hell with riches*

'This Oxford business isn't working,' he added in a manic letter to Catherine, with just five days to go before he saw her. He indulged in a fantasy about taking her off to Romania and living for months and years. Intoxicated, he quoted Yeats to her:

> *One careless look on me she flung*
> *As bright as parting day;*
> *And like a hawk from covert sprung*
> *It pounced my peace away*

Switching to the Irish poet J.M. Synge, Greene introduced the aspect of religious guilt, jealousy, and sexual possession that was to brand their love:

> *Now by this window when there's none can see*
> *The Lord God's jealous of yourself and me*

'Cafryn, I'm so much in love,' Greene ended. Under his name (he usually preferred to end his letters simply 'Graham';

occasionally it would be 'your husband Graham', or 'your lover Graham'), he added: 'Is *this* a love letter? You are going to be so involved soon, you won't want another soul. You are in love & I'm in love & we are going to meet Thursday.'

may i borrow your wife?

'Let's have more than a fortnight,' Greene urged Catherine before their second visit to Ireland in July 1947. 'Do you remember how cautious we were the first time against deciding on more than a week?' And after finishing *The Heart of the Matter*, Greene wrote to say, 'I want to begin the next book with you in Ireland – if possible at Achill.'

The next book, which he referred to as his 'I' book or the 'Great Sex Novel' was to become *The End of the Affair*. But, importantly, he did not say he wanted to *set* the novel in Ireland. This is partly because Greene's time there with Catherine was to become sacred for him. He didn't want it sullied by public exposure; it became part of his 'private universe', a phrase used by Greene to describe Henry James's 'religious aspect' in a penetrating essay on James, from whose classical prose technique he learned much. When Greene wrote to Catherine from Canada to say that he wouldn't be including in *110 Airports* the experience of her hair falling into his face in the plane from Cambridge, it was partly for this reason. It was just too private.

Greene had been happy to help Catherine's poet/IRA general friend Ernie O'Malley with introductions in London. Had he known that Catherine had rented her cottage in Achill to be close to O'Malley's family house on the northern coastal road to

Westport, he might have been more reluctant to get his address book out.

Burrishoole is just a few miles from the eighteenth-century sea-port town of Newport, about fifteen miles from Achill Sound. Hanging in the Georgian marble hallway of the charming Newport House Hotel (where Catherine and Greene used to dine) are two framed black and white photos of Grace Kelly, wearing Chanel shades, and Prince Rainier of Monaco, who stayed at the country-house hotel in the late 1950s. In April 1956, Greene and Catherine booked rooms at the Hotel de Paris in Monaco in order to watch their royal wedding; not as VIP guests, but as spectators joining the thronging crowds that lined the streets. As a special holiday treat, they had taken along Catherine's thirteen-year-old son Oliver, a pimpled Etonian who was besotted with the blonde American actress. Since the princess's 'fairy-tale' wedding, and tragic death, it has greatly helped the Newport tourist industry to note that Grace Kelly's ancestors came from the nearby village of Drimurla.

But for the locals themselves, the ancestry they are most proud of is their connection with the legendary sixteenth-century pirate queen Grace O'Malley, a sort of mythical Irish Boudica figure, whose second husband, Richard Burke (known as 'Iron Dick'), built the solitary and beautiful Burrishoole Abbey, whose ruins stand on the east bank of the river that drains Lough Furnace. Just across the water from Ernie O'Malley's house, it is down a single track road.

Referring to Achill in a letter to Catherine whilst on his depressing trip to Ireland with Dorothy, Greene wrote: 'I miss bread-making, candles, motor licenses, graveyards . . . more than I can say.' Catherine and Greene would almost certainly have visited the ruined abbey, and it is the first thing she would have seen from her bedroom window when she was staying with Ernie.

The desolate medieval ruins, surrounded by their broken-walled graveyard, are among the most beautifully 'peaceful' – the word that Greene used to symbolise Achill – and remote settings on the west coast of Ireland. As the drops of rain fell on the slate-grey water, on the ruined cloisters, medieval tombstones, and overgrown graveyard – including the tomb of the Achill priest who was executed for talking to the French troops at Newport in 1798 – one cannot but be struck by its still, quietly intense, romantic grandeur.

As a boy I was obsessed with Arthurian literature. The ruined Irish abbey at Burrishoole, with its rusted iron gate, crumbling Celtic crosses and wildly overgrown dark tufts of grass, comes the closest to my image of where one might find the mythical Lady of the Lake. With the fading afternoon light falling across the murky green surrounding water, it is – as Greene said – the sort of place you want to see when you are in love.

I wanted to stop off briefly at Burrishoole on the way to Achill to illustrate an important point about Greene's experience there. The west coast of Ireland was an exhilarating romantic adventure for Greene. The third verse of the love poem, 'After Two Years', describes the almost metaphysically sexual and 'religious' communion between them that began in April 1947 and refers to the importance of Achill in Greene's imagination:

I who learned Ireland first from you

He was being taught about a new place, by a beautiful American, and he discovered new vistas in both his heart and his imagination. Shortly after his return to London from Achill in August 1947, he admitted to Catherine: 'Ireland is breaking in on me irresistibly.' He had tramped across Liberia to write *Journey Without Maps*; he had travelled across forbidding borders whilst in Mexico to write *The Lawless Roads*; but it was in Achill that he felt himself journeying – in his early forties, and perhaps for the first time in his life – into that dangerously uncharted territory for the creative man of high intelligence who marries too young: adult love.

After returning from their second Achill trip, he wrote: 'Catherine dear, I long to have you lazily stretched on an Achill sofa with a book & a pencil and interrupt you every ten minutes with something I want to talk about & every twelve minutes I was in love. How it makes me hate the *smell* of other people.' Achill saw the beginning of the affair, but it was also the reason for its continuation, as Greene discloses in a letter written from St James's Street on Friday 24 September, 1949: 'Somehow I feel an awful reluctance and ache of heart when I address the envelope to Achill. That was where we began [. . .] we probably would never have done more than begin if we hadn't had these weeks, but only an odd couple of days in England [. . .] I wish I could make you feel, not just by faith, how missed you are the moment the door closes and how life begins when the door opens.'

Ireland as a whole was opened up to Greene by Catherine as they explored the west coast in her old Ford, driving from pub to pub, church to church, up to Galway, Westport and Shannon. Greene seems to have had a deeply sentimental affection for her old car. On their first romantic journey together from Shannon airport to Achill, Catherine had turned to Greene, taking her hand from the wheel, and said, 'You know, I don't *like* being driven by somebody I haven't slept with.'

It was a typical Catherine remark, and Greene was to quote it back to her approvingly in a subsequent letter. He would write saying that he longed to be driven by her; that he longed to be just looking out of the window, watching nothing in particular as the Ford bumped along; and to 'annoy' her by saying whatever leapt into his mind.

Whilst the Achill Greene was shown by Catherine was freshly intoxicating, like a new emotional cocktail that caused a delirious hangover for months, for Catherine it was more like a bed that had been shared with other lovers. Catherine didn't just choose a cottage in Achill because it was a pretty coastal spot (the cottage was rented for about twenty shillings a month by her rather than Harry); it became the place to which she liked to take her men. Vivien Greene described a chat she once had with a priest at Ampleforth (where her son Francis was educated), when he let slip that Catherine Walston (whose son

David also attended the school) had invited one of the monks on holiday to the west coast of Ireland – not such a strange occurrence at the old-fashioned Benedictine public schools.

But in Mrs Walston's case it wasn't that straightforward. Vivien informed the priest, 'It's only a small cottage you know, it'll just be him and her alone.' After this information, the Ampleforth priest 're-considered' the invitation.

Certainly, anybody who had visited the Walstons' luxurious Thriplow, with its 'more bathrooms than bedrooms' as Waugh had noted, sliding panels and Arab stud, or later the grandeur of Newton Hall, would have been startled by the contrast with Catherine's cottage in Ireland. When Cormac O'Malley visited Newton Hall, he experienced a vast difference between his childhood home in Ireland with no electricity and indoor plumbing. 'I had to walk an hour and a half to get the drinking water . . . to go from that to a 3,000-acre farm where there was a cook . . . and there was the Bentley and the chauffeur and a children's wing in the upstairs floor of this mansion and a German governess. It was mindblowing.' Catherine felt just the opposite, and Achill's primitiveness appealed to Greene as well. Whilst in Hamburg in 1950, Greene yearned for the quiet that Achill afforded him: 'I so long for somewhere like Achill or Capri where there are no telephones,' he wrote.

In addition Catherine's cottage had – and still has – no address. When I arrived in the last few days of summer, and crossed the bridge at Achill Sound, I had no idea where to start looking. All I had to go on was the name of a village on an envelope from the Black Box that Greene had written in 1947: 'Mrs Harry Walston, Dooagh, Achill, Co. Mayo'.* The one-line entry in the *Blue Guide to Ireland* was not promising. 'W. of Keel is the village of Dooagh, with workshops of the St Colman knitting industry.' The guide added a warning: 'Below lies Keem Bay with its deserted coastguard station. On the S. side of the mountain amethysts are found: on the N.W. sheer and overhanging cliffs rise 1,950 ft above the sea and care should be taken when nearing the edge.'

It was getting dark by the time I drove through Keel, having travelled across Ireland from Dublin. Being the end of the season all the cars had been going the other way. When the task of finding somewhere – anywhere – to eat in the sleepy fishing village proved tricky, I became even more gloomy about the chance of finding a nameless old crofter's cottage the following day. As I entered the village of Dooagh, a line of new ugly, modern, white holiday bungalows sprawled along the winding coastal road. Most looked empty, and were built in what is known as the 'non-traditional' style (i.e. concrete), in an attempt to lure summer holiday-makers. I read in a copy of the summer 1999 *Achill Island Journal*: 'For many years (since the Great Famine), we have lived in the shadow of failure and disappointment. The holiday home building boom which has taken place over the last couple of years is a mixed blessing. It is great to have top quality holiday accommodation, but what do you do when you have too much?'

Catherine's old place had probably been knocked down years ago, I thought, or else turned into an £18-a-night bed and breakfast with knotted-pine double-beds from the Westport discount furniture warehouse and a white plastic tea-making machine in the bedroom. Norman Sherry's description did not offer much hope either: 'The cottage at Achill had a corrugated roof, no running water and only a cold tap outside.' There was one other detail. In a letter to Catherine, Greene referred to hearing the swinging of a rusty 'broken gate' at night. No Greene biography contained a photo of the cottage, although Sherry includes a snap of Greene, in his Achill knitted sweater, sitting on the sand at Keem beach, watching the fisherman dragging in their nets.

I stayed at Joyce's Marian Villa (the Metropole of B&Bs along the sea-front) in Keel; everywhere in Dooagh looked closed. The one local restaurant still serving past 9pm had a novelty form of wine list: a few bottles from the local Spar were displayed on a table as you walked in, with the supermarket prices still attached. It also had a gift shop where I bought an island map. Before going to bed, I dropped in for a drink at the one place in

Dooagh that was still very much open – 'The Pub', located directly opposite the rocky beach where oarsman Don Allum landed his boat on shore after being the first man to row the Atlantic in both directions.

It was 10.45 on a Friday night and the locals – old fishermen, ex-sharkers, unemployed builders, Achill salmon-mongers, B & B owners – were in festive mood. As I felt in my pocket for my notebook, I was reminded for one uneasy moment of that wonderful 1973 horror film *The Wicker Man*, about a mainland policeman (Edward Woodward) who flies to a remote isle to investigate the mysterious death of a child. After asking too many questions in the local pub (where Britt Ekland is the barmaid), and witnessing a nymphomaniac nude fertility dance, he ends up becoming the victim of a pagan sacrifice, burnt alive with pigs inside a vast pyre on top of a high cliff-top overlooking the Atlantic.

After ordering a Guinness, I began talking to the oldest people I could see. I was looking for somebody of at least eighty. Holding court at a table by the bar, wearing a thick brown cardigan and with a wad of lavatory paper sticking out of a cut ear, was a wizened old character called Paddy Kelly. He wore thick glasses that had been repaired with tape, and his remaining tufts of wiry white hair badly needed brushing down. His veined nose suggested he had always enjoyed a drink. When I mentioned the name 'Catherine Walston' his watery old eyes lit up.

'I knew Mrs Walston indeed,' he said. 'She was a fine woman indeed. A real lady. Wonderful gait. I used to push her car when she ran out of petrol. Always ran out of petrol . . .'

Back in the 1940s, it turned out that Paddy Kelly – who also used to work at the Achill Basking Shark Fishery – operated the old single petrol pump in Dooagh, when petrol was strictly rationed. It was just opposite the pub. Mrs Walston liked to drive, and had plenty of money, so one expects they came to some kind of an agreeable arrangement (aged eighty-five, Paddy still has a sharp head for business). He told me that he once played bar billiards – 'just there', he said, pointing in front of us –

with Graham Greene. Greene wasn't any good. Paddy had thought he just came up to Achill for 'writing holidays'. He 'did well', somebody once told him.

'What did they do?' I asked.

'Kept to themselves,' he said, adding, 'If I'd known what was going on indeed I might have fallen out with her. Not given her the petrol.'

'Where was her cottage?'

'Up the road, over the little bridge, first house on your left.'

'Is it still there?'

'Bein' knocked down, I think. There's a new bungalow next to it now.'

It was too dark to look. The next morning, after a walk along the deserted, stony, shingle beach at Keel (Keem is further up the island) I went to investigate. I parked by the side of the road next to a hideous new grey-white stucco bungalow. Set behind it, across what looked like a builder's rubbish site, stood a crumbling traditional Achill seaman's cottage with a sloping grey-slate roof; many slates had been blown off by the fierce Atlantic winds but it was certainly not made of corrugated iron. The cottage stood about fifty yards from the stony beach in a patch of weeds, nettles and overgrown grass.

There was no longer a gate; just some loose rusty wire fencing. An ugly blue gas cylinder sat hunched by the wreck of a front porch, the white paint so badly flaked off it revealed the rotten plaster beneath like a lacerated septic wound. The cobweb-matted outer windows of the grey porch were broken. Ripped sacks of cement were piled up against one wall, an old rusty mixer standing neglected in the weeds, along with pieces of torn-up plaster board, cigarette boxes and abandoned sections of pipe. The outside walls were the colour and texture of lumpy grey porridge.

Seagulls squalled and circled overhead. The late August morning sky was a moody, mackerel grey. I had reached what had once been Greene's equivalent of Dove Cottage, only to find it was a squalid wreck. Whilst the ruins of nearby Burrishoole

Abbey now stand peacefully still, its fifteenth-century stone foundations threatened only by the lapping tide, Catherine's Dooagh cottage – where Greene had written parts of *The Heart of the Matter* and *The Fallen Idol* – was soon to be visited by a local council bulldozer. No longer to exist as a literary relic or curiosity, in the future it would only inhabit the imagination. As Bendrix says when, sentimentally, he revisits Arbuckle Avenue, where he first took Sarah after dinner at Rules: 'Half of it was gone – the half where the hotels used to stand had been blasted to bits, and the place where we had made love that night was a patch of air.'

But poetry, at least good poetry, is as much a physical experience as an imaginative one – one should *feel* one is holding a delicate Sèvres jar, not just thinking about one – and the second verse of 'After Two Years' reveals the paradoxical nature of the truths revealed to Greene after making love to Catherine on the bare cottage floor, in front of the turf fire:

> *In a plane your hair was blown,*
> *And in an island the old car*
> *Lingered from inn to inn,*
> *Like a fly on a map.*
> *A mattress was spread on a cottage floor*
> *And a door closed on a world, but another door*
> *Opened, and I was far*
> *From the old world sadly known*
> *Where the fruitless seeds were sown,*
> *And they called* that *virtue and* this *sin*
> *Did I ever love God before I knew the place*
> *I rest in now, now with my hand*
> *Set in stone, never to move?*
> *For this is love, and this I love,*
> *And even my God is here.*

I knocked on the door of Catherine's replacement stucco bungalow. A washing line of faded old jeans, t-shirts and sheets blew in the back-garden. A dog barked. The cheap caravan-like aluminium door handle turned. Annie O'Donnell – the old owner of the abandoned cottage, and now its nearest neighbour – took me over to the filthy entrance porch, which led to an unlocked front door. In the hall was a very dead pot plant, its thin branches stretched out like a withering old bamboo cane. Walking into the cottage, I had to immediately run out again: the rancid stench of damp, moulding, rotting furniture and walls made me retch.

The place in which Greene and Catherine had hooked up a turf bucket above the fire, and cooked eggs in a pan, and made bread, was now an abandoned squat.

In a new cottage about a hundred yards up the road lives Mary Gielty, the daughter of the former owner of the Clew Bay Hotel, a three-minute walk from Catherine's cottage. Ernie O'Malley and Catherine often used to sit up late drinking at the bar there.

'I know it was shots,' Mary said. 'I know it was whiskey because I tell you we didn't sell much of it then because the locals would drink pints because they wouldn't have the money for whiskey.'

She wasn't just the bargirl at the Clew Bay Hotel; in the morning she also cleaned the rooms.

'Where would Ernie and Catherine go after their drinks?'

'Well,' she said, '. . . he would stay in the cottage with her.'

'What did you think?'

'I suppose we were very innocent here then and we just thought they were good friends and that was it. He was well known to be a ladies' man, Ernie O'Malley.' She added, 'They're going to knock down that house, which is a shame.'

'Why was it allowed to get into such a bad state?'

'It's not an old house, it's a good solid building, but they just let it go, you know, they didn't do any repairs on it for years. Carelessness probably . . . they didn't want to spend the money.'

Mary said she didn't remember Greene 'at all'. Indeed, when I was in Achill, several elderly locals remembered Mrs Walston but spoke of her as O'Malley's companion rather than Greene's. Greene was far from being any sort of fool, and it wasn't long before he twigged what was – or certainly had been – going on between Ernie and Catherine. Ernie was seven years older than Greene; he turned fifty on 26 May 1947.

But it took Greene a long time to shrug off his pose of indifference, pretending to act like a man of the world who didn't care who she slept with. Writing to Catherine in early 1958, Greene revealed a real sense of loss about the state of their affair (each had had numerous other lovers by this time). A few days before, she had called Greene, and he had cried afterwards in the bath. On 15 January 1958, he wrote: 'There's been no release only sadness. I think the answer is quite simple. I think that you are so lovely and so nice that I was always afraid of losing you – even the first times on Achill, I was jealous of Ernie. I'm sorry. It's the way I am.'

When Greene returned to England in August after the second Achill trip, he became entangled in a bizarre triangle concerning a woman he referred to as the 'Mystery Girl' whom he first met through Peader O'Donnell, an old friend of Ernie. She was an Irish Catholic widow, former secretary to Herbert Read, with two children; in Greene's eyes she would normally have been ripe for a casual affair. 'Very lustrous and slightly wrong in the teeth & in accent,' wrote Greene. Only she was expecting 'Ernie' over soon from Ireland; O'Malley had invited her on holiday to Aran. Greene was taking her to lunch the following week. Of course, all of this amounted to no more than a veiled threat to suggest to Catherine that if he couldn't see *her*, he could have whom he wanted elsewhere. However, he admitted that, if the lights 'dimmed', he didn't think he could actually go through with it with Peader's Mystery Girl. Although, Greene added, it would be 'fun to cuckold Ernie'.

Greene went on to say that the Mystery Girl was going over to Ireland in September and had 'wondered whether I might not be over too', but he 'regretfully' declined. 'I feel this will give you another good laugh over your peaches and cream', Greene ended, adding the jab, 'It would be nice however if Ernie would be supplied with a bedfellow & not bother anybody else.'

As I drove along the empty coast road towards Westport, past Burrishoole Abbey, and on towards the Old Head Hotel at Louisburgh, I began to realise why the Achill locals remembered Ernie O'Malley rather than Greene.

To become a legend in Ireland, Ernie not only had to be a leader of the 1916 Easter uprising, he also had to be shot to pieces, jailed, and endure a forty-six-day hunger strike. Playing around on the Berkhamsted Common with a starting pistol loaded with blanks isn't quite the same. Greene could keep up a tough pace with Gurkhas on a march, but he was never any sort of romantic soldier-rebel. He may have been an intellectual revolutionary at heart, but he couldn't stand the sight of real human blood (a Greene family trait). Greene knew he had every reason to be wary of Catherine and Ernie; the former IRA general, and author of *On Another Man's Wound*, was the real thing.

One of Greene's most serious fantasies of the late 1940s (in addition to walking across Ireland with Catherine and dragging her off to Romania) was of retiring from writing books, marrying Catherine and them both buying the Old Head Hotel, just outside Louisburgh. Yet, as with Achill, Catherine had first been introduced to this beautifully located old-fashioned Irish country-house hotel by Ernie O'Malley. When Ernie was first married in 1935, his family house was on a little cliff overlooking the silver-sand beach at Old Head.

Ernie's son, Cormac O'Malley, remembered the Old Head as being a quaint, run-down, relaxing sort of place, 'relatively spartan, things were not prim and proper, they were just nice and dowdy, but you could get your sandwiches and walk out'. When they lived at Burrishoole they would sail over Clew Bay for lunch. The hotel wasn't grand, but very comfortable in a slightly down-at-heel way.

Below it lay one of the most romantic beaches of the west coast. Guests could walk down to the sea through the landscaped garden in only a few minutes. In the late 1940s and 1950s, the hotel was run by an English character called Alec Wallace, a renowned Byzantine scholar and authority on the early Greek alphabet. Regular guests in the summer included the Poet Laureate Cecil Day-Lewis, along with his young son, Daniel Day-Lewis. The bar was excellent, with Wallace holding court every night on Irish poetry, arts, history and politics, into the early hours.

In *On Another Man's Wound*, O'Malley's brilliant Irish Revolutionary memoirs, he evoked the lyrical magic of growing up against such a backdrop, a gritty love of the sombre, grey-black, craggy beauty of the Atlantic west coast that he passed on to Catherine, who in turn 'taught' Greene. As Professor English put it, the 'rapture of the sea and the lyrical depiction of the Irish countryside were to be important themes in the O'Malleys' world, and their roots lay in these childhood experiences':

> In rain or sun we loved this country; its haunting impersonal bareness, its austerity, aloofness, small lakes, the dispropor-tionate bulking of the mountains, smells of shrivelled seaweed rotting in grey dirt-spume, brine, storm-wood, tarred rope and riggings, sea-wrack, and mud after an ebb tide . . . Our life was ringed by the Bay; it was a huge world to us.
>
> [*On Another Man's Wound*]

Greene's own equivalent of this imaginative ring of water was, of course, the brick-walled garden of Harston House, just a few miles from Thriplow, where he had spent his summers play-ing in the garden; mapping out hidden paths ('Wild Walk'), spying on croquet matches, and hiding in the potting shed. But Edwardian kitchen gardens and the memory of serving ice-cream to soldiers heading off to the trenches of World War I was pretty tame stuff compared to the rich grandeur of the imagina-tive world evoked by the crashing Atlantic that sprayed the rocks around Achill and Westport.

After being with Catherine in Ireland, it's easy to see why

places such as the Old Head came to rest like stones on the bed
of the 'Cousteau-like' underwater world that Greene felt they
had created together. Ireland not only inspired him to write
some of his best poetry, it also forged open depths to his creative
imagination in a way that was never matched by the places that
were to became later symbols of their love: the Paris Ritz; the
Hassler Hotel above the Spanish Steps in Rome; Florians in St
Mark's Square in Venice; his beloved Rosaio villa in Capri, along
with Gemma's restaurant and the Capri to Naples boat.

Writing to Thriplow in 1949, on Monday 11 April at 8.45am,
Greene was suddenly overcome by the realisation of the contrast
between what was simple, and for that reason fundamental, in
Achill, and the fake experience of staying in luxury hotels: 'and
now in the middle of shaving I'm overwhelmed with a longing
for Achill, when I first began really to love you, and whitewash
and the Atlantic smell and candle and peat and the broken gate.
For 18 months we've only been together in "luxury hotels" and
now I begin to feel we are doomed to them. Achill means more
sentimentally perhaps to me than you, simply because it's associated only with you: hotels seem to be associated with all the
other people who have stayed in them.'

I planned to stay the night at the Old Head Hotel. Driving
towards the ramshackle town of Louisburgh, the coastal road
passes through desolate moorland and peat bogs. The tiny town
is unusual as being one of the few examples of a town on this
side of the Atlantic named after its American counterpart.
Following a traditional white road sign pointing to 'Old Head',
I turned off the Westport road, along a narrow lane that dipped
down and around towards the sea. To the left was a drive leading
to a large country house. Beside it was a sign: 'Old Head Luxury
Holiday Apartments'.

I parked outside a large Georgian-looking white stone house.
There were no other cars. The hotel had been closed for years.
It had been converted into flats, and the exercise did not look to
have been a complete success. The only part of the hotel in use
was a bar – not the original bar – in a new annexe that doubled

up as a disco. The old bar area had been knocked down to build a dining-room. The fireplace had been boarded up, and was surrounded by pink wallpaper. Above it were two kitsch purple china jugs and some garishly gold-framed prints of ducks. The dining-room tables stood empty, dust gathering in the small wine glasses. There hadn't been a wedding for years. There had been no calls for a 2000 New Year's Eve party.

Nobody had any objection to me walking around to see the old rooms of the original hotel that Greene had dreamt of buying up and retiring to. I couldn't quite imagine him setting *May I Borrow Your Wife, And Other Comedies of the Sexual Life* in Westport, but who knows?

After I got up early the next morning to walk along the beach at The Old Head, I began to understand why Ernie played such an important role in the early phase of Greene's affair with Catherine. The letter of 1958 about Greene being 'jealous' of Ernie does not simply refer to sexual jealousy. By Cormac O'Malley's own admission, his father did not have a high sex drive (indeed, Cormac is sceptical of whether they had an affair at all). It was more a jealousy of his experiences.

Ireland was a key link between Catherine and the underworld of Greene's subconscious. Small things such as Catherine's 'red dressing gown' and his 'Achill sweater' took on a major symbolic importance that he returned to in letter after letter as their affair was swept into more dangerous and stormy waters.

After the second Irish trip in the summer of 1947 – Catherine gave him a present of a Cuala Press limited edition of Frank O'Connor – Greene wrote to her incessantly about how Ireland had affected him and his creative imagination. When Greene got back to London he gave the manuscript of *The Heart of the Matter* to his friend John Hayward, whose opinion he greatly respected, to deliver his verdict. The last part – written at the cottage – was 'good', he knew. 'If you'd taken me to Achill two years ago, it would *all* have been good perhaps.'

One cannot underestimate the obsession with Ireland that gripped Greene in the next year or so. Within a month of being

back in London at his offices at Eyre and Spottiswoode, he wrote
to Catherine to say that whilst trawling through some author's
manuscript, the memory of the 'view of Galway harbour' forced
its way into his thoughts 'and I fell in love . . . It's odd and pleasant how one can go *falling* in love with the same person . . .
sometimes several times a day'; a week later he wrote to say that
'all last night I was catching a plane to Shannon in my sleep'.

But the dreams weren't always so happy. Writing from
Belgium a week after getting back from Shannon, Greene talked
morosely of what had become his 'absurd, complicated,
grotesque life'. The night before he had dreamt they had parted,
that the last five months had been 'wasted'.

'Do you think we *only* like each other in Achill?' he asked. 'I
hope not. These are just the notions that stick when one is so cut
off. This place is very pretty, very clean, very kind – I think it
must be rather like Limbo [. . .] I prefer Achill & the choice of
Heaven or Hell.'

Back in England, life was becoming more 'tense' by the month.
At Gordon Square with Dorothy, he came 'face to face' with a
giant rat when he opened the clothes cupboard. He killed it by
clubbing it with his shoe. Catherine had gone off to America –
to the family farm at Wilton, New Hampshire – and Greene was
feeling flat and morose. The following, quoted from Donne,
was 'nice':

> *My heart is of dejection, clay*
> *and by self-murder, red*

With Catherine in America, he said it was like the court of
Denmark when Hamlet was away in England. He was praying
hard. Unable to detach himself from Dorothy, he was urgently
hoping she would take another lover. To alleviate his private
hell, he busied himself with reading. A biography of J.M. Synge
reminded him of her. Reading Gide cheered him up: it made
him think *The Heart of the Matter* wasn't such a bad book after all.

'It's a damned sight better than his,' he reported; re-reading *The Brothers Karamazov* left him severely 'disappointed' by Dostoevsky.

Greene had sent Catherine the manuscript of his novel and she had marked it with corrections. Her literary education had proceeded faster than anybody could have guessed; Greene was now moaning that he wished she hadn't been so 'acute' as a critic. He also wanted her to help him write the lecture on 'Christianity and Civilisation' that he was giving with Mauriac in Brussels. Of course, much of this was sexual flattery. 'You are an awfully good typescript reader. I'd like to be married to you.' As his work mounted up, so did his earnings – and his tax liabilities. He was off to see his accountant about forming a limited company (it was named Graham Greene Productions). 'Can you love a limited company?' he asked her. 'Perhaps you'd like to be a director?'

Catherine did.

Another request in the same letter was more unusual. The 'important' cigarette burn on his skin had vanished – it 'must' be renewed. On a Sunday afternoon, after a very 'boring' Mass at Blackfriars, he admitted that he only seemed to get anything out of Mass when he went with her. He was, he said, a much better Catholic when he was in a state of 'mortal sin'; or at least he was more aware of being one: 'the dark night for me is dreariness, inertia, boredom: with you I don't feel that – or despair either.'

Back in Oxford with Vivien and the children, it was another story. Francis and Caroline would shout up the stairs as he tried to work in his top-floor study on a *New Statesman* review, or other work. But the moment he began clacking away on his type-writer in Beaumont Street, he found himself thinking of her. 'Directly, I write to you, Cafryn, I fall in love. Even on a typewriter. I wish you were here. I wish taxis still didn't always go up St James's Street [when they did he was reminded of her]. I wish I didn't miss you. I wish I could hear your strange telephone voice saying "Good Morning" at 4.30 in the afternoon.'

Catherine used a special 'interrogative' voice when she wanted to 'talk' theology with Greene when they woke up.

Greene always maintained that his dreams often had a prophetic and powerfully subconscious quality to them. In Beaumont Street especially, he often dreamt of her. Writing on 2 September 1947, however, he said he had had a sleepless night. He supposed, he added, *trying* to sound unconcerned, that she was with 'Lowell' in America.

His rival's name was Lowell Weicker, (referred to as LPW in Catherine's diaries) an American general with whom Catherine had also been having an affair. Greene was clearly upset, but was trying not to show it. As he invariably did, he retaliated in kind. On Monday, he wrote that he had felt rather 'restless' without her. He had got rid of his energies, he said, in the 'usual way' (presumably he had walked up to Shepherd Market, or some other brothel location). 'The trouble is that it is a poor substitute in my case,' insinuating that he hoped the same was true for her. 'I suppose you are out of the Church again and I wish I was the only one who put you out! And how I wish we'd just have each other & no one else – anyway – for a few years.' Although Greene found his own jealousy very hard to control, he was less understanding of others, especially Dorothy's possessive feelings towards him. A few days later he wrote that he had had a long chat with Dorothy, prior to packing her off for several months to West Africa on the 'Elder Dempster' cargo ship, and she was now 'much more ready to accept that one can love two people!'

With Catherine away, Greene became moody, insecure and restless. Francis had been taken to Brighton, his 'girlfriend' was being sent off on a long holiday; he wanted to do something *he* liked for a change. He hoped Catherine did too, but was nervous about seeing her on her return: 'maybe you'll be getting too American to want do the same things anymore . . . Anyway this is one letter that isn't a love letter – or is it? Perhaps in its dull way it's more of one than the others.'

Shortly afterwards, there was a long 'sandwich and whisky' session at St James's Street with John Hayward at which

Catherine was 'thoroughly analysed' and discussed. 'It seemed odd – and rather disagreeable that you weren't there.' He ended on an ebullient, self-congratulatory note: 'O, the Greene stock is booming. *This Gun for Hire* revived at the Plaza, reprint of *Nineteen Stories* announced, two more of uniform edition & hope enthusiasm for script of *Basement Room*.'

And there was another project on the horizon: a literary biography of his distant cousin Robert Louis Stevenson, based on unpublished letters owned by a man living in Nice. Greene strongly identified with his mother's cousin. Writing on Stevenson in the *New Statesman* in early January, Greene commented that Stevenson had learnt to suffer for literature ('for suffering like literature has its juvenilia – men mature and graduate in suffering'). The main purpose of mentioning the project to Catherine, however, was to dangle the hope that the research trip could double-up as an exotic Gauguin-like holiday to the 'South Seas'. 'I wonder if you'll be still interested in coming too? Or whether I'll have to fall back on a local girl with flowers in her hair.'

As always the subtext was clear: I can fool around too. But his cocksure stance betrayed his true feelings. He was determined to marry her. To complicate matters further, Greene was himself in America in October 1947 on Eyre and Spottiswoode publishing business, taking Vivien along in a guilty effort to give her – one senses – a final holiday. A cocktail party was to be held for him at the Cosmopolitan Club in New York on 10 October. Showing his more sensitive side, Greene said that he wished Catherine could be there but that it wouldn't be 'fair' to Vivien on her first day in New York ('I don't want to risk spoiling her holiday').

Yet that is not how Vivien remembered the trip to New York. She claims she was left to fend for herself. 'I was put in a hotel, very smart, I was left there,' she said. 'I was told my food and everything was all paid for. And he went off. I think he was meeting publishers. I was just left in the hotel. But I was accustomed to it.'

Her memory is clear enough to remember that she found a

companion – an Englishman from Camden who had written a novel, apparently called *Cards of Identity*. The introduction was made when she saw he was reading a copy of *Old Possum's Book of Practical Cats* by T.S. Eliot. The stranger had a poky 'cold water flat' (i.e. no hot running water) somewhere in Manhattan; 'anyhow, it was lovely to have somebody to talk to'.

The Greenes were staying at the Gotham Hotel in New York. A few days before they left for England, he wrote to Catherine again, this time trying to sneak in a rendezvous, if only for an hour. The letter sounds a note of serious disappointment. Greene had already planned a third Achill trip for 1947, booking and paying for passages to Shannon airport for 31 October. He was desperately looking forward to visiting Ireland again, partly as a way to fill the dark hole that had been left by the finishing of his novel. The day after sending the manuscript of *The Heart of the Matter* to Heinemann he wrote: 'I feel very empty and played out because . . . I have no idea for another book and feel I never shall. This is always the way when a book is finally cleared. It affects one badly, so that even one's religion doesn't mean a thing. The only thing in the next month or two that could mean anything or that would bring one alive is loving someone. So I look forward to Ireland like an escape from Purgatory.'

Yet for some reason – possibly to do with Ernie O'Malley – Catherine wrote to Greene from America to say that Ireland was off. 'It seems a pity if we have to give up going to Achill together,' he wrote despondently. 'It's got under one's skin. Only yesterday I was longing to push that rusty gate and see it swing.'

This was a blow. Greene felt very 'dark nightish'; 'how I long for a spot of peace again. Cafryn, sometimes I feel homesick for your bush with the Atlantic blowing in through the top of the door & that feeling of freshness and dampness on the skin when one goes out in one's pyjamas. Don't let us give it up.'

Trapped in his hotel suite at the Gotham with Vivien, the only thing that Greene had to look forward to was his firm 'date' with Catherine at Rules on 28 October (life without 'plans' would be simply intolerable, he used to believe).

But ten days seemed like a century away.

What was discussed at Rules that night is unknown. Greene was now obsessed by the idea of winning Catherine away from Harry, and then fate intervened. The next chapter of Greene's life began with a phone call.

Vivien was in tears. She had just opened a letter. An impassioned love letter.

The Times forecast for Thursday 20 November 1947 was 'dull and misty with occasional drizzle'. As the early morning fog lifted on the morning of the royal wedding of Princess Elizabeth to Philip Duke of Edinburgh at Westminster Abbey, the Oxford postman delivered a letter to Beaumont Street. It was addressed to Mrs H.D. Walston in New York, in Greene's spidery hand, and marked 'return to sender'.

Vivien knew Graham would never marry Dorothy. But since he had met Mrs Walston, her husband had changed. He had become harder. (Aware of this in himself, he actually inscribed a book to Dorothy 'from Graham the bastard'.)

Fearing the worst, Vivien opened the envelope. Her face dropped.

'My son (Francis) was sitting at the breakfast table,' said Vivien. 'And he watched me for a minute and he said, "Is something the matter?" And he got up and stood by me. Because my face must have told him.' Francis was a day boy at the Dragon School near Summertown and would have left the house by about 8am.

Devastated, Vivien walked up to St Giles and through Cornmarket to try and see her friend Father Tom Corbishley at the Jesuit Campion Hall. Before the 11.30am service Oxford was already heaving with undergraduate excitement; banners and flags were flying across the Turl, indeed the celebrations, reports maintained, were the 'gayest' the town had seen since the war. Tipsy students, some dressed up in costumes and swigging on bottles, handed out glasses of champagne to passers-by as a toast to the bride and groom.

Just over a year before Vivien had drunk champagne on the lawn of Campion Hall to celebrate Catherine's reception into the Church. Walking through the cloister in the damp November morning, it must have been difficult not to have thought back to Catherine's 'radiant' smile . . . her New Look Dior outfits, her money, her diamonds . . .

When I asked Vivien what sort of Catholic she thought Catherine really was, she replied, 'I don't want to think about her really. She was right outside my province. I've never met anybody like that. I thought it was awful, as if she wanted to pull down or destroy the best that she could find. Two priests and writers, Graham wouldn't have been the only writer. For all I know, painters. She was completely oblivious. But the more serious the person, the better it was. She wouldn't have been bothered by an ordinary person.'

Father Corbishley, dressed in his dog-collar and priest's black cassock, had been listening to the royal wedding on the wireless 'I said to Tom, don't you want to listen? I can wait to talk to you.'

'No, of course not,' the Jesuit replied.

Then he read the letter.

'Afterwards,' said Vivien, 'he said [again, this is Vivien's version], "Divorce him." That was very unusual for a priest to say.'

They talked for a while.

Meanwhile, events around Westminster Abbey were proceeding – or had proceeded (Vivien can't remember the exact time of her visit to Campion Hall) – with military precision. At 11.16am, a 'tumult of cheering' greeted the arrival of Prince Philip and his groomsman, Lord Milford Haven, who slipped in through a side door at Poets' Corner 'in the inconspicuous manner of any ordinary wedding', as *The Times* reliably informed its readers.

After the service ended with the final blessing by the Archbishop of Canterbury, the Orlando Gibbons's Amen and the National Anthem, a riotous party of over-excited Oxford undergraduates, led by a Scottish piper, stormed the Oxford Union. The proctors were called as eightsome reels were danced along

Cornmarket and the Broad. Fireworks were let off as more champagne was handed out in the streets.

When Vivien got home to Beaumont Street, she telephoned Greene at Eyre and Spottiswoode.

'I've read a letter you sent Mrs Walston,' Vivien said. 'A love letter.'

'That doesn't mean anything. You know how one writes.'

'No, Graham,' replied his wife. 'I know what real feeling is and this is real.'

Pause.

'I am going to leave you,' Greene replied. 'We'll be going away together.' Click. He said he would come home later that day.

The ending of Vivien's marriage on the future Queen's wedding day was a particularly brutal blow. It was a day that Vivien had looked forward to for weeks.

Wirelesses around Oxford had crackled with the Archbishop's austere ('actual') voice: 'You have made this great promise willingly and gladly because you have given yourselves to each other in unselfish love. Love must always be unselfish, and unselfishness is the true secret of a happy married life . . . And thus you will learn to bear one another's burdens as you walk on the road of life, making the journey together with happiness and hope . . .'

By late afternoon, as Greene travelled from his office at Bedford Square to Paddington Station, the news-stands were loudly hailing the Royal wedding with a special issue. On street corners around Tottenham Court Road, bags of hot chestnuts were selling quickly, along with the evening paper and official programmes. All day in London, as reports put it the following day, the streets took on a 'carnival air'. At Harrod's, Heal's, shops along Mount Street, Bond Street, and St James's Street, windows displayed official Royal photos. Despite the cold November weather, a 'dense throng' surrounded Trafalgar Square, Pall Mall and crowded outside the gates of Buckingham Palace, forming a semi-circle banner to watch the couple parade by in their horse-drawn carriage.

It says something about the effectiveness of media censorship back in 1947 – or the desire to hear only good news at a time of such depressing austerity – that so little was made of the fact that by the time Greene caught his afternoon train, at least 2,500 people had been injured in the crush around Trafalgar Square. This merited just four lines in *The Times* at the bottom of a page.

But as Greene sat back in his train seat and looked grimly at his reflection in the compartment window, he was in no mood to either celebrate or read about the forty royal watchers who ended up in hospital. As the train passed through the grey English countryside, one can imagine him thinking back to VE Day, 7 May 1945, when Princess Elizabeth and Princess Margaret had been permitted to shake hands with the crowds outside Buckingham Palace. Greene had stayed in London to celebrate the festivities with Dorothy.

And it had been Dorothy not Vivien – who at the time had been moved to rooms at Trinity College – with whom he had lived through the Blitz. In *The End of the Affair*, Greene describes Sarah and Henry holding hands in St James's Park to watch the firework display that Greene had taken Dorothy to. By 1945, Greene's love – for both his wife and mistress – had turned to a form of pity

Surrounded on the train to Oxford by faceless men in dark suits and bowler hats, perhaps getting home a little earlier because of the wedding, Greene knew he was about to pass into the most important new frontier of his life. As for so many Oxford graduates, those sixty-odd miles to London were not simply a familiar train ride: they had become coupled to the experience of his life. The journey was a crossing of the border between youthful undergraduate innocence – the cloistered walls of Balliol and digs in Summertown – and the world of manly experience.

Shortly after leaving Oxford, Greene penned notes of mad longing to see Vivien, always trying to defeat the train times to squeeze in extra minutes. Yet within weeks of his marriage he was slinking off to London to visit favourite prostitutes like

Annette; on the return journey to Oxford he would sit alone in the back of the carriage, with the remains of the sandwiches his wife had made him and his guilt.

From Oxford Station, it is less than a ten-minute walk, past Worcester College, to the bottom of Beaumont Street. Vivien met him on the doorstep.

'I handed him the letter and he said what he said before, "Oh well, you know, this is just a sort of love letter," and I said, "No, it isn't."'

He went upstairs and packed several suits into a case. A few days later he sent a man from London to collect his things, packing them all into tea-chests. 'I was with Francis and a little man came and took all his clothes and all his books. And we just watched him as he packed Graham's clothes and books. Took them away.'

A final 'talk' was attempted in the drawing-room, but it was hopeless. This 'Oxford business' had to stop. He had made up his mind: his future lay with Catherine. Then he hurried downstairs. Vivien heard the thud of the front door slam as Greene walked out into the street.

Looking down from the window on that fateful November night, she saw her husband standing alone in the early evening darkness. With his overcoat collar turned up, Greene stood beside his small suitcase.

'You saw him from the window?'

'Yes, I saw him walking away,' Vivien said. 'All very painful. He looked behind. Yes, I think he did turn.' Before disappearing into the night, clutching his case like a newly released prisoner.

As Norman Sherry has pointed out, Greene was to later use the experience in *The Quiet American*, when the British journalist Fowler is tormented by the random nightmares of the painful memories of his life: 'the body of a bayoneted Malay . . . my wife's face at a window when I came home to say goodbye for the last time'.

The end of her marriage came three days later at Sunday Mass at Blackfriars on 23 November 1947. When the offerings basket was passed down the aisles, Vivien began to loosen the ring Greene had given her before they were married, twenty years earlier, in 1927.

I had noticed two glittering diamond rings on Vivien's hand when I had sat down. 'These are mine,' she said, holding them up for me to see. 'Not engagement rings. When Graham came and said "I'm going to leave you permanently and live with Mrs . . ."'

Her voice tapered off to a near whisper, as if repeating the name remained painful.

'. . . Walston, after that – I mean it was a dreadful thing – I gave my engagement ring to Blackfriars at Mass. These [she held up her hand] are all ones that I inherited, or saved up and bought.'

'You gave away your engagement ring at church?'

'I put it in the collection.'

'Because you thought . . .'

'It was . . . finished.'

the edge of the desert

The handcuffs may have been removed but Greene knew he was playing a dangerous game of Russian roulette with his future. He was now determined to make Catherine his wife (he used to write the name Catherine Greene on scraps of paper and in the margins of his books); and yet he knew the chance of a divorce from Vivien was minimal. If he even wanted it. Vivien told me that Greene, in fact, had a 'horror of divorce'.

According to Vivien, it was the one subject over which Greene badly lost his temper with her. 'In those days divorce was embarrassing,' she said, with Francis going to Ampleforth and Lucy at St Clothill's convent. 'One day he came out of the blue and threatened me and said, "If you divorce me, I'll never see the children again." And that was going to be such a material and spiritual loss, I never thought of it again.'

Tellingly, when Greene and Vivien later went to see a priest to discuss what should be done about the terms of their separation in the eyes of the church, they went to see Vincent Turner SJ, who had received Catherine into the Church, rather than his colleague at Campion Hall, Father Corbishley, who had read Greene's letter to Catherine. Greene's one hope was an annulment. 'I mean the Church would have simply laughed at the idea,' said Vivien. 'Two children and all these years of living together when we were quite poor.'

Although Greene was certainly no longer poor, the trouble was that Catherine – after sorting out an arrangement with her husband years before – was very reluctant to leave her children to run off to Ireland or Romania or the South Seas with a forty-three-year-old homeless self-confessed 'manic-depressive' writer who was prone to possessiveness and fits of jealousy, never mind the complications with Dorothy (whom Greene was to keep seeing for many years). As Vivien said, 'She [never "Catherine"] was quite comfortable where she was. Because her husband gave her everything she wanted. Didn't mind who she slept with.'

In *The End of the Affair*, Sarah's civil servant husband Henry is a very different sort of character. The idea of Harry Walston asking Greene to hire a private detective to trail Catherine is absurd. Yet Greene legitimately shared with Bendrix a sense of grievance over one undeniable aspect of both Catherine and Sarah's character, 'so again and again I returned home on other days with the certainty that I was only one of many men – the favourite lover for the moment.'

'Last night I had felt friendship and sympathy for Henry,' says Bendrix the day after first making love to Sarah, 'but already he had become an enemy, to be mocked and resented and covertly run down.' Greene thrived on twisted, conflicting emotions and was certainly unsure – at the start – about how he felt towards Catherine's cuckolded husband. His feelings seemed to have gone beyond pity, jealousy, guilt, or a desire to bully or humiliate; the acutely sensitive novelist viewed Harry Walston with an almost scientific sense of detachment. He seemed to Greene to be curiously devoid of ordinary human emotions. In his *Times* interview in 1994, Oliver Walston described his father as 'rather boring, an emotional free zone. He never got angry or sad or cried or shouted.'

The dramatic exception to this was one emotionally explosive weekend at Thriplow, when Catherine confronted Harry about her deep love for Greene. Just as Sarah makes up her mind that she is going to leave her dull husband to marry Bendrix in *The End of the Affair*, so in real life Catherine was on the point of walking out on her husband. Catherine lost her nerve at the very last minute, however, after Harry broke down and cried all night.

Greene simply couldn't understand how Harry could be so nice to him. He even went so far as to invite Greene to spend Christmas 1947 with the Walston family at Thriplow. It almost irritated him. At the Mauriac party Harry hadn't kicked up a fuss when Greene sat talking to Catherine all night by the sand-pit.

Greene's nature, on the other hand, inclined towards the misanthropic. His friend Michael Meyer confirmed this to me when he described how Greene had once said to him: 'Never forget how lucky you are in two respects. You like people unless you have a reason to dislike them, and you're happy unless you've a reason to be unhappy. I'm the opposite.'

To begin with, however, Greene did try to *like* Harry Walston; or so he wrote to Catherine before lunch with him in late December 1947. 'I do think he's one of the nicest people who ever lived.' But Greene was probably just carried away by a magnanimous – as well as diplomatic – pre-Christmas-at-Thriplow spirit.

The set-up at Thriplow was ideal from Greene's point of view; his own children weren't there which, frankly, was a relief (rather reluctantly, one feels, he did read the Walston children bedtime stories). So ideal was the arrangement that he was careful not to make any public scenes for fear he wouldn't be invited back. He obviously behaved himself for the most part. Throughout January he was back again. He told Catherine, 'I fell in love walking in a field, playing Wide World, sitting on the floor with an egg.'

Writing to Catherine on green copperplate Thriplow Farm headed stationery on Monday 29 December – he was still at Thriplow – Greene said: 'Darling, I have loved this Christmas.' There does seem, however, to have been some rationing of onion sandwiches. 'Don't think of my irritable outbursts – mere symptoms of night starvation . . . My dear, I love you & begin to miss you so much before I leave even.' It seemed 'so natural' to have her around as he worked, upstairs, sitting in the next room, talking in the kitchen. 'I am in love with you,' he repeated. 'I wish I could turn my ring and make time move.'

The next day he was back in London at his desk at Eyre and Spottiswoode. It was a lovely cold 'silvery day'. One might imagine that at 9.30am on a Tuesday after Christmas, a publisher would have plenty of work to clear. But taking up his fountain pen, Greene first pulled out a sheet of off-white note-paper from his desk drawer. He was feeling 'happy' for the following reasons:

1. They were in love with one another.
2. He was still a Catholic without 'any difficulty whatsoever'.
3. On the train down to London he had become excited about his new short story (which finally became *The Third Man*), which he had hopes of off-loading onto Korda for a film. He wanted to go somewhere warm – preferably with her – and get it done.
4. Dorothy claimed to be 'happy' and had been converted to the idea of independence. Apparently she no longer felt jealous. A few weeks later he added, 'I feel terribly sorry for her – physically the whole thing shows, but as for love (in the f—sense) we are two corpses'.
5. He had walked to the office.
6. On the way to Bedford Square he had passed a film poster of *Brighton Rock* with his name prominently displayed ('I never get tired of my name in print!').

Greene ended by saying that he now felt overwhelmed by a feeling of indifference about 'poor' Vivien; a feeling that he had done all the worrying of which he was capable.

'My love for you is getting out of hand but that's my problem,' Greene wrote from Brussels after giving his lecture on Christianity and Civilisation with François Mauriac. In the first hint that Greene had begun to see his love affair as inevitably doomed, however, he added, 'I love you unwisely and in the long term rather hopelessly but I like it and long to see you.'

This brooding sense of tragic loss and waste – the idea that a grand passion represents just a 'stage' in one's life – was to haunt Greene's idea of love for most of his 'grotesquely complicated' life. Not just in terms of the way he saw the patterns of his own series of betrayals and failures, but in the narrative of other people's as well.

In the winter of 1981, the seventy-seven-year-old Greene received a huge package at his flat in Antibes. It was postmarked Rome. Inside was a typed 800-page manuscript called *Style* that had been sent by a man called Justin Behrens. A covering letter of recommendation had been written by the painter Caroline Hill, who had painted Greene at his flat in Antibes.

The unedited manuscript originally sent to Greene was an extraordinarily intense autobiographical account – often inchoate, at times very intensely moving – of the man's fourteen-year love affair with an exotic and strikingly beautiful Hungarian *haute* bohemian sexual adventuress called Ursula. In the late 1970s, unable to find satisfaction in the merely sensual or aesthetic – or in adultery – she had committed suicide in the Sudan's Western Darfur, shooting herself in the head with a .22 revolver after failing to slash her wrists with an open razor. The manuscript later formed the basis of Justin's brother, Tim Behrens' account of their love, *The Monument*. One of Ursula's last diary entries reads: 'I have had enough of everything, sex included'.

Greene was often sent unsolicited manuscripts to read. But this one – with its settings of Rome, Paris, London and Greece, its themes of obsessive jealousy, betrayal and taboo-breaking sexual lust, clearly captured his interest. Greene and Walston viewed love and sex as an extension of religion. The theological question Greene addresses most directly in his love poems to Catherine – almost as if God is looking after his shoulder as he writes on the roof in Anacapri – is, can you love God through a woman? Can you love God through sex? Greene certainly believed so with Catherine.

After reading about the extraordinary passion between Behrens and Ursula, Greene's reply was perhaps self-revealing: he said he would have published the book if he had been a publisher but would also – just as he did with Sarah's diary – propose 'severe cuts' in the wife's diary in a way that 'would enable the sad story to proceed towards its tragic end with a sense of inevitability'.

This is precisely what Tim Behrens did in re-working the diary into *The Monument*, which has become a literary classic about an obsessive love affair. Its dust jacket explains:

> There were once lovers who became completely exclusive of the outside world. At the same time, their appetites for novelty, travel, beauty and art impelled them to far reaches of the globe. Making their bases in Rome and Greece, their days were dedicated to a maximum of pleasure with a discipline most people associate with work. For seventeen years their love for each other was obsessional and willingly doomed.

Greene certainly felt his love affair with Catherine was inevitably doomed from about 1948. His letters to her a year into their affair indulge much of the same impulsive, high romantic, Wagnerian desire to escape the world, and doubtless one's self. The moment Greene arrived in snow-covered Vienna on 12 February 1948 – to find a plot for *The Third Man* – he stuck a photograph of Catherine up in a letter rack near his bed at the Sachus Hotel as though he was 'an undergraduate in love for the first time'. That the airport had been covered in snow had added to his sense of romantic longing. Thinking, perhaps subconsciously, of Cambridge airport, he reported to Catherine: 'There was snow on the roofs as we came down to Vienna.' After dinner he posted a letter to her. When he got back to his room, he fired off another, saying that he was overwhelmed by an urge to say things to her – 'uninteresting banal things' – as they came into his head.

Sometimes I wish you were unhappy & not a Catholic & I'd say send me a wire to meet you in Rome, Paris, Dublin, London, Galway, Prague, anywhere in the world & I'd write damned good books and I'd love you and boast of you and proclaim 'she's my wife' – can you trump all that? or we'd do a hell of a lot of things, sit up talking till 2am, have parties with all the people we really liked, do a bit of —ing & —ing.

He added that the letter was definitely not one she could file away in the Black Box (she did anyway).

But sometimes I become hopelessly sentimental and wish that the world knew that you loved me. Because you do, as soon as I'm there, you know.
   I love you . . . Miss me or I'll wring your neck!

Of course, all doomed lovers – especially those with literary or artistic sensibilities – like to delude themselves that they are unique; or if not unique, at least as romantically ill-fated as the familiar cast list of literature, ranging from Tristan and Iseult (to whom Bendrix refers) to Ted Hughes and Sylvia Plath.

There is the clearest evidence that Greene very deliberately looked out for literary connections – taken from his vast reading – through which he identified his passion for Catherine. Every year from 1949 until at least 1955, Greene gave her for Christmas an ordinary hard-backed exercise book 'love diary', in which he went to the extreme lengths of hand-writing a literary quotation just below each day of the year; each quote reflected an aspect of their shared literary and religious interests.

Rivalling W.H. Auden's 'Commonplace' book, *A Certain World*, and Cyril Connolly's *The Unquiet Grave*, in its width and breadth of literary references and allusion, from Plato to Péguy, Emily Brontë to Thomas Lovell Beddoes, the quotation entries include thousands of extracts from poems, novels, works of theology and the gospels, as well as other writers', painters' and philosophers' diaries, letters and biographies, making up an extraordinary record of how a powerful creative mind like Greene's tries to understand itself, as well as the nature of an obsessive love ('I love you wildly, hopelessly, crazily'). In the diaries, Greene reveals an intensely personal shared imaginative discourse with a reference library of literary thought, tradition, poetry and language.

The love diaries he gave to Catherine each Christmas are intensely revealing, not so much for the actual entries – which are rather matter-of-fact, ranging from, say, recording that the children went to the pantomime in Cambridge, or that she had lunch with the Longfords and Victor Gollancz at the Savoy Grill – but for what Greene, perhaps unconsciously, reveals about himself, and the sources of his literary self-identification as he was writing *The End of the Affair*.

In *Ways of Escape*, Greene referred to the 1950s, with laconic understatement, as 'a period of great unrest'. Any attempt to understand the complex layering of personal and creative influences on Greene leading up to, and during, this dangerously volatile – yet also highly productive – period of his life cannot ignore the pages of Catherine's love diaries. The first book Graham gave her was a hard-backed aquamarine exercise book. Beside a sticker of Father Christmas, possibly from a cracker, is the simple inscription: 'My dear. My dear. My dear, Anon. For Catherine with love, from Graham 1948.'

Read in conjunction with what Greene wrote about the literary genesis of *The End of the Affair* in his autobiography, it is obvious that the novel is very far from being a 'human soap opera', as the British media – aided by Shelden and Sherry – seemed to enjoy deducing in 1994. As Christopher Hawtree was alone in observing in *The Times*, instead it is a highly complex literary narrative that draws on a remarkably deep well of literary sources, including Proust, Dickens, St Thomas Aquinas, the theological criticism of Baron Von Hugle, T.S. Eliot (his *Four Quartets* were published in 1944), his friend Evelyn Waugh's *Brideshead Revisited*, and Ford Madox Ford, whose 'end-of-the-affair-ish' (a phrase used by Greene in letters to Catherine) novel of pre-war adultery, *The Good Soldier*, was described by Greene as one of the best of the century. In addition, he had been reading Scott Fitzgerald's letters to his wife Zelda. In *Ways of Escape*, writing of this tumultuous period in his life, Greene quoted a line from Fitzgerald: 'A writer's temperament is constantly making him do things that cannot repair . . .'

Diary quotation for April 16:

Wear that gold hat if that will move her
If you can bounce high, bounce for her too
Till she cry, 'Lover gold hatted, high
Bouncing lover
I must have you

Another literary coral to be found on a close reading of the theme of guilt and human redemption in *The End of the Affair* is Coleridge's *The Rime of the Ancient Mariner*. Bendrix comes close to experiencing an understanding of 'grace', through love, as well as through hate. The strange mercy of God was an obsession with Greene; the more unlikely the recipient the better. Bendrix's intense ability to hate is, as Father Martindale pointed out to Greene in a letter written just after the novel came out, really an admission of his equal ability to love. Significantly, the *Ancient Mariner* is slyly mentioned by Greene in the novel as the 'random' poem that a performer is challenged to recite at Clapham Common's Speakers' Corner.

The diary seems to have been filled with quotes from books as he was reading them. So it offers a fascinating looking-glass with which to slowly watch the sea-change that takes place in his own imagination, transforming the raw flotsam of material into the subterranean citadel of words that the novel becomes. Greene always kept a record of the books he read each month at the back of his Hermès pocket diary.

As I started to compile a list of the literary influences (only some of which are named above) with which Greene seemed to identify around 1948–50, I realised that almost all the authors shared with Greene their own very unhappy personal histories of marriage, usually involving adultery; and yet – as with Greene – the adultery, or failure of marriage, became a source of literary re-awakening. I refer to Eliot, Waugh, Scott Fitzgerald, Ford Madox Ford, Dickens; Proust was certainly unhappy in love, but, of course, not married. Exactly the same creative debt to adultery is apparent in the major novels of Greene.

It seems likely that Cyril Connolly's *The Unquiet Grave* had a direct influence on Greene's creation of Catherine's diaries. It was a book that Waugh, incidentally, disliked for its self-pity. In it, Connolly fuses the quotes with journal entries that recollect a year of guilt, remorse, self-indulgence, sloth, literary escapism, and other intellectual sins. Connolly was not Catholic, but his elegant classical prose glistens with tension, as do Greene's letters to Catherine, between the pull of a pagan world of beauty and pleasure and the call of a guilty Christian conscience. Many of the locations of the Greene–Walston affair – those 'places' that haunt his memory and spill again and again into poems such as 'After Two Years' – are exactly the same as Connolly's; even the restaurants are the same: Paris, Italy, London, the Côte D'Azur, the Amalfi coast.

In the new introduction to the revised 1951 edition of *The Unquiet Grave*, Connolly talks about the creative genesis of what is really a personal dream diary, a cycle of seasonal meditations on literature, art and love blended with a dazzling collection of little marble-like quotations. Greene, of course, also kept a dream diary – it was his last published book, edited by Yvonne Cloetta. In it, he writes again and again to Catherine after they have separated – throughout the 1960s – of how many times he has dreamt of her during the year. In 1964, for example, there were twenty-eight entries under Catherine. Like Connolly in *The Unquiet Grave*, Greene put an index in his dream diaries (as he also did in Catherine's diaries).

The last section of Palinurus's (Connolly's *alter ego*'s) journey towards redemption opens with a series of passages inspired by

the streets of Paris, recalled by the autumn mist in London,
'Mediterranean harbour scenes are followed by Atlantic sea-
scapes' with topographical allusions to Baudelaire at Honfleur,
Proust at Houlgate (Greene was reading *A La Recherche du Temps
Perdu* whilst writing *The End of the Affair*), and 'Flaubert at
Trouville, where he met his "fantôme" and dark inspirer,
Madame Schlesinger'. 'About the fortieth birthday of Palinurus
the catharsis occurs,' adds Connolly, 'he relives the early stages of
his love-affair' (just as Greene was to return again and again in
the narrative of his letters to his early memories of his love for
Catherine). For Connolly, as for Greene, returning to the scenes
of a real adult first love appears essential for continued creativity.
Other loves are mere self-illusion.

> We love but once, for once only are we perfectly equipped for
> loving: we may appear to ourselves to be as much in love at
> other times – so will a day in early September, though it be six
> hours shorter, seem as hot as one in June. And on how that
> first true love-affair will shape depends the pattern of our
> lives.
>
> [*The Unquiet Grave*]

Perhaps this is why Greene could not stop himself writing to
Catherine. Connolly's marriage to Jean Bakewell, like Greene's
to Vivien, broke down after repeated adulteries on his side. The
mistress – unlike Greene he succeeded in making her Mrs
Connolly – that Connolly ended up trying to turn into his
Madame Bovary, was called Barbara Skelton. She seems to have
shared some characteristics with Catherine. She had become a
rich man's mistress in her teens, caused a court martial in India,
then joined the *Horizon* set. She became involved with King
Farouk of Egypt, writing in her diary after dining with him, 'I
am deadly tired, and ache all over from a flogging last night on
the steps of the Royal Palace. I would have preferred a splayed
cane, but instead had to suffer a dressing gown cord.'

That one of Bendrix's previous books is actually called *The*

Grave on the Water-Front (a clear allusion to *The Unquiet Grave*) suggests the extent to which Greene, in the writing of *The End of the Affair*, acknowledges his creative debt not just to life but to the narrative of literature. Indeed, the darkly comic scene when Waterbury, the black corduroy-wearing and tediously self-important journalist, interviews Bendrix before Sarah's funeral is a sharp cautionary warning against critics, or readers, assuming that Bendrix and Greene are the same (Sherry: 'Bendrix, in some senses, reminds me powerfully of Greene'). Significantly, the interview is in a bar off Tottenham Court Road, close to where *Horizon* was edited from Bedford Square.

'A funeral in Golders Green,' Waterbury exclaimed. 'How like one of your own characters. It would have to be Golders Green, wouldn't it?'

'I didn't choose the spot.'

'Life imitating art.'

The question of Sarah's 'faith' in *The End of the Affair*, is mirrored directly in many of the quotes with which Greene chose to illustrate Catherine's diary for 1949. Since they would have been written in towards the end of 1948, we can see how the character of Sarah was forming in his mind. Take the quote for 15 January 1949, for example (the theologian is unclear): 'Life is not long enough for a religion of inferences; we shall never have done beginning if we determine to begin with proof . . . to act you must assume & that assumption is faith.' Sarah holds exactly this idea in *The End of the Affair*, when she says, 'I believe the whole bag of tricks, there's nothing I don't believe, they could subdivide the Trinity into a dozen parts and I'd believe.'

By the end of the novel, Bendrix too is afflicted by this idea, although differently.

'For if this God exists, I thought, and if even you – with your lusts and your adulteries and the timid lies you used to tell – can change like this, we could all be saints by leaping as you leapt, by shutting the eyes and leaping once and for all: if *you* are a saint, it's not so difficult to be a saint. It's something He can demand of any of us, leap. But I won't leap . . . You're a devil, God, tempting us to leap. But I don't want Your peace and I don't want Your love . . .'

Bendrix ends up like Conrad's Marlow, the unreliable narrator of *Heart of Darkness*, who peers over the edge into the darkness of the Congo but cannot bring himself to take that leap, like Kurtz, into the world of beyond, the New World of limitless possibility that is – temporarily, at least – opened up for Bendrix by the act of adultery. For Scobie, the physical taste of lipstick after kissing his new mistress felt 'like something he never tasted before. It seemed to him an act had been committed which altered the whole world.'

But Bendrix, who professes to hate God, does not see the world as a supernatural or spiritual universe in which a personal act – such as Sarah's pact with God to stop sleeping with Bendrix if he survives the bomb blast – can change the world. Bendrix does not live in the blind world of faith. Like Marlow, who cannot 'kick himself loose of the earth', he is too weak an individual to risk stepping ashore. Both Marlow and Bendrix step back at the last minute from the abyss.

Over ten years after writing *The End of the Affair*, Greene himself remained haunted by this very question of plunging into the unknown. It frightened him. A revealing letter that Greene sent from Antibes to Catherine at the Walston's St Lucia estate in the West Indies in January 1962 – their affair had reached its dark night of the soul – explains that he feels as if he is clinging onto the end of a 'long rope' and that there seems little left to do except to take a 'blind leap back into faith for what I haven't the courage to do'. He is referring to his relationship with Yvonne Cloetta, and how – although he realises it is over between himself and Catherine – nothing can take her place in his life. He feels robbed of her 'companionship'. To take the 'blind leap' would mean 'pushing a fond object back into the stream from which I fished her, in a bad moment [when he was writing *A Burnt-Out Case*], for an "adventure" . . . I feel so finished . . . that it seems it must be the end or the beginning. But then the damned years of responsibility begin. Somehow in our generation we've lost the nerve never to be cruel and kind, so we become kind and cruel. I love you as I love no one else and I worry you with these outpourings . . . and at the moment I'm not talking of sexual love, which at the moment [he has flu] I don't feel for anymore'. He was to stay with Yvonne until his death, and she was to become another great love, but such an 'outpouring' was typical of Greene, using his letters to Catherine as an attempted form of narrative therapy.

The idea that it takes courage to leap into the unknown waters of faith is one that Greene long struggled with. In his first letter to Catherine – before he had even met her or thought about having an affair – he wrote that he thought her decision to become a Catholic was 'extraordinarily courageous'. Yet, typically, it was courage he was all too aware of lacking himself.

Greene always used to carry around a picture of Padre Pio in his wallet. Back in 1949, whilst writing *The End of the Affair*, he had taken Catherine to the small remote hill town in the mountains of northern Italy where the alleged stigmatic priest was only allowed to say Mass at 5am (so as to discourage coachloads of religious tourists). Greene told Sherry that the Mass – which he had been warned took two hours – seemed to pass in about twenty minutes; during the service Catherine and himself saw the clotted blood on his wrists, and witnessed that he seemed to be in great pain. Afterwards Greene and Catherine were invited to meet the priest. Greene declined: 'I did not want my life to be changed by meeting a saint.'

The paradoxical possibilities of the 'appalling strangeness of the mercy of God' – a theme that was to obsess Greene – is also an idea that Samuel Beckett, another articulator of twentieth-century moral anxiety, so acutely confronts in *Waiting For Godot*, with its seemingly despairing vision of human justice. Like

Greene, Beckett lived simply (they resided quite close to each other in Paris) and wrote about the down-trodden, losers, failures, life's cast of dispossessed. In *Godot*, the bored, lonely tramp Vladimir refers to St Augustine's line about how one should not presume to know which thief crucified with Christ at Golgotha was saved, and which was damned. Yet Beckett – like Greene in *The Heart of the Matter* – views their fate with a sceptical mind. Likewise, we do not know whether Scobie is damned when he commits suicide.

A similar question was to ignite a storm of controversy when *The Heart of the Matter* was published in 1948. Greene's fellow Catholic and friend Evelyn Waugh, who found it impossible to conceive of a world without God, and adhered to the rigorous orthodoxy of his faith with unswerving loyalty, denounced Greene's theological thinking as a 'very loose poetical expression of a mad blasphemy'. Greene's attitude towards Waugh's inflexible intellectual logic on this question was reflected in what he once wrote about François Mauriac. 'If my conscience were as acute as M. Mauriac's showed itself to be in his essay, "God and Mammon", I could not write a line.' He added that his continued membership of the Catholic Church 'would present me with grave problems as a writer if I were not saved by my disloyalty'.

Although in an interview with *The Tablet* in 1985 Greene said that he did not believe in a biblical sort of Hell, he was certainly somebody who thought a good deal about damnation. Diary quotation, 30 March: 'Why this is Hell, nor am I out of it' (Christopher Marlowe). Very early in the diary, Greene quoted Eliot's famous credo from his essay on Baudelaire: 'Most people are only a very little alive; it is only when they are so awakened that they are capable of real Good, but that at the same time they become first capable of Evil.'

This idea was crucial to Greene's conception of Catherine – it is a central theme of 'After Two Years' – but quite irrelevant to Bendrix, who (at least to start with) only despises God. The 1949 *Observer* profile of Greene eloquently describes the uneasy conflict between Greene's strong belief in sin and his more dubious one in salvation. 'Seldom able to control the world', Greene's characters 'are buffeted about in it like plaintive puppets: all they have to rescue themselves with is a soul and a sense of purpose . . . his heroes are lonely figures who have come to terms with their conscience and work and their salvation in their own way.'

One can reliably say the same about Greene. The very first quote he writes in Catherine's diary bleakly reflects the paradox between, on the one hand his rapidly growing fame and on the other, his uncertain love with Catherine. He was often (so he said) driven close to suicide over her refusal to leave her wealthy husband to marry him: 'Literature as a rule is the refuge of the miserable. The happy seldom write for writing's sake; they are fully employed in living,' runs one quote; a few days later, 'We are only like dead walls, that ruin'd, yield no echo'; often it is almost impossible to read the author's name scratched beneath in his tiny ink hand. But again and again, the quotes Greene wrote in Catherine's diaries reflect the very same themes – of love and hatred – that afflict Sarah and Bendrix in *The End of the Affair*.

22 January: 'How easy it is to hate myself. True grace is to forget'; 9 April: 'The priest says this is all sin. The women, like astonished deer, seem to say with their velvet glances, "that's not true"' (Paul Gauguin); 13 May: 'The sinner lies at the very heart of Christianity . . . It is a city. A good citizen belongs to the city. A good stranger does not' (Charles Péguy); 14 June: 'Better sin the whole sin, sure that God observes . . .' (Robert Browning); 13 August: 'With the disappearance of the idea of Original Sin, with the disappearance of the idea of an intense moral struggle, the human beings presented to us in both poetry and prose . . . tend to become less and less real' (T.S. Eliot).

Eliot was a critically important influence on Greene, who was rarely in awe of other writers. Waugh he greatly respected; Eliot he revered. The film-set designer Jocelyn Rickards, Greene's mistress of the early 1950s, clearly remembers how Greene would practically shake when he would occasionally see Eliot at his flat at 19 Carlyle Mansions on the Chelsea

Embankment. It was a source of serious literary pride to Greene that his novels, before they were sent to his publisher, were first read by his wheelchair-bound friend John Hayward, who was such a good critic that T.S. Eliot not only used him too (he edited much of Eliot's *Four Quartets*) but also actually invited him to live with him.

The foundations of *The End of the Affair*'s complicated narrative scaffolding could also merit footnotes. In Catherine's 1950 diary, shortly before the novel was published, she records a conversation with Greene in which a title under serious consideration for the novel was 'The Edge of the Desert', which has a T.S. Eliot echo to it. It is certainly no coincidence that Greene chose to set the novel around the edges of a bourgeois south London common. In the original hand-written manuscript at Georgetown, one can clearly see that Sarah first lived in central London at Warwick Avenue; but Greene wanted to be able to mine the symbolism of the common as a suburban version of Lear's heath – a limbo of lost commuter souls pelted by the dark London rain.

From the opening lines of *The End of the Affair*, Bendrix declares himself an unreliable narrator; he starts off as an atheist, and he is about to embark on a record of hate, yet he makes a point of saying he 'chooses' this moment to start: free will is of course the essential doctrine of a Christian, not the determinist atheist that he professes to be. *The End of the Affair* begins:

> A story has no beginning and end: arbitrarily one chooses that moment of experience from which to look back or from which to look ahead.

and itself looks back to the opening of the last section of Eliot's 'Little Giddings':

> What we call the beginning is often the end
> And to make an end is to make a beginning.
> To end is where we start from.

John Hayward was to become a very close confidant of Greene regarding Catherine. There are photos of him sitting on the New England-style white porch at Thriplow at this time, laughing, as Greene is buried in a copy of the *News of the World*. At the lunch when Greene arranged for Catherine to meet Evelyn Waugh, John Hayward was the only other guest present. Waugh records in his diary for 28 September 1948:

> To London by early train in order to be in time for luncheon. Graham Greene suggested the meeting and refused to come to my club. The idea was Catherine Walston's who was curious to meet me. Graham's flat is next to hers at 5 St James's Street. The paralysed John Hayward was there, tenderly and candidly petted by Mrs W. Luncheon plainly had been brought from her flat for there was no salt. She sat on the floor and buttered my bread for me and made simple offers of friendship. Twice a year she and her husband give a great feast primarily for Hayward. I was asked to the next, in January. Finally, I was asked to go with her to the country. I couldn't that afternoon as I had to dine with the editor of the *Daily Express*. Very well they would pick me up after dinner. I couldn't do that as I was lunching with Father Caraman next day. Very well she would send a car for me at 2.30.

The next day Waugh awoke 'with a pleasant sense of having an interesting time ahead'. After saying 'prayers' at the very 'old Roman' church in Maiden Lane in which Sarah sits down and sobs after lunching with Bendrix at Rules after two years apart – Waugh went to a press screening of Greene's film *The Fallen Idol* which he thought clever and original. Waugh records that at lunch with Caraman, 'We talked about *The Month*'. It's likely that Greene's 'friendship' with the recently converted Catherine Walston was also discussed. Like most priests, Caraman enjoyed a gossip. Then the Walston car arrived. Waugh recorded he was 'driven by a lout' who did not know the way so he was hours late arriving for dinner at Thriplow.

Her house has been confiscated by the socialists so she lives in a farm building, one storey, modern, wood. A living-room with modern books and gramophones and wireless and modern pictures, a little dining-room, magnificent Caroline silver, a kitchenette, a bedroom, two bathrooms, two dressing-rooms. No servants except a nurse called 'Twinkle' who dined with us very neatly dressed as a nurse and talked about masturbation, incest, etc. Three children out of five were at home. Mrs Walston barefoot and mostly squatting on the floor. Fine big eyes and mouth, unaffected to the verge of insanity, unvain, no ostentation – simple friendliness and generosity and childish curiosity. Two bottles of champagne before dinner in silver goblets . . . We talked all the time of religion. She and Graham had been reading a treatise on prayer together that afternoon. Then she left the room at about 1 and presently telephoned she was in bed. We joined her. Her bedside table littered with books of devotion.

The next day Waugh woke after four hours' sleep and to work off his bad hangover went for a walk over the Walstons' 'flat, well kept, fields among Arab horses'. When he got back Greene and Catherine were in 'pyjamas' (Catherine wore cream silk piped pyjamas that Greene gave her, monogrammed with his initials) and having coffee in her bed. 'Perhaps they felt the effect of drinking more than I,' added Waugh, still – almost incredulously – not seeming to grasp what was going on.

It is not impossible that Catherine had thought of adding Waugh to her list of conquests, but, like most other beautiful and sophisticated women that came into the Wavian orbit, (as Acton used to refer to Waugh's shocks of social electricity), he preferred to remain at a safe distance. When Anne Rothermere enquired about the nature of Greene's friendship with Catherine, Waugh replied: 'My opinion is valueless on their sexual relations. I have no nose for such things and am constantly bowled over to learn who does & who doesn't go to bed with whom.' Indeed, reading through the original Waugh diaries in Texas, I came across a naive journal addition on his visit to Thriplow that, for some reason, was edited out of his published diaries. After climbing out of bed with Catherine and Greene, and noting the religious flavour of the books by her bed, Waugh actually ends his entry for the day: 'I think her affair with Graham is platonic.'

The exact nature of Greene's relations with Catherine was a subject of intense speculation amongst Waugh's circle of friends. It took until December 1949 – two years – for the gossip to reach Nancy Mitford. This came via Lady Diana Cooper who, in passing, had mentioned escorting 'Graham Greene's mistress to the station'. 'Has he one? Did you know? I was riveted,' replied Mitford.

Slowly Greene introduced Catherine to his friends. They began to see a lot of the Earl and Countess of Huntingdon. Jack Huntingdon was married to the writer Margaret Lane. On a tour of Newton Hall with Margaret, Catherine once pulled open a drawer in her bedroom to reveal a large supply of various-sized condoms. Margaret was to act as an important go-between when the affair turned ugly, suggesting to Harry that Catherine be allowed to live with Greene for a trial 'six months' (in the end the exact reverse happened; after *The End of the Affair* was published Greene was banned from seeing her for six months). She helped negotiate peace settlements between Harry, Greene and Catherine, with Greene occasionally being allowed to take a 'holiday' with Catherine, although remaining exiled from their house.

It wasn't until 1950 that Nancy Mitford herself met Catherine. 'I was *surprised*, having pictured scruffy Bloomsbury' she wrote to Waugh. Having quarrelled in print over adultery in *The Heart of the Matter*, and with Waugh recently having been introduced to Vivien Greene on a visit to Campion Hall in Oxford, Graham had to tread carefully so as not to cause an embarrassment between them over the subject of Mrs Walston. The purpose of the first lunch at St James's Street may well have been to seek Waugh's tacit approval of their illicit relations. Greene cared very much about Waugh's opinions; in 1948 he wrote curtly to Catherine, who appears to have lost a letter from his friend, 'Have you found the Evelyn Waugh letter yet?' Finally, after the overnight visit to Thriplow, Greene, in his rather tortured and awkward way, owned up to Waugh. Waugh was saddened but understanding. 'You relieved my mind enormously', wrote Greene from St James's Street in early October 1948, 'Thank you so much.'

Rather than naively compare Bendrix to Greene, it may be more useful to be reminded of Charles Ryder, in *Brideshead Revisited*. Ryder, a jaundiced middling-to-good professional artist, like the author Bendrix, looks back on his failed illicit wartime affair with a woman he fervently hoped to marry but who suddenly breaks off the affair. Julia, like Sarah, cannot continue to live in sin, a problem, as we shall see, that was to beset Graham and Catherine with some very serious confessional difficulties of their own. Ryder's rather crowded adulterous ménage à trois between Julia, himself and God (He finally wins) bears many thematic similarities to that of Bendrix and Sarah. Ryder, of course, would never be seen dead in a cheap Paddington hotel, although, when abroad, he seems to have shared Bendrix's interest in prostitutes.

Greene was incapable of writing Catherine out of his life. There is nothing new about this. Ted Hughes was arguably afflicted by a similar reluctance to let go of Sylvia Plath. Many of the poems in *Birthday Letters* seem to have been written by the end of the 1970s. After that the poet's friends say he became burnt out creatively

Catherine certainly drove Greene to the edge of suicide several times. Greene's diary quote for 15 February 1949 makes this clear. It is the 'Suicide Last Letter' found on the body of Thomas Lovell Beddoes after taking poison:

My dear Phillips
I am food for what I am good for – worms. I have made a will

here which I desire to be respected. W Beddoes must have a case of champagne, Moet 1847 growth to drink my health in . . . Life was too great a bore.

In *Ways of Escape*, Greene reflected on his own suicidal impulses: 'So it was that in the fifties I found myself tempting the end to come like Bendrix, but it was the end of life I was seeking not the end of love. I hadn't the courage for suicide, but it became a habit for me to visit troubled places, not to seek material for novels but to regain the sense of insecurity which I had enjoyed in the three blitzes on London.'

Catherine's nature seems imbued with a remarkable lack of guilt, or a monstrous form of self-absorption, depending how one looks at it. She does seem to share with Sarah a remarkable sexual candour: when an act was done it was done. The havoc she caused by sleeping with other women's husbands, and later with priests, was not something she seemed to trouble herself with. Yet not even the Jameson's Irish whiskey, which she later came to depend on, could successfully numb the effects of the often wilful way she chose to live. Her friend Diana Crutchley said to me, 'She had a lot of money, but, you know, she wasn't very happy. She told me she really disliked herself.'

Greene's conscience, on the other hand, remained fettered by the heavy iron weight of his guilt. That is one reason why he often wrote to Catherine – especially at the beginning of their passion – saying that he wished they were 'pagan', and could live like pagans in Greece, or wherever, oblivious to the responsibilities of other people.

Greene never had an especially high opinion of human nature. He preferred to spend his time alone, reading. For Greene, his books were his real world. As soon as his affair with Catherine became really serious, he began re-acquainting himself with Henry James's Kate Croy; then he re-read the nineteenth-century Russian authors. In August 1947, for example, Greene wrote to tell Catherine that whilst 'book-hunting' he had bought an Everyman edition of *Oblomov* by Goncharov.

Before that he had read Tolstoy's short stories on the train to London (he thought they were 'brilliant').

Greene's affair with Catherine lasted – physically – until the early 1960s; but continued emotionally for many more. There is now scientific evidence from studies in evolutionary biology to suggest that 'erotic love' only has a natural life span of between one to three years, based on the infant's early attachment to the mother. After that time, scientists suggest, *eros* naturally subsides into the calm of *agape*. Greene's continual attempt to creatively reclaim the intensity of the early two or three years of his love for Catherine arguably bears this out. Indeed the opening lines of 'After Two Years' suggest this directly:

> *I have only two years to give,*
> *But they are yours,*
> *Of all the lives a man has to live,*
> *From the obscure word*
> *In the cradle heard*

Greene, in order to help him understand Catherine – and himself – attempted to answer the same question. Indeed, he never stopped. Until her death, he kept returning in his letters to the early, intense days together, almost, it seems, as a way of keeping alive the narrative blood of those first precious years. Examining his life one can say that for Greene, adultery was a means by which he grafted vital new Proustian experiences – what Greene liked to describe as experiences a man never forgot – into the vaults of his imagination. To remember requires an act of imagination. To imagine is to create.

Anybody investigating Greene's creative influences during the most prolific period of his life cannot fail to pick up on the fact that all his serious mistresses were foreign. This is important. For any Englishman who has an impassioned love affair with a beautiful, intelligent American, part of the appeal – especially if they are half-English – is that the two can never understand each other; indeed, part of the attraction in the Greene–Walston affair was an unwritten truth that they *could* never understand each other.

The whole appeal of love is that it is irrational; and Catherine was one of the most irrational people Greene had ever met. Religion and love are very similar in that respect.

Greene also clearly liked slightly dominating female types. He almost seemed to derive a gleeful satisfaction from always referring to Catherine as his 'mistress'. There was the occasion, for example, in 1952 when Greene, Catherine and Waugh attended a dinner party at Carol Reed's King's Road house in Chelsea, at which Waugh had been offensive and cruel to Sir Alexander Korda, who had brought his girlfriend with him. Greene was trying to help Waugh out by steering a Reed script assignment his way ('Not very exhilarating work but he promises good wages,' as Waugh wrote to Nancy Mitford in a letter on 1 June 1952). The next day, sharing a taxi, an annoyed Greene had challenged Waugh as to why he had been so rude. Korda, Waugh said, had no right to bring his mistress to Reed's house.

'But,' replied Greene, 'I brought my mistress.'

'That is quite different. She is married.'

Greene was always attracted to experience, especially in a woman. He found innocence, or the idea of the willowy English rose type, as emotionally precious as a Wedgewood bone china service, deeply unappealing. He preferred the sound of plates smashing, and an undercurrent of high-voltage emotional and sexual energy. There is a scene in his 1959 play *The Complaisant Lover* that is possibly self-revealing. Like *The End of the Affair*, the play was dedicated 'To C'.

Anne: Have you loved a lot of people?
Clive: Only four. It's not a high score at thirty-eight.
Anne: What happened to them, Clive?
Clive: In the end the husbands won.
Anne: Were they all married?
Clive: Yes.
Anne: Why do you choose married women?

Clive: I don't know. Perhaps I fall in love with experience.

Anne: One has to begin.

Clive: Perhaps I don't care for innocence.

I don't want to labour the details of the often quite bizarre sexual role games Greene played with Catherine Walston, but one does get the sense, reading his letters to her, that he seemed to privately entertain some sort of schoolboy fantasy about his 'Mistress Catherine' running a disciplinary salon for the sexually imaginative.

In the beginning of their affair, Greene would often write to Catherine as if she was his mother, ending by saying, 'only five more days to the end of term' (meaning until he saw her). When Greene was an adolescent, his first infatuation was with his family nanny, a much older woman whom he curiously refers back to in his impassioned 1947 letters to Catherine. He often made a subconscious sexual link with female authority figures. When Greene managed to get himself taken away from Berkhamsted School, aged sixteen, and psychoanalysed in London by Kenneth Bell, he became sexually obsessed with Bell's wife, a curvaceous woman years older than himself. The Bells lived in Bayswater, near Paddington Station. It is likely that Greene's first experience of prostitutes – what he liked to call the 'brothel life' – began during those impressionable six months in London.

As Greene got older, of course, his preference for older women was substituted by an inevitable desire for younger companions. But he still liked them married. When I went to Antibes to interview Yvonne Cloetta, Greene's mistress of over thirty years, it was evident that she was certainly no ingénue. Greene finally left Catherine for Yvonne in the early 1960s. Far from being Greene's petite, poodle-like Cote D'Azur 'companion', as she has been portrayed, Yvonne has an immediately apparent, feisty, no-nonsense, sexual authority – bordering on the bossy – that Greene clearly seemed to like.

The moment I met Yvonne, it was very clear that she must

have had a powerful hold over him. In addition to looking almost eerily like a female version of Greene, with grey-blue eyes and the same mischievously cherubic face, she certainly had the streak of gentlemanly feminine chic that Greene seemed to find so essential in his women.

He liked women to be able to take the initiative, to take control. As he told Marie Françoise Allain, 'With women, I've usually needed to be shown the green light.' The red light district of his interests, of course, was quite another matter.

Whilst in Vienna to research *The Third Man* in February 1948, he was chaperoned by Elizabeth Montagu, who worked as Alexander Korda's personal assistant. Trips were arranged to tour the Russian zone across the canal; interviews were set up with the American police chief, playboy Austrian counts, Austrian Catholic publishers, and a 'hideous hawk-like American woman who won't take "No" for an answer. My dear, I'm so bored, but I think I've got the main point for the story & so I promise not to be late with our date.'

He was referring to a rendezvous he and Catherine had arranged in Rome. Greene had persuaded Korda to fly him to a luxury hotel to write the short story/treatment for *The Third Man*. 'You bring whisky & silk pyjamas. Italy won't wipe out Achill – nothing would. But it will be a lovely alternative.' They planned to stay until April, visiting Rome, Venice and Assisi.

Greene finally got his story 'tapped', as he put it, after Montagu set him up to meet with Peter Smollett, Vienna correspondent of *The Times*, whom he may already have known from his secret service days. Whilst plying Smollett with Scotch, Greene learnt about the black market penicillin racket that was the cause for Harry Lime's disappearance.

Whilst in Vienna, Greene spent an admirable amount of energy firing off Byronic letters of obsessive infatuation to Catherine, staring dreamily at her photo by his bed and telling her how he was nervously counting down the seconds before arriving in Rome (via Prague) where they were meeting up ('of course I shouldn't begin to believe in it until the day before'). He called her once on the phone but it cost £2 and he confessed he was 'getting mean'.

But there was a typical Greene paradox about his research activities in Vienna. When Greene wasn't scribbling love letters, he was asking Elizabeth Montagu to accompany him as he trawled around the local brothels. What surprised her was not so much his appetite for the Viennese brothel life but his apparent choice of the most haggard-looking women he could find. Elizabeth told me that Greene never once mentioned the name Catherine Walston when he was with her in Vienna.

When Elizabeth asked him one night how he could reconcile his interest in the local prostitutes with his Catholicism, he said, 'I have my ways.' Greene was to later enjoy taking Catherine to brothels. The role-playing side of their relationship certainly became unusual.

Italy – perhaps it was the cocktail of love and religion – always seemed to bring out the erotically imaginative side of Greene and Catherine's relationship. Whilst in Venice, after the last day's filming of *The Stranger's Hand*, which Greene had scripted for his friend Mario Soldati, Greene requested a make-up artist to come over to his hotel. The film was having its wrap party that night in a Venetian brothel. 'There is a certain lady I've got in the hotel who I've always wanted to take. Could she come dressed up as a boy?' said Greene, his friend Guy Elmes told Michael Shelden. Catherine joined the party dressed up in a large cap with her knotty dark hair tucked away underneath. 'And she came in with us and enjoyed it as a man . . . she had a whale of a time – roared with laughter – thought it very funny. I can still hear her laughter . . .'

With Catherine, certainly much of the appeal to Greene was that their natures complemented each other. Greene was exceptionally intelligent and had an over-active imagination. For all his Hemingwayesque talk in Vienna of dining with a party of 'foreign correspondents' (that will be 'tough and drunken'), Greene really had quite a feminine nature. He could never drive; he certainly didn't shoot or hunt – although he was handy with his slipper swiping at cockroaches in Freetown – and was in fact, for all his practical jokes, quite shy. As he told Marie Françoise Allain, he usually put on an 'act' for people. Catherine was a natural athlete, an exhibitionist, opinionated without being intellectual or especially well read, sexually domineering and – in contrast to Greene, whose obsessive need to feel that he was of 'use' to his lovers was often a form of twisted egotism – frankly unrepressed.

Catherine's striking beauty was clearly another part of the attraction, yet, interestingly, in his letters there is only the odd instance of Greene complimenting Catherine on her looks. He was a compulsive reader of theology and it is probable that he was more interested in the theological and aesthetic philosophy debate about beauty as a form of divine revelation. When Keats, in May 1819, wrote his *Ode to a Grecian Urn*, with its famous final couplet,

> *Beauty is truth, truth beauty – that is all*
> *Ye know on earth, and all ye need to know*

he could hardly have expected his premise to become the subject of serious late-twentieth-century *scientific* inquiry that has recently pulled science and religion together, not apart.

Although Catherine had an intuitive intelligence about men, Vivien could also be highly perceptive, as Greene was aware. In *The Heart of the Matter*, there is a wrenching scene shortly before Scobie finally leaves 'literary' Louise. Scobie declares that the truth 'has never been of any real value to any human being – it is a symbol for mathematicians and philosophers to pursue. In human relations kindness and lies are worth a thousand truths.' That might be a noble sentiment for a non-believer, but it is a fairly hopeless one for a Catholic; or as Greene put it with Scobie, a 'vain struggle to retain the lies'.

'Don't be absurd, darling. Who do you think I love if I don't love you?'

'You don't love anybody.'

'Is that why I treat you so badly?' He tried to hit a light note and it sounded hollowly back at him.

'That's your conscience,' she said, 'Your sense of duty. You've never loved anyone since Catherine died.'

The last letter (that was kept) that Vivien wrote to Catherine is undated and the 'Dear Catherine' has been dropped. Elizabeth Rothenstein had just come to lunch. She had been 'very sweet' but had frightened Vivien, saying 'she was afraid of losing you . . . I don't usually repeat what I'm told, as you know – it's so exhausting! I do believe we together are doing a wise *interim* thing. She, E. [Elizabeth] thinks the same will happen to you as to the others [presumably this is referring to Greene's other mistresses], but I don't believe it because I don't think that life will *satisfy* you for very long.'

Once Greene had his story notes for *The Third Man* safely locked up in the smart new briefcase that Catherine had given him for Christmas, he couldn't wait to meet her in Rome. Italy was to become Graham and Catherine's second Achill. Indeed, in many ways, Anacapri was to actually replace it. 'In Italy I wrote the treatment for *The Third Man*', wrote Greene in *Ways of Escape*, 'but more importantly I found the small house (in Capri) where all my later books were to be at least in part written.'

Finding the Villa Rosaio was a stroke of luck. He discovered it was on the market for around £3,000 'within hours' of arriving on the island with Catherine in the early spring of 1948. He bought it largely with money made from the sale of the film rights of *The Third Man*.

Before making his 'date' with Catherine in Rome, however, Greene planned to drop in (probably on secret service business) on Prague, where he hoped a revolution was about to break out. He was anxious 'not to miss' it. When the snow was finally cleared at Vienna airport, he stayed in Prague for about a week. But, disappointingly, there was no major military coup.

Italy, when Greene finally got there, was a working holiday. He liked to read out his work to her as she sat up in bed in the hotel suite. As Greene says in the introduction to *The Third Man*, he always found himself incapable of writing a film script unless he wrote it as a short story – or novella – first. All he had shown to Sir Alexander Korda so far were a few lines he had written on a scrap of paper: 'I had paid my last farewell to Harry a week ago, when his coffin was lowered into the frozen February ground, so that it was with incredulity that I saw him pass by, without a sign of recognition, among the host of strangers in the Strand.'

Writing to Catherine from his publisher's desk just after this first visit to Italy, Greene seemed – for once – at ease with himself. He had finished the story and was already now beginning to think about his next novel. 'My dear I love & miss you more than I've ever done. I want you to do mad things – & I'd try to make them seem quite sane and sensible, exciting and peaceful, reasonable and eternal as soon as they are done.' He couldn't bring himself to write to her about the 'dreary' hell of his continued saga with Dorothy. Oddly, Greene had decided the best way to end it with her was to take her on a long holiday. 'I'll take her to Africa but the end is nearly on us – it's going to be a pretty miserable time . . . How peaceful Venice was & Ravello & that sloping field beyond Anacapri. I want you and peace, Cafryn, with no more decisions to be made & no more ointment to put on.' He longed to be doing his writing and 'to belong to oneself'.

Whilst Greene was in Italy with Catherine, Dorothy had been left alone in London to confront the truth that many middle-aged women must fear: Greene was seriously in love with another woman. He had given her an address in Rome (c/o Thomas Cook) but had not – perhaps deliberately – bothered to pick up any letters. Dorothy's letter was forwarded to the Hotel Europa in Venice. Why Catherine had the letter in her Black Box remains a mystery. The letter had been torn into three pieces. It is the only letter from Dorothy to Greene that seems to have survived, and is dated 14 April:

Heard little except the story of you and Walston for an hour and a half. Everyone from Douglas [Jerrold, with whom Greene shared his office at Eyre and Spottiswoode] to the packers [at the publishing firm] it seems know you are behaving like a fool over an American blond as you have made no attempt to disguise it from anyone, everyone you know in London is talking about it too! Charles [the chairman of the firm] supplies the directors with information (he is in great demand as he has become part of the set up and drinks with you all) and your secretary deals with the lower orders and so on. They also know that you are prepared to break up Oxford for this woman. Although they guessed it all as far back as last April it was not until this Autumn (while I was away) and the affair seems so strong and you completely lost your head that they are sure, you have been foolish to tell Charles so much.

They are of course 'very sorry for the other woman' who they regard as a kind of Graham Greene specimen – something to be kept in a pint of wine and never seen or mentioned. It appears that when you are not with Walston you are 'babbling' on the telephone to her – I suppose the operator listens in. The general idea is that you are going out of your mind as no man in his right senses would behave as you do over an American blond with a yearning for culture!

They also know that she has returned to Italy with you – this I checked when I came home to see how far any of the story was true I find she flew over the day after and then went back with you I suppose and will return at the end of the month – on the 26th I've no doubt.

So you see my dear there is little use in trying to build up any kind of life not even the one I suggested you are not to be trusted to help make one in anyway. I suppose we will go on living together for a while checking our bags in and out and sleeping there between times I feel I don't care either way life has been so completely unmarked for me during our time together and so much has had to be lost that nothing matters very much any longer. I'll go on with it all as long as the parent lives of course but I'll be glad when its over.

Dorothy went on to say, in her garbled prose, that his attitude towards her since she came back from Africa had puzzled her. His 'excuses about a lot of trips were so thin' but she had no idea how far a journey he had already made 'in the other direction'.

There seems little point in our holding on dear a week or two with me will fall very flat after three months with a woman you are so madly in love with so cancel it if you like it could be awful too to lie with one woman when all your thoughts are on another. I am glad I know all this as otherwise I would have tried to perk things up again with us in several ways now I simply live my life apart from you.

I have written this to you because it's impossible to talk to you I don't want a repetition of the last revolting utterances with you, one only spits at someone you regard as a pretty low creature and a woman who has lived so long with you and through so much.

When you come back please don't mention Italy or your film.

I will arrange as soon as possible for us to have separate rooms as I know you will prefer it you couldn't of course suggest it as it would have meant telling the truth.

If at any time you want to make a life we can share or this thing with Walston breaks tell me but any advance now I'm afraid must come from you.

But he didn't want to think about Dorothy. Achill had meant peace, but in Italy, on that first trip, the sense of inner peace he found with Catherine – *away* from Dorothy and Vivien – was even greater. Like the still music that lies in the 'heart of light, the silence' that T.S. Eliot describes in *The Waste Land*, when the Hyacinth girl, her 'arms full' and her 'hair wet' appears almost as a mystical apparition in the Hoefgarten. As Greene had hoped, they stayed in Italy until spring. In April, after visiting the church of San Francesco in Venice, and monasteries in Assisi and Padua, Greene wrote a love poem to Catherine about how their great *pace* was perhaps more human than the sanitised peace of the monasteries they visited:

'Il pace, il pace', *the Friars invariably said,*
Meaning Peace, their Peace,
Complacently stretching a hand that covers
So many acres of vine and garden,
Offering the sense of release
And of pardon
To the obsessed, the foreign lovers,
Who betrayed themselves by a halting glance, an inflexion of voice,
'You see', they said,
'We have cause to rejoice.'

Out of reach, out of reach, the heart invariably said,
Is pace, *your great* pace,
Of cloister and well, the plaster image for prayers.
But love is a little peace as well as a little death:
In an hour our pulse shall cease,
Stopped like a breath,
Our bodies thrown down like clinches on a chain,
Abandoned like choice.
You see, the heart said,
We too have cause to rejoice,
Here is 'Il pace, Il pace'.

April 1948

martinis before lunch

Below the date 9 January 1949 in Catherine's new aquamarine diary, Greene wrote the following quotation from the French philosopher Léon Bloy: 'Man has places in his heart that do not yet exist, and into them enters suffering that they may have existence.'

This was, of course, to be the epigraph chosen by Greene for *The End of the Affair*. In *Ways of Escape* he records that the novel 'first came to life' in December 1948 in a bedroom at the Hotel Palma in Capri shortly before he moved into the Villa Rosaio.

Much of the novel was to be written in Capri over the following three months. Catherine and Greene arrived on the island on 26 January, having driven from Rome with their film director friend Mario Soldati. Catherine had plans to write a novel whilst she moved Greene (who was hopelessly undomesticated) into his new villa. Her young children – and later her husband – were to join them in time.

As Catherine records in her diary, Greene – who had been suffering from a severe bout of manic depression – gave her the love poem 'After Two Years' on the afternoon of 31 January 1949. He wrote in pencil after lunch on the roof terrace. The night before they had had their first supper alone together at the new house. They ate bread and butter and drank a bottle of wine, sitting by a large vase of scarlet and yellow fresh flowers.

The third verse read:

> *There was a second year.*
> *I who learned Ireland first from you*
> *Learned Italy too.*
>
> *Rome and Venice, street shadow and water light,*
> *And the sense of a world that grew more dear*
> *Because of the feet that walked and the tongue that spoke*
> *And the breath how quiet in sleep.*
> *And my joy that woke*
> *In Rome, Ravello and Capri,*
> *Sienna, Venice, every day*
> *Touching you where you lay,*
> *And knowing you are here.*
>
> *My dear, no more to say,*
> *But another year . . .*

The poem was too personal for Greene to include in *A Quick Look Behind*. The tiny hand-written copy he gave to Catherine includes the note: 'Villa Rosaio, Anacapri, February 1949. A letter written on the roof in the sun after Mass while you wrote another letter.'

For tax reasons, Villa Rosaio was bought in the name of Greene's film producer friend Peter Moore, a Korda crony, who signed a private document saying that Greene actually owned it. This was to cause serious problems later when Peter Moore found himself liable for years of unpaid local taxes. After trying to track down Greene for months, the matter was finally solved through an appropriately Greeneian coincidence, when they encountered each other in an infamous French cabaret club. 'It certainly was a surprise to bump into you at The Crazy Horse in Paris last week . . .'

Moore was technically the legal owner of the Villa Rosaio until the late 1960s. It had originally been built by Edwin Cerio, scion of an aristocratic family who owned (or used to own) a palazzo near the little cathedral in the main piazza. His sister, Laetitia Cerio, was a well known artist. Edwin Cerio wrote one of the best books ever published about the island, called *The Masque of Capri*. The book gracefully chips away at the clichés encrusted like barnacles on the old tourist face that the island put on to lure its summer visitors. Cerio reveals the bare, unsentimental and often tragic history of the island – from where the Emperor Tiberius ruled the entire Roman Empire at the time of Christ – whose literary association dates back to the Iliad. Greene said Cerio's 'fine' book captured the 'magical' essence of Capri.

Apart from the sun, and its beauty, Italy had other advantages over damp, wet Achill. When Yvonne Cloetta first visited Greene's villa in Capri in 1965 – having been so special to Catherine and Graham it took several years before he could share it with another love – Greene turned to her and said, 'It's very odd to be in the house that I love so much, leading a completely different life from what I used to.'

'What sort of life did you live here before?' asked Yvonne.

'We used to go over to Naples with friends and spend three or four nights at the Excelsior there.'

'Doing what?'

'Oh, we would go to a bordello every evening,' Greene had answered.

'Did he ever make a similar suggestion with yourself?' I asked Yvonne.

'Once . . .' she said, laughing.

'You mean once was enough?'

'*Oui*. And we nearly broke up over it.'

'You nearly ended the relationship over going to a brothel?'

'Ah, *oui*, so he never tried again.'

'Do you think he had dark sexual needs?'

'*Non*, there I think it was Catherine who needed something

extra, you know. Why I don't know. My interpretation would be that she had problems there, but I don't know.'

Greene was made an honorary citizen of Anacapri. The ceremony was held in the charming little town church of San Michele, whose floor is entirely covered with a sea of pale washed blue and white ceramic tiles depicting paradise on earth, with Adam and Eve surrounded by unicorns.

In his brief address – the hand-written original is held at Boston College – Greene spoke of how Anacapri had become his own private Arcadia in which to write: 'All my books of the last 30 years have felt the influence. Here in Capri in 4 weeks I do the work of six months elsewhere. For me there is a quiet and happiness in Anacapri which I have found nowhere else in the world. I have been a restless traveller – in Africa, South America, the Far East. I will always be restless. But Anacapri more than my native land is home and like a pigeon I always return,' he said.

Greene always spoke of the Villa Rosaio as much more than a holiday house in his letters to Catherine. Writing from Stonyhurst College in April 1950, Greene talked of how 'in spite of all the temporary poison [she had been seeing another favoured lover] & bitterness & desire to hurt, I need you more than I've ever needed you'. They had been quarrelling seriously. 'What a wretched two months it's been,' Greene wrote, saying that he had experienced the 'worst' pain since 'when I made up your mind for you that there was to be no annulment and no marriage. Pray for us very hard and go on forgiving me the work! . . . Please try to look forward to Italy. It will be all right when we get home to Anacapri and quiet. Your lover, Graham.'

For a man who – as Vivien Greene put it to me – couldn't stay in the same place for more than 'two weeks', Anacapri with Catherine was the closest he had to a family home. After finally splitting up with Catherine in the 1960s, Greene still identified 'C' so much with the Villa Rosaio that he very nearly sold it. But he just couldn't. Despite no lack of offers to relieve him of it, and many sleepless nights debating whether he should sell up, it wasn't until 1990 – the year before he died – that it was finally sold.

Much of the appeal of Capri was its timeless quality. When Catherine and Graham holidayed in the villa they lived as if they were married. In a letter sent from Kuala Lumpur in January 1952 (a year after *The End of the Affair*), Greene wrote: 'Nothing with me is changed. I love you in exactly the same way – only perhaps more deeply still after this "beastly time". Let's see more of each other in 1952 than we did in 1951. All my love. Your lover and your "husband" – Graham.'

In the Six Days War letter sent in 1967 from Tel Aviv, when Greene was nearly killed during the Arab-Israeli conflict, he refers to a squabble he had with Catherine over the fact that Yvonne had been mistakenly thought of as Mrs Greene. Catherine was clearly upset. Greene tried to explain. Yvonne always 'knew' about their Capri but she had a temperament that made concierges, butchers and bakers fond of her and possessive. 'They romanticise her as a sweet wife, she couldn't care less (as a Catholic) whether we are officially married or not; like you once in Italy she finds herself unwittingly accepted in a false role.'

Indeed, a July 1947 *News Review* article on the 'literary invasion' of Capri's famous colonists gives a potted history of the Villa Rosaio, 'looking out over the glittering sea'. Edwin Cerio had sold the house to Compton Mackenzie (whose old black velvet upholstered customised 'writing chair' stands in a lonely corner of the manuscript library at the Harry Ransom Humanities Research Center). Other writers who have lived or stayed at the villa include Thornton Wilder, Hugh Walpole and Maxim Gorky. 'The walls of Il Rosaio seem to guarantee success,' the *News Review* added, 'for now Graham Greene owns it – and lives there most of the summer with his wife and two children.'

Not exactly. The journalist was clearly talking about Mrs Walston, who did bring along her young children in the summer holidays. In *The Spectator* article of 1994, Oliver Walston described in detail his first holiday with Greene in Capri as a young boy in the 'spring of 1948'. According to Catherine's diaries, however, he arrived on 3 February 1949 with his nanny

Twinkle, younger brother Bill, and sister Susan. They flew from Northolt to Naples.

> For three months we sat in the sunshine of Capri, playing in the walled garden of Greene's white-painted villa. In the mornings we were confined to the furthest corner of the garden and told to be quiet because 'Graham works in the morning' . . . In the evenings we would stroll down to the piazza of Anacapri and eat a dish which, for a boy who lived in dreary, rationed post-war England, was unspeakably exotic. It was called pizza . . .

As Capri holiday treats, continued Oliver Walston, they would go on boat trips to the Blue Grotto or else trek over to Capri to see friends such as Gracie Fields. Catherine had some Victorian framed prints of tourists in the 'Grotto Azzura' in her upstairs study at Newton Hall, which she later gave to her personal maid, Miss Bittorf. They now hang in Miss Bittorf's sitting-room, near a glossy, tassled souvenir guide to the Houses of Parliament's Speaker's House, the official residence of the Right Hon. Betty Boothroyd, who at one time was Lord Walston's political secretary.

Reading Catherine's 1949 diary one can see how easy it would have been for anybody to have assumed that Greene and Catherine were married. On 7 February 1949, for example, she is out ordering a new chestnut dining-room table and an Italian double bed, and arranging Italian lessons for the children. Oliver Walston wrote that he remembered Greene as a 'distant figure who appeared to tolerate children but never to enjoy us. He must have looked on us as the price he had to pay to have my mother's company . . . Throughout our stay on Capri it never occurred to me that Greene was anything more than a good friend of my mother's. The complexities of human relationships, still more the concept of adultery, meant nothing to me.'

I did not need to visit Capri to see the Hotel Palma, or the

Villa Rosaio, because I had seen them both on previous occasions. Although the Villa Rosaio is quite impossible to find, up a maze of narrow unmarked streets behind the little town of Anacapri, I can close my eyes and walk there right now. Aged twenty, before I had ever heard of Catherine Walston, I drove to Naples for reasons that now seem rather odd. Before starting at university, I had the crazy idea of writing an historical novel about Tsar Alexander I in Italy. Hoping for inspiration one day – it was March, I think – I hopped over to Capri (leaving my car in Sorrento) to see where Greene had worked and lived (I had been reading *Ways of Escape*). It was raining very hard. Gushing torrents of muddy water flowed down the rough-stoned streets as I darted into an Anacapri café where the locals were huddled until the downpour stopped.

When I finally got to the house – after being directed by a local to a modern phone box standing by a locked green iron gate – I remember being surprised how very small it was. I hadn't been expecting an old palazzo like Gore Vidal's down the coast near Ravello, but I was deflated. Peering through the gate at the white-washed walls, it looked no bigger than a small hotel bungalow. I tried to imagine Greene writing at his rough grained wooden desk, in a bare upstairs study no larger than a monk's spartan cell. But something wasn't right.

It wasn't until I came back many years later, on a cold day in May 1998, that I realised I had made a mistake. There are actually two houses next to each other. The small one is a guest-house. The main villa, set back from the road, and protected by a high wall and iron gates, is a comfortably sized traditional Italian villa with landscaped garden, and a spacious colonnaded roof terrace scattered with large garden urns and pots, where Greene and Catherine would lounge, laze, work, drink and make love.

Writing to Catherine in October 1954 at the Crompton family farm in Wilton, New Hampshire, Greene says of being alone in Anacapri: 'I love you and your traces are everywhere: the dead butterfly in the Madonna's hands, the little cactuses in their bright pots, the shell ashtray – everything is yours – the pictures of Brighton. Come very soon.'

One line that often re-appears in his letters is what Catherine said to him on the first Achill trip when they drove in the old Ford from Shannon to Achill: 'I wonder what would happen if we *really* fell in love?' Writing in April 1950, just before they met up again in Italy, he said he now had the answer: 'Nothing. So let's be cheerful and sunbathe. Anyhow I love you a lot and I wish you'd fall in love with me in Italy.'

There is a photograph taken by Catherine of Greene sitting on a white stone wall seat on the roof, wearing a hugely over-sized fluffy white towelling robe, reading a book through his owl-like tortoiseshell glasses. On the roof he would read out the poetry of, say, Robert Graves, or Cafky, or write her a poem after lunch, or doze as she tried to either write her own novel or her letters. Greene was keen to encourage Catherine as a writer. Before they left for a holiday in the West Indies in the late 1950s, he gave her a new manuscript notebook. 'For Catherine, you have to start on a new story with this in Jamaica, love Graham' (it contains no story).

'Now I love Anacapri when there are no press-men and tele-phones,' Greene wrote in April 1950, after being ambushed by journalists at Hamburg and subjected to six hours of water-torture-style interviews ('Sometimes I literally want to lie down and scream'). He told Catherine that he might have enjoyed the attention when he was young, adding: 'But now one wants peace. I love Italy and Ireland because nobody bothers us that way.' In June 1951, three months before *The End of the Affair* was published, Greene wrote of Capri in his poem for Catherine, 'In the Restaurant Car':

> *I want peace and quiet,*
> *I want to play with you*
> *every day the self-same way,*
> *the same siesta in the sun and after*
> *(I might even learn laughter)*

sometimes love and sometimes lust
and sometimes just
a walk down the dull Anacapri street,
but mostly sleep.

★

The four-star Hotel Palma is behind the Quisisana Hotel in Capri, and has a fine majolica-tiled lobby. It dates back to 1822, and I definitely remember not being able to afford to stay there.

When he bought the Villa Rosaio, Greene turned over the job of decorating the house to Catherine. In letters, he refers to it as 'her' house. After buying his Paris flat in January 1952, he wrote to Catherine: 'It seems a bit eccentric having three houses. But don't let's give up Capri. It's my favourite with the curtains and rooms you chose and the holy statues from Naples. But I can't go there till we go together.'

Greene may have been a brilliant intellectual, but he was no decorator. On the back of a postcard from 'Gemma's Ristorante Pizzeria' – Greene and Catherine's regular restaurant – there is a shopping list in Catherine's hand-writing for furniture for the Capri villa. It lists a living-room chair, three outdoor chairs, outdoor cushions, two pillows, one mattress, and so on. When Greene was away from the villa, it was looked after by the owner of Pensione Aniello, a simple family hotel in Anacapri. Whenever work was needed on the house – Greene was to put in new electricity, and new boilers – Aniello would negotiate on his behalf with the local plumbers and electricians.

Capri may seem to be a paradise. But there is always a darker side to island life. People who seek refuge in islands are not usually happy. They are often not just escaping the mainland of life, but escaping from themselves. It is not just a coincidence that Greene's two favourite refuges, Achill and Anacapri, were both islands. Greene may have been obsessed with the idea of crossing borders in his fiction, but in his life he preferred to live where he could control his borders.

On the island, Greene and Walston were to live as an

eccentric extended family, of which the Villa Rosaio was the centre. The group of close friends included the writer Shirley Hazzard, her husband Francis Steegmuller, and a sex-crazed local doctor called the Dottoressa Moor, to whom Greene had first been introduced by Norman Douglas. 'The best of my two doctors, my dear. She doesn't try to stop me drinking like the others,' Douglas had said to Greene early in their – somewhat unlikely – friendship. The Austrian Dottoressa was the only doctor used by the local peasants and farmers, who paid her in fish, bottles of wine, or a few lire. They would certainly never have gone to Alex Munthe, physician to the Queen of Sweden and author of *Villa of San Michele*, who plundered the island for Graeco-Roman treasures in order to turn his villa into a private museum. 'Selfish to all except her patients (to them a bit of a bully), egotistical, self-pitying often, she could drain friends dry for the sake of her own survival,' wrote Greene of the Dottoressa in the epilogue of her remarkable memoirs, *An Impossible Woman*, that he – in his seventies and one of the most acclaimed writers in the world – edited and found a publisher for.

Catherine and Greene found her quite maddening, but, more importantly, fiercely loyal and a Capri original in her 'quality of passionate living'. Greene used her as a model for Aunt Augusta in *Travels With My Aunt*. Sex was a frequently discussed subject. The Dottoressa and Catherine's personal secretary, Miss Bittorf, also an Austrian, became good friends, bound by their zestful appetite for physical passion. Just as the Greene–Walston papers contain a hardly legible list – written on Europa Hotel notepaper, from their 1948 visit to Venice – of all the women Greene could remember having slept with (there was another list for prostitutes), so he included in the Dottoressa's memoirs a list of the men that the old doctor could recall passing through her bed. The list ran to thirty-two names, and included the Capri pharmacist, the local teacher, sailors, flying officers, doctors, peasants, a Russian tenor and Edwin Cerio. When the Dottoressa was too ill to continue her practice, and had to leave the island, Gracie Fields sang at the little harbour as the boat chugged out of Marina Piccola.

On Capri, Greene became a sort of honorary consul figure, using his international influence to help locals settle various disputes. For example, when he heard reports through his friends on the island that the parish priest at the cathedral in the Piazza was turning into a dictator (not unlike the priest responsible for the downfall of Monsignor Quixote), Greene wrote a letter rebuking him. (The priest had committed the unwise sin of being rude to Gemma, the proprietor of Greene's favourite restaurant.) The letter was pinned up in the square. Greene went so far as asking the Vatican to intercede.

On Catherine and Graham's early visits to Capri, they became close friends with Norman Douglas whose novel *South Wind* was an elegantly brittle evocation of the sybaritic life on Capri. Catherine, in particular, adopted him, and her photos from the late 1940s include many of Douglas, Greene and herself, draining another bottle of local wine and playing drunken party games (in one, Catherine has removed some of her clothes). Greene was naturally indisposed towards homosexuals – at Oxford he deliberately avoided the Harold Acton aesthete set – but, of course, he was always willing to make an exception for anybody with a creative enough mind who didn't bore him. Through Douglas, Greene also became friends with the Italy-based photographer Islay Lyons.

As with Ernie O'Malley, whose financial affairs were always a mess and who was, for a time, reduced to living with Cormac in just two rooms at Burrishoole, Catherine tried to help Douglas out by sending over to Italy a steady supply of wine, books and presents. These included a jersey and expensive shaving soap. Douglas always wrote back with a deep sense of gratitude. On 10 April 1951, for example, he wrote to Greene: 'Much love to C, I am wearing the yellow pullover at the moment . . . I have enjoyed the book so much.' A month later, in response to a Greene postcard about sending tobacco: 'Any kind of tobacco would do . . .'; in July he wrote again: 'It's very naughty of Catherine to take so much trouble about sending things. Please thank her ever so much!'

But other letters to Greene and Catherine from Douglas were not so happy. After Greene had used his literary influence to get Douglas's long essay on *Paradise Lost* published in England, there was a hitch over the agreed terms of payment. But he couldn't 'bother any more' about the hope 'of extracting an extra quid', since he was in a very poor state of health. 'You might let him [Frere, Greene's publisher at Heinemann] know that he had better lose as little time as possible over the proofs . . .'

In Greene's epilogue to the Dottoressa's memoirs, he describes in some detail why Norman Douglas took an overdose of sleeping pills in 1954. A few years before, in a cautionary letter about the perils of exotic Far Eastern travel, Douglas had written to warn Greene: 'Look out for syphilis . . . I am in a pretty groggy way myself. In addition to all my other complaints I have now got erysipelas: no fun. If I can now get Babylonian itch, and a tape-worm or two, the collection will be complete.' The Dottoressa signed his death certificate and the nature of his death was secretly buried.

Until Greene unscrewed his Parker pen. Greene was occasionally something of a happy hypocrite when it came to the double standards he applied to vigorously protecting his own privacy whilst invading other people's for his work. But he remained loyal to Douglas. In his 1987 letter to me, dictated from Antibes thirty-seven years after Douglas's death, he was still defending his friend. One of the points in my letter had referred to the Imagist poet and biographer Richard Aldington – a friend of T.S. Eliot and Ezra Pound (beside Greene's death-bed in Switzerland was a copy of Pound's *Letters*). Another of my early literary projects was my hope of publishing a small volume of Aldington's selected poems, writing an introduction myself. I asked Greene if he had known him. 'I never knew Aldington and I thought his book attacking my friend Norman Douglas was despicable,' he replied.

Later, I was amazed that Greene had not ripped my letter up the second he had seen the name 'Aldington'. Indeed, in an odd way, his brief, curt remark, in the context of an otherwise warm letter, only reinforced my early opinion of his possessing a natural and very real generosity. What I had not known was that Greene had led a vicious and ugly literary assault on Aldington after he published an excoriating biography of Douglas (following his death in 1954) called *Pinorman*. Aldington – who has since been clearly vindicated – was the first to cast (in a fairly restrained way) light on Douglas's sexual appetite for Italian children, in addition to lobbing a few well-aimed javelins at the already tarnished and tatty sails of his literary reputation.

A carbon copy of Greene's original review can be seen in the 'Douglas' file at Boston College. It is so personally hostile towards Aldington that it was flatly rejected by the *London Magazine* on the grounds of libel. Greene then wrote to Aldington, challenging him to allow publication anyway; Aldington refused. A nice example of Greene's talent for literary double-crossing ensued. Having horse-whipped Aldington for being a moral coward who 'has seen fit' to publish after Douglas's death to escape the courts, Greene subsequently did exactly the same thing by publishing his review – a decade later – after Aldington's death in 1966.

There is another colourful twist to this story. In the 'Walston' file at Boston College, there is a letter to Greene from young Oliver Walston, written in 1966 from America where he was working as a publisher. Whilst recently in England, 'Mum' had given him her copy of Norman Douglas's smutty limericks. In her diary for Sunday 6 February, 1949, Catherine records how, after Mass, followed by a lazy lunch with Norman Douglas and his American friend Kenneth Macpherson, they sat around drinking Scotch and reading out his poems until 6pm.

By way of example:

> *There was an old man of Stamboul*
> *With a varicose vein in his tool*
> *In attempting to come*
> *Up a little boy's bum*
> *It burst, and he did look a fool*

Oliver Walston thought the limericks funny and offered his services – and contacts – in the cause of trying to get the pornographic verses published in America. He added that he felt strongly that any contract should include some remuneration to the Douglas family. Where should he send the cheque?

Greene's response was sharp: 'Dear Oliver, Surely it is not a question of feeling strongly that some payment should be made to Norman Douglas's estate but a legal obligation . . .'

Another visitor to the Villa Rosaio was Harold Acton, the half-American owner of the famed Villa La Pietra outside Florence. Greene and Acton had been at Oxford together but had badly fallen out – two new razor-sharp swords slashing at each other's egos – over a failure of shared aesthetic taste regarding the subject of poetry rather than sex. Greene had been editor of the *Oxford Outlook*. Much to his annoyance, Acton used to make a habit of dropping off his latest poems to the porter's lodge at Balliol, or to Greene's digs at Thorncliffe Road in Summertown, with astonishingly pompous and self-important covering notes scrawled in a florid ink hand: 'Please do not print it all if you will not give it the first and most important position in the paper . . .'

Greene printed Acton's work. But Acton drew blood – Greene's first real taste of literary failure – towards the end of their final term at Oxford, when he reviewed Greene's first volume of poetry in *The Cherwell*. The review is caustically insulting and must have wounded Greene's ego. '*Babbling April* is a diary of average adolescent moods,' he declared. On reading a poem about Greene's (probably invented) experience of Russian roulette, standing alone on Berkhamsted Common, 'with eyes blind and fingers trembling', Acton was seized by the urge 'to throw down the book in disgust, to cry aloud: "For God's sake, be a man!"'.

Although Greene attempted a retort by noting the absurdity of aesthete Harold Acton – a youthful portrait of him drawn by Pruna in 1925 has him sitting in a grey flannel suit wearing a lavender-pink double-breasted waistcoat – appointing himself a 'professor of Manliness', the damage was done. A few days later,

Acton finished off the already bruised Greene, saying he should have dismissed his little book in a few words appropriate 'to the vast contempt I feel for Mr Greene'. He was still licking his wounds when yet another pummelling by Acton was dished out. Greene called this a 'gross impertinence'.

It took decades for this passage of arms to be forgotten and the scars to heal. Still, it was impossible to ignore Greene as a literary force, whilst Acton's own career had drooped like an old waterlily. He clearly liked Catherine (who was half-American like himself), and invited Greene and his mistress up to La Pietra. In August 1962 (note the date: well after the 'we were lovers for twelve years' line cranked out by Greene to Mark Amory), Acton wrote from his Florence villa: 'You and Catherine were the kindest and most considerate of hosts, and my visit to you was vastly refreshing after the hotel life and mineral baths which left me a bit fatigued' (he was referring to a holiday he had taken on the nearby island of Ischia prior to staying in Capri). Another postcard, depicting a Neapolitan girl in a skimpy bikini, describes 'the jolliest weekend I've enjoyed for many a year. I only hope I did not try your patience with my idle chatter. Love to Catherine. When may I return your hospitality?'

It is not known who made the first offering of peace. A letter from Greene to Acton at La Pietra, suggests it may have been Sir Harold; Greene's ego had an unforgiving side when it came to literary feuds. And he had clearly not forgotten.

Dear Harold,
Thank you so much for your letter which made up for those unfavourable reviews. Catherine and I always remember that very happy day we spent at your villa. What ages have passed since those squabbles in Oxford . . .

Yet, as so often in this investigation, that is not the whole story for that day. Catherine's diary entry for the visit in March 1949, shows the cracks in her and Greene's relationship were starting to widen by the month. After a grimly depressing dinner and argument that lasted until the early hours of the morning, Greene drugged himself to sleep.

There is one bizarre story – and yet another strange coincidence – that earns Greene a footnote in Capri's decadent homosexual history. I wrote earlier that I had twenty-six file boxes of abandoned research notes for my LA novel (stored in a lock-up at Santa Monica and Vine). One of the boxes is titled 'Capri'. The plot of my would-be big LA novel involved the downfall of a disgraced Hollywood talent manager who ends up fleeing to Europe. I had decided – two years before starting this book – to imagine him being discovered by his former wife (on holiday with her new husband or boyfriend) working as the manager of a small hotel on Capri. When I went to the island in 1997 to research the chapter, I couldn't find a hotel that seemed right. Then one morning, after climbing up the treacherously steep, three-mile mule path that leads up to the Villa Jovis, at times having to crawl through the scraggy undergrowth near the sheer rock face where Tiberius's unlucky victims were flung hundreds of feet to their deaths on the rocks below, I walked past an empty, derelict white villa with a gold-leaf freize and marble colonnaded entrance. It looked as though it was being renovated.

Inquiries established that it had once been owned by Count Jaques Fersen, a wealthy homosexual Swedish-German count who had written a long decadent poem in praise of the Marquis de Sade. I decided that I would use it as the hotel in my novel.

Many, many months later, whilst reading the Dottoressa's memoirs, I found a brief section devoted to this derelict old villa. It turned out that the old count was quite a character. Compton Mackenzie included him in his book *Vestal Fires*, whilst Roger Peyrefitte's book *The Exile of Capri* is also about Fersen. The Dottoressa, in her jumbled way, describes the house: 'Like the Palace it has a precipice which drops straight down. There in a green garden stands the house, quite in the wilderness, and the garden has become a jungle out there on the rock.' She went on to describe an old Swiss hunchback who used to smoke opium with Fersen in an exotic 'oriental retreat' that Fersen had built as his personal opium den. Before the count died of a drug overdose during a homosexual orgy at the villa, he had, according to the Dottoressa's memoirs, given her a small tin of opium.

Years later, when Greene once mentioned he had enjoyed smoking opium in Indo-China, she gave him the tin. And so it was that about thirty years after Count Ferson died, Greene opened the tin late one night to smoke opium with Catherine back at his Albany flat off Piccadilly. Although a lot dripped on the bed – Greene had a king-size blue bed with a large photo of Catherine above the headboard – and the building reeked of the drug (other residents included Kenneth Clark, Harold Nicolson and Terrence Rattigan), they managed to smoke several pipes each. Graham later told the Dottoressa that Fersen had the most 'beautiful opium'.

the r e p l a c e m e n t l o v e r

'Forty-five today, darling, I'm racing you to the end,' wrote Greene to Catherine on his birthday, Sunday 2 October, 1949. The sight of John and Elizabeth Rothenstein at the early-morning Mass at Farm Street in Mayfair made him miss her 'bitterly'. He felt starved and half-witted without her. Vivien had sent him Burton's *Travels in West Africa*; Dorothy gave him Clare's *Poems of Madness*; his son Francis an electric torch; and, rather oddly, his daughter Caroline a thermometer.

Catherine, meanwhile, was staying for a long weekend with her husband at The Old Head Hotel, near Westport, breakfasting in bed – so she records in her diary – reading *Madame Bovary*. As he entered middle-age, Greene was lost at sea without an anchor. Writing – and drink – were increasingly his only palliatives; his only means of salvation. Even though he was not taking Benzedrine, he said he felt so numb inside that he may as well have been. Like Balzac's lonely gambler, his wet feet freezing in the mud, Greene knew the odds on Catherine leaving Harry were quietly stacking up against him. His letters in late 1949 and early 1950 refer again and again to images of a desperate blackjack player. 'I have laid the cards on the table. Do play them straight & with courage. I love you. I want you as a mistress, and much more as a wife [. . .] I want to trust you to tell me the truth even when it is unpleasant. There's no future in half truths. God bless you. Pray for me'.

As Greene clung on desperately to the hope that their affair wasn't 'dead', his career continued its never-ending roll of success. He had taken Catherine to the 'first night' of *The Third Man* on 2 September. Two months later an *Observer* profile-writer – Greene looks suitably grim in the photograph – described Greene as 'tall, slim, long-fingered, reticent: a man of 45, slightly worn looking, and with pale eyes that seem to be contemplating an inner joke. He dresses demurely, speaks quietly, enjoys such refined sports as winning under another name the *New Statesman* competition for a parody of his own style. The course of his outward life has been as untroubled as his appearance would suggest . . .'

Inwardly, however, Greene felt that if he lost her, he lost everything. On 16 April 1953, when Catherine didn't come up to London for the opening night of his play, *The Living Room*, he sat glumly watching the stage. He had the money and acclaim he had once craved, but now that he had achieved success, he could no longer look forward to it. After the play, the delighted audience gave a frenzied standing ovation, with eight curtain calls, and shouted 'Author, Author,' dozens of times. Greene refused to shuffle onto the stage. A journalist caught him afterwards, as he was trying to leave the theatre. 'Do not call me a success,' said Greene. 'I have never known a successful man. Have you? A man who was a success to himself. Success is the point of self-deception. Failure is the point of self-knowledge.'

By the summer of 1949, Greene was facing his worst fears. In childhood it had been the 'green baize door' that divided his life; now Greene was to be tormented by the idea of an 'iron curtain', or 'semi iron-curtain', about to drop between himself and Catherine. 'Nobody can make a curtain between us but you,' he wrote to her. Always lurking in the back of his mind was Catherine's impending move from Thriplow Farm to the stately grandeur of Newton Hall, just a mile or so up the road. If she was to leave her husband, Greene knew perfectly well it was not going to be just as she had installed herself as the chatelaine of a vast, fully serviced, five-star mansion that was run almost like the Ritz. This was something even her closest friends couldn't help but notice. 'My father always said that money was very important to Catherine,' said Lady Selina Hastings, daughter of the Earl of Huntingdon, who used to stay at Newton Hall as a young child. 'It was very much upper-class left-wing intellectual.'

In 1949, Selina's mother, Margaret Lane had proposed a scheme whereby Catherine would live with Graham for just six months, and then return to Harry. Writing to Catherine after the proposal was rejected, Greene said, 'I feel Margaret was right and if only one could have six months one could live on it after all . . .' Lady Selina explained why her parents would have been perfectly suited as mediators between Harry, Catherine and Graham. 'They would have loved it,' she said. 'They would have liked the role. They had long adulterous affairs themselves, they would have been particularly sympathetic. Their sexual morals were very free and easy.' Indeed, a confessional letter that Graham sent to Catherine in 1951 owned up to the fact that 'I've told you everything after a bit, even the kissing of Margaret . . .'

The tone of his letters about Thriplow weekends is now dour. 'Don't worry about me and Harry,' he wrote two weeks after his forty-fifth birthday, suggesting that Harry's acquiescent stance on his wife's adultery with Greene might have altered. He had also been attacked in the Catholic press. 'Adultery is adultery,' Bishop Brown had railed of *The Heart of the Matter*, 'whatever attempts may be made to disguise it.' Greene was collecting a lot of 'enemies'. He admitted to Catherine that they couldn't all be wrong.

But however played out he felt, he struggled on with *The End of the Affair*. A press cutting dated 28 October 1949, kept by Catherine, referred to a discussion of Greene at a *Brains Trust* programme — a sort of 1940s equivalent of *Question Time* — broadcast from Kingston-on-Thames. 'Graham Greene ought to be introduced to some really nice people,' advised panellist Dr Letitia Fairfield after a question was asked about Catholic novelists who specialise in the seamy side of life.

Greene didn't want to meet anybody new. He only wanted Catherine. He was still indulging wild schemes to lure her away so that they could both live together and write their books. Addressing her desire to earn her *own* money, Greene made the crazed suggestion that she become his literary agent in place of Laurence Pollinger. He wanted her to meet his 'mum'. He suggested – like the young Coleridge – that they run off to a revolutionary commune together. Another letter suggested they found a Christian mission in Africa. What 'nonsense' this all was he finally admitted, 'because I know I'll *never* win you'.

He clung on, however, to the idea of persuading her that she would only get the most out of her life if they lived and worked together. Images such as her 'red dressing gown', and combing her knotty hair by the window of her Achill cottage on their first morning together back in April 1947 began to rear up in his thoughts once again. Without her, his memory became like a cage.

Airports and Africa continued to exert their pull. In transit in December 1949 at Dakar airport, he wrote on Air France writing paper that he loved no part of the world as he loved Africa and he loved no other woman as he loved her. He loved her smell as he loved the smell of Africa; he loved her 'dark bush' as he loved the dark jungle: 'You change with the light as this place does, so that one all the time is loving something different and yet the same. I want to spill myself out into you as I wash.' He added: 'You're my human Africa.'

By this time it had become too much. On the morning of Sunday 18 December, Greene was back in Paris. He had managed to put a call through to Thriplow in the morning, but it had only made matters worse. After Mass, he walked across the River Seine and 'stupidly' found himself 'crying in the Tuileries Gardens', where they had once been so happy together. He now described their love as a form of epic battle campaign: 'You captured Rome and Dublin, and now on the second assault you've captured Paris.' He used to like being alone, but now when he thought of her that inner sense of 'peace' was cracked with uncertainty about their future. All he could think of was sitting on the floor in their 'old suite' at the Ritz with his head resting between her naked legs, fresh and warm from the bath. The sight of a telephone made him itch. But it was no good. Whisky was the only respite from the pain.

Earlier, on her thirty-third birthday on 12 February that year, Greene had written a light poem, nostalgic of their happy time in Paris when, in the Rue de Provence, they had stayed in a brothel for fun and heard the local whores reciting their menu of 'thirty-two positions' of sexual delight:

> *But the thirty-third is between me and you,*
> *On the thirty-third year,*
> *A secret that you only can understand,*
> *A secret for you only to wear.*

By the late autumn his tone was very different. In a poem 'And Afterwards Common Sense', written on 22–3 October 1949 he wrote:

> *At my sadness you always feel surprise,*
> *never foreseeing how after the sun inevitably comes the rain,*
> *And one day, after one of these goodbyes,*
> *We shall not see each other again.*

The second verse likens the forthcoming year between them to the gradual pruning apart of two saplings from each other. Greene now spoke only of counting 'our love in months'. By Christmas Greene's mood was even bleaker. On Boxing Day, they went for a walk together near Harston House. Afterwards they had a drink at the Old English Gentleman, a Harston pub that served – and still does – Greene King beer (Greene was always proud of his family connections to the brewery). The following poem – far removed from the flushed romantic excitement he had felt driving past the pub on the way to Cambridge airport almost exactly three years before – was written when they got back to Thriplow.

> *The stripped trees and the grubbed fields*
> *and the passive sky and the craving for death:*
> *O You who gave Man too the blessing to die,*
> *Shorten the term of our breath.*

'Walking Back After Drinks Together at The Old
English Gentleman' (December 1949)

★

Six months before, on the hot summer's feast day of St Peter and Paul on 29 June 1949, Catherine and Graham had gone to the same pub for beer and fried eggs, whilst Harry and young Oliver (who was bought a sailing dinghy a few days later for learning to swim) had gone to the Norfolk County Show. In the pub, fortified with Greene King, Graham had fired off another barbed letter to *The Times* complaining about how the Bank of England, in a desperate effort to curb inflation, had turned down his request for the normal businessman's allowance of £10 per day whilst he visited New York to write a Broadway dramatisation of *The Heart of the Matter*. It seems this Rodgers and Hammerstein production idea was regarded as a 'bad risk'. Greene sneered that the Bank of England 'still appears to regard (writers) as an inferior race, or at least distinct outsiders . . .'

Greene was ranting but he had been in good spirits. With money pouring in from his screen projects and the bestselling success (over 100,000 copies in hardback) of *The Heart of the Matter* – which had been banned in Ireland – Greene had bought a yacht, the *Nausikaa*, moored in Portsmouth, which he planned on sailing to Italy. He had also, it seems, tried his hand at painting. On 4 July 1949, Catherine recorded in her diary that Greene made his first stab at being an oil painter; in the evening he turned cook, boiling some eggs for supper. The following night, Father Thomas Gilby – the Dominican priest who was to exert a most powerful influence on Catherine's life after Greene – came for dinner. They all sat up talking until midnight.

But Greene's mood swings were now becoming more frequent and more violent. Two days later, after driving to London in the yellow Rolls-Royce – Catherine had an appointment to see Ernie O'Malley at the St James's Street flat – she came across Greene in a dreary depression, drinking morosely with an Italian film director and plotting to quit London and buy up an island in the West Indies. Greene suddenly flew into a rage at Catherine for showing up late. That she had been seeing O'Malley may well have had something to do with it. When Twinkle the nanny later called Greene, he swore angrily down the phone at her.

A week later, after recording that she flew to Dublin on an early-morning flight, Catherine's diary suddenly stops, other than to record that Harry and Twinkle flew over to Dublin as well on 16 July and that James Walston, her fourth 'son', was born at 39 Percy Place on 18 July. What really happened in Dublin between 14 and 29 July 1949, when she arrived back in London with two Irish hams smuggled in her luggage, remains a intriguing mystery in which Greene played an important role as accomplice.

If you look up Hon. James Patrick Francis Walston in an old *Kelly's* or *Debrett's*, the entry will state that he was born on 18 July 1949, educated at Ampleforth, and that he is the fourth son of Baron Walston. But no mention is given of his mother. In the 'Walston' file at Boston College there is a letter from James Walston to Greene in Antibes, towards the end of Greene's life, asking whether he could come and see him on a very private matter. It referred to his having reached the age when he sought answers to 'long repressed' questions. Greene replied, of course he could visit. Only, as the correspondence continued over the months, it looks as if Greene may have been deliberately evasive (he was unwell) about a suitable time for the visit.

As Norman Sherry has unearthed, based on 'impeccable sources', James Walston was not Catherine's son at all (although she is recorded as his mother in the Dublin Registry of Births and Deaths). In what would have become a high society scandal at the time, Catherine Walston 'faked' her pregnancy with James Walston by putting pillows under her dress. This was confirmed by her friend Diana Crutchley, who remembers having tea with Catherine in Cambridge and her taking the cushions out. It was all a bit of a joke.

Yet James was certainly born on 18 July 1949 at 39 Percy Place in Dublin. Greene sent a telegram of congratulations to Harry at Thriplow. He also wired a telegram to Catherine saying that he had written to her at the Lansdowne Hotel and the Shelbourne Hotel but, oddly (or perhaps not so, as she wasn't the mother), he did not 'congratulate' her.

There had always been a rumour that Greene had been the father of one of Catherine's children, according to Lady Selina Hastings. 'My father loved good stories and this was one of his favourite ones,' Lady Selina said. When she was researching her biography of Evelyn Waugh she got to know Father Philip Caraman quite well, and was given permission by him to read through the 'restricted' Greene–Caraman correspondence held in the vaults at Boston College. When Lady Selina asked Father Caraman about Greene's hinted-at paternity of one of the Walston children, he replied that it was 'absolutely categorically untrue, they are Harry's.'

Although Greene had a complicated and often uneasy relationship with his own two children, he was very serious indeed about wanting to have a child with Catherine, even if he couldn't marry her. On 24 March 1950, for example, he wrote about a visit she was making to Ampleforth to see her sons David and Bill. What 'fun' it would be, he added, if they were going up *together* as parents to take out 'our' own boy. In September 1951, writing to Catherine at Newton Hall (she moved from Thriplow around December 1950, as Greene was correcting the final proofs of *The End of the Affair*) he repeated this wish: 'If you would marry me, I'd want to do so much (for God) in return. If without bad danger to you we could have a child, I'd love a child with you.' In another letter that month he boasted about what an 'intelligent' child they could have.

Catherine, I was told by a confidant who knew her well, also desperately wanted to have a child by Greene. Sadly, however, Catherine had been warned by her doctor that having another child could be extremely hazardous – if not impossible – because of medical complications that had arisen with the birth of one of her other children. Hence Greene's phrase 'bad danger'. Diana Crutchley, a regular visitor to Thriplow at the time, confirmed to me that Catherine had seriously considered 'adopting' another child, partly for this reason.

Sherry also dismisses any idea that Greene could have been the father of James by asserting that the real mother was, in fact, a close 'friend' of Catherine's who had been sleeping with Harry, although she had apparently also been sleeping with somebody else. What he does not specify – and what has never been solved – is the name of the intimate friend of Catherine who she was prepared to go to such unusual lengths to help out, in addition to raising the son in her own house as one of her own children. It is a serious criminal offence to fill out a false maternity registration form.

When I went to visit 39 Percy Place in Dublin, there were certain elements of the Sherry story that didn't quite fit. Sherry states that 'presumably the biological mother was staying at Percy Place and at birth the baby was moved secretly to Catherine's room and the pillows dispensed with'. Possibly this might have been feasible if Percy Place was a private house and a tame Dublin doctor had been used. But, as I discovered, Percy Place is a smart Georgian terraced street about fifteen minutes' walk from Dublin's Shelbourne Hotel, just the wrong side of the canal; in 1949, No. 39 was not a private house at all.

Above the dark green front door is a faded old original glass panel in which you can faintly read the words 'St Bernard's' in white paint. Further inquiries to the current owner established that in the 1940s the house was a private maternity hospital used by well-to-do Irish women who found themselves pregnant and wanted to have their child without questions being asked. When they moved in twenty years ago, the guest-house was full of maternity scanning equipment, and the upstairs bathroom had a special midwife's bath. The top floor was a professionally run maternity ward. There is no way Catherine could have just waltzed in with her cushions, taken a maternity room, and pretended to the nurses and sisters that she was pregnant.

Catherine, it seems, actually stayed at the Shelbourne. Who then was the real mother at Percy Place? One possible candidate who cannot be ruled out is Twinkle, the Walston nanny. She flew over with Harry on 16 July, only two days before James was born; she was a close, intimate friend of Catherine. Visitors to Thriplow and later Newton Hall were always rather baffled by her role in the household. Certainly, as Oliver Walston has suggested, she was like a surrogate mother for the Walston children anyway. Why Greene swore at Twinkle down the phone is unknown, but he certainly knew exactly what was going on. Catherine's diary for 19 June records that Twinkle had been extremely ill during the night; possibly this was related to her pregnancy.

The identity of James Walston's mother is a guarded Walston secret, and I found nothing in my enquiries to support the suggestion that Twinkle was involved. However, when I brought up the subject of James Walston with Yvonne Cloetta, she informed me that Greene had once let it slip out that the 'nurse of the [Walston] children' was 'probably' his mother. There is no reason why Greene would have wanted to make this up to Yvonne, yet he may have been mischief-making. Then, of course, according to Sherry, the father may not have been Harry. Like Greene, Ernie O'Malley also certainly knew the truth. He crops up in Catherine's diaries as having visited her in Dublin on both 27 and 19 July. In a letter to Catherine, Greene mentions that when he next saw O'Malley: 'Curiously he never said a word about you or the recent event.' It was typical of Catherine to enjoy keeping the various men in her life guessing about what each other knew about her secrets. The 'event', as Greene put it, was transformed years later into fiction in *Travels With My Aunt*.

Lady Longford, who is James Walston's godmother, remembered Twinkle as 'a sort of icon figure in the Walston family. Nobody could really question anything that Twinkle did.' Yet by 1951, two years after the birth of James, things had sharply changed. One day Twinkle simply left Newton Hall and nobody knew where she had gone. She reappeared, but the diaries then become loaded with references to her hysteria. On 23 March 1951, Catherine and Twinkle had a major row. On 7 April 1951, Catherine received a twenty-page letter from her. On 18 June Catherine had a firm talk with Twinkle about dates for her leaving, noting that she is totally unable to comprehend the situation.

Thirty-nine Percy Place wasn't the only Walston address in Dublin behind whose front door lay a scandalous secret. About fifteen minutes' walk from Percy Place, across the canal, on the right side of Dublin, was Catherine's basement flat in Fitzwilliam Square where, in the 1950s, she conducted her long-term affair with the Rev. Donal O'Sullivan SJ, a highly distinguished Irish Jesuit who was head of the Irish Arts Council from 1960–73.

On 29 April 1949, on a trip to Dublin with Greene, and staying at the Russell Hotel – long since torn down – at the corner of St Stephen's Green, Catherine (before Greene's arrival) drove down to the Jesuit house at Tullabeg to have lunch with Father O'Sullivan. After lunch Donal O'Sullivan showed Catherine the five large, beautiful stained glass windows by Evie Hone that she had designed for their St Stanilaus College Chapel, built in 1946. The *Irish Times* described the windows as 'probably the most perfect stained glass presentation in Ireland, for it can always be seen without the competition of daylight from any other source'. The introduction probably came through Ernie O'Malley, who was an early champion of Evie Hone's stained glass work.

That the 1949 April visit to Ireland was not as idyllically 'peaceful' as the previous trips is suggested by a poem Greene wrote afterwards. His brooding imagery of 'wet salt', 'torn letters', dug-up graves and fatal wounds – 'incisions on every tree' – suggest his growing sense of inner torment. His memories are now 'stacked like tins'.

> *But why with images conceal*
> *My pain and my loss,*
> *Why in similes disguise*
> *The new nails in Your cross?*

Catherine's diaries for the Achill trip contain the usual references to The Old Head, where they stayed on 27 April, running out of petrol in the old Ford, and the inevitable lurking presence of Ernie O'Malley. Greene, likewise, had been seeing Dorothy Glover. On 7 April, she had dinner with both Graham and Hugh. The following day Catherine noted in her diary that Graham sounded dejected on the phone; she suspected he had spent the night at Gordon Square. Not even the once magical spell of Ireland could lift his spirits. On 26 April for example, Catherine recorded that Greene did no work. On 30 April they quarrelled until 2am. Greene's continuing dark fits of jealousy may well have been behind this.

On 4 May 1949, the day's quotation for Catherine's love diary is taken from Logan Pearsall Smith (to whom Cyril Connolly dedicated *Enemies of Promise*): 'I love to lie in bed and read the lives of the Popes of Rome. I am ready to read anew, with even renowned astonishment, the outrageous doings of those Holy & obstinate old men.' Six days after being shown the Evie Hone windows, Catherine was lunching again with Father O'Sullivan – this time at the Russell Hotel. Also in the party were Greene and her old ringer, actor Bobbie Speaight. After lunch they all strolled down to the Dawson Gallery to see a Jack Yeats painting ('A Man Entering a City At Night') that Catherine wanted Harry to buy. Harry, as it happened, couldn't stand the picture – nor, later, could he stand Father O'Sullivan – so Greene bought it instead.

When in Dublin, Catherine, of course, always stayed at either the Shelbourne, the Lansdowne (now demolished) or the Russell. But when her friendship with Father O'Sullivan became more than simply a shared enthusiasm for drinking Irish whiskey and 'discussing' modern art, it was obvious that they could not take a room at a smart Dublin hotel. Father O'Sullivan was a well known figure.

The cottage in Achill had been rented for a pittance. But one couldn't pretend that filling up a turf bucket had quite the same romantic appeal in the cold Irish capital. Fortunately, during the 1950s, Catherine had been left a considerable amount of money by a Labour MP (Dick Stokes). The basement flat in Fitzwilliam Square became her private refuge; her equivalent of the Achill cottage, a place where she could be herself, and take who she liked.

Father O'Sullivan was an opinionated, handsome man. Born in 1904 in Dunamark, Co. Cork, in the same year as Greene, he was ordained as a Jesuit at Innsbruck in 1937 and was Rector and Master of Novices at Emo Park, Portarlington – the training college for Jesuits in Ireland – from 1947 to 1959.

When allegations that the whisky-drinking Father O'Sullivan had shared a ravishing, titled American mistress with Catholic novelist Graham Greene first surfaced in 1994, there were cries of outrage from within the Irish Jesuit Province. Lawyers were, or were going to be, consulted to see what possible legal action could be taken against biographer Michael Shelden. But when older members of the Jesuit order in Ireland began talking amongst themselves, it became clear that legal action would be a serious mistake, only serving to fan the flames that had already mysteriously burnt all of O'Sullivan's private letters from Catherine Walston shortly before he died in 1977 (his medical records are 'restricted' as to the cause of his death).

One highly regarded senior Jesuit Irish priest who had been a novice under O'Sullivan in the late 1940s told me that the matter of taking legal action was 'dropped' after he felt it was his duty to pass on to 'the powers that be' certain information he had been told over the years by another Jesuit priest concerning Father O'Sullivan's aberrant moral behaviour. 'What I knew was sufficient to warn me that every word that the fellow [Shelden] said might have been true, so I passed it on, saying, "Shut up, don't make a fuss, just let the thing die, because I have enough evidence to substantiate the possibility that it was true". And they did. Not a word was said. If they had brought this fellow to court, Jesus, the thing would have blazed in lights across the sky.'

Perhaps a warning sign was already visible when Father O'Sullivan, back in the 1960s, launched a highly controversial exhibition in Dublin of the work of Irish artist Francis Bacon. Bacon's interest in crude nude forms seems to have been shared by O'Sullivan. A highly placed Jesuit told me a very bizarre story about Father O'Sullivan's libertine behaviour one night after the claret had flowed at a smart literary dinner party in a country house in Ireland. The assembled guests, and the host, were mortally shocked when Father O'Sullivan – apparently very much the worse for drink – stripped off his dog-collar and cassock and began running naked around the house chasing after the sixteen-year-old daughter of his host.

This story sounds fantastic but it was told to me as an example of just how high the flames could have danced in the sky had Jesuit lawyers decided to try dragging Shelden through the courts. The O'Sullivan affair with Mrs Walston was all the more embarrassing because it wasn't the first time that the Jesuit Master of Novices had led by a very poor example. Another Jesuit priest who served as a novitiate under O'Sullivan told me that the head of novices before Donal had also turned adulterous. 'He went off with his woman and married her, from the novitiate. I mean he was Master of Novices, can you think of anything more crazy than that?' he said. 'A man is supposed to be forming these people in the religious life and at the same time having an affair with a woman; the mind boggles.'

But other Jesuits I spoke to defended O'Sullivan as a man who, in the words of Cyril Barratt SJ (a philosophy and theology don at Campion Hall who also knew Father Martin D'Arcy and Vincent Turner SJ) was 'way ahead of his time'.

The *Irish Times* obituary of O'Sullivan did not mention any scandalous affair, but they did note that 'long before the modern post-Vatican council stress on the liturgy' O'Sullivan had helped revolutionise the liturgical presentation of the Mass in Ireland, and the revival of ecclesiastical art. Indeed, he was a man acutely sensitive to the beauty of modern art, being the pioneering force behind the Irish Arts Council's patronage of many fine twentieth-century Irish artists, notably Evie Hone. Catherine seems to have enjoyed being a link between O'Malley, who launched Evie Hone's first major exhibition in Ireland and O'Sullivan, who was one of her main patrons. Hone's work combined the rich sensuality of the medieval ecclesiastical world with the influence of modern French painters like Roualt. Catherine – who herself collected an extremely valuable collection of Henry Moore's sculptures, paintings by Jack Yeats, Lowry and John Piper – often depended on Father O'Sullivan's advice before making acquisitions of her own.

It was an odd relationship. Harry Walston did all he could to prevent Catherine giving O'Sullivan money to buy more whisky; or whatever else he wanted. As a priest, of course, Father Donal was unable to own any paintings of his own; in Catherine he could at least come close to feeling that he owned his own Picassoesque woman. As Father Barratt admitted, 'Oh, I've seen her photo many times and she would have attracted me. There is a type of woman who likes to seduce priests as part of their rebellion against Catholicism.'

This seems close to Tony Tanner's idea that literary heroines such as Madame Bovary who commit adultery 'find a devious way back to an experience of the sacred'. The idea that an illicit act can offer an open window back into the world of meaning certainly held appeal for Catherine. It is easy to see why she identified with Madame Bovary and re-read the book several times. Both heroines felt that the narrative of their life had been temporarily stopped through a marriage that had become a sham. The tragedy of Madame Bovary's life is the realisation that she almost wilfully slowly closes the door on the world of 'sacred' meaning. With each new – and more casual – lover, she finds it more difficult to be satisfied with life, exactly as Vivien Greene had once percipiently written to Catherine.

When Catherine finally moved into the grand family house at Newton Hall, her diary entries often read rather pathetically, not to say tragically, as she sat alone, surrounded by gilt opulence in her upstairs sitting-room with her parrot, or in the downstairs 'Long Room' with her Jameson's Irish whiskey. Having arrived in Newton Hall, the future Lady Walston recorded in her diary how she felt as if her life had turned into a sort of chromium-plated façade, cut off from passion. Indeed, back at Thriplow in March 1950, she complained in her diary of sitting alone in the house, consumed by an overwhelming sense of luxury and bore-dom.

When I suggested to Father Barratt the idea that Catherine may have slept with priests and committed adultery with count-less lovers because – in the absence of Harry's disapproval – she wanted somebody to object to her actions (that person being God), Barratt replied, 'Oh absolutely.' He told me that he had known several former students who couldn't get any 'kick out of sex unless they were committing adultery'.

I said that Greene seemed to have the same problem, and quoted his seemingly paradoxical line that he felt closest to God – and the truest he had ever felt as a Catholic – when committing adultery with Catherine.

'Well, you see, this all makes theological sense,' replied Father Barratt, seated in the Randolph Hotel (we were less than fifty yards away from 15 Beaumont Street). 'I mean when you do a wicked thing of course you become close to God because you're doing something you shouldn't do and God disapproves of and therefore God is at the forefront of your mind.'

Brian Wormald (now a Catholic) was a regular visitor to Newton Hall. Sitting in his book-lined Cambridge study, wearing a fishing-style waterproof waistcoat and rolling his own cigarettes, he explained that despite having 'affairs with endless people', 'the Catholic thing' was very important to Catherine. 'Anybody who talks about religion being superficial to either Graham or her is quite, quite wrong,' he said.

Indeed, in 1950 she went so far as to ask various priest friends of her to see if they thought either of her sons, David or Oliver, were suitable to be trained as priests (her third son, Bill, who lives in Cambridge, later nearly became a priest). Diary entries record how David and Oliver made up an altar in their bedroom from which Mass could be served at Thriplow. Later, at Newton Hall, the house was equipped with its own private chapel.

Why did he think that Catherine had what amounted to almost a fetish for Catholic priests?

'That I don't know. She was always surrounded by priests. She collected them.'

'Did having priests around somehow help validate her adulterous and "sinful" affair with Greene?'

'You can't just explain these things. The affair is serious, your religion is serious, you periodically go to confession.'

Yet, according to Wormald, the 'books of devotion' that Waugh observed scattered around her bedroom, and bulging from the cases of her study, were not read as theological self-help books. In 1950 she was reading the journals of Baudelaire, the letters of St Thérèse of Lisieux and St Thomas Aquinas. 'One always knew she was intelligent but not intellectual at all,' said Wormald. 'She had a huge collection of books. I don't think she understood any of them. In fact she gave a lot of them to me. How can I explain Catherine? She was immensely attractive, she was powerful, she was a genuine person, there was no sham.'

Writing to Catherine in April 1950 after a 'bad' day's work on *The End of the Affair*, Greene prayed that whilst some people had a vocation to love God, others had a vocation to love another human being. Please, he prayed, let not this vocation be squandered. Sounding not unlike Sarah's journal – which he was writing at the time – he said a prayer. 'I've proved it badly in the past but this time I've entered Orders for Life. Don't let it be wasteful. It's a bad prayer but even bad prayers may be heard.' He added that he knelt all the time in his room at the feet of St Thérèse and repeated the prayer: 'I love Catherine. Please let this love go on through all this life and be complete.'

St Thérèse of Lisieux (1873–97) was a virgin French saint who became a Carmelite nun and assistant to the novice-mistress of her convent in 1893. She died of tuberculosis aged just twenty-four and would have vanished into obscurity had it not been for her letters and, more significantly, her short spiritual autobiography, *L'Historie d'une Ame*. Catherine was obsessively reading both at exactly the time Greene was writing *The End of the Affair*. On Thursday 23 March 1950, for example, on the day Greene set off for a business trip to Germany, Catherine spent the evening reading a translation of *L'Histoire d'une Ame* in front of the fire in her living-room. According to the *Oxford Dictionary of Saints*: 'the special appeal of her cult lies in her extreme artless simplicity' and for her saint-like 'miraculous cures'.

In *Ways of Escape*, Greene informs the reader that *The End of the Affair* was directly influenced by his reading of Dickens, Proust and Ford Madox Ford, so it is slightly odd that he does not refer at all to the writings or letters of St Thérèse. Perhaps it was just too personal; or possibly he didn't want people to know just how important an influence St Thérèse had been during the final months of writing the novel, when Sarah herself is turned into a miracle-curing saint. Indeed, on a three-day trip to the Ritz in Paris in early March 1950 – a 'holiday' negotiated with Harry after a weekend of rows at Thriplow – Graham and Catherine took a car to Lisieux in order to visit her basilica and shrine. They found it deplorable. Then a French priest they encountered became over-excited when he recognised Greene as the author of *The Power and the Glory*. Fleeing back to Paris, they had yet another morose dinner, until Greene came up with the suggestion of visiting a 'Negro night club'. Unlike the basilica, that at least was fun. The next evening – after cocktails at the

Ritz bar, lunching at the Ritz grill and dinner with Greene's French literary agent Marie Biche – Greene and Catherine ended up in a lesbian sex club.

It might seem strange for both Graham and Catherine to pray to a young virgin saint to intercede in helping them through a rough swell in their adulterous love affair. But sex, suffering and religion were always important and potent ingredients of Graham and Catherine's illicit affair. Through his veneration of Catherine's unholy brand of what he saw as her dangerous goodness, Greene was able to explore an exotic range of sexual fantasies that with Vivien – or most women for that matter – would have been unthinkable. Yet, in Catherine's case, her own imagination clearly needed little stimulation. Her diary entry for Saturday 25 March 1950 – the day after she had begun reading St Thérèse's autobiography – reveals the truly bizarre depths to which sex and religion were tied in her imagination. That night (one can only speculate on the influence of her Parisienne sex club visit, exactly a week before) Catherine not only dreamt of St Thérèse of Lisieux but – so she clearly writes – had an 'orgasm' in her presence.

Whether Catherine's broad range of sexual libertinism included lesbianism is uncertain. Certainly Greene and Catherine enjoyed going to Paris brothels where lesbian sex was performed. During this trip to Paris with Catherine, whilst he was visiting Cartier, Catherine had gone shopping for some 'fake' jewellery for her close friend Margaret Huntingdon, probably as a present to wear at the grand dinner party for ten she was throwing at St James's Street the following Tuesday. There is a small possibility that Catherine (who admired writers) and Margaret (the biographer of Beatrix Potter and a left-wing bohemian intellectual) had some sort of Carringtonesque love affair. As Waugh noted on his visit to Thriplow, lesbianism was freely discussed around the dinner table.

We certainly know that Catherine wrote intimate letters to Margaret. On one occasion Greene mentions he had just got off the phone with Margaret – he was booking a date for the four of them to have dinner together – who had told him 'about your love letter . . .', referring to a Vita Sackville-West-style outpouring from Catherine to Margaret.

When I read this out, Lady Selina Hastings replied that Pat Frere (the wife of Greene's publisher at Heinemann), always 'used to rather insistently say that my mother was one of the few women that Catherine really loved and she implied there was a rather emotional relationship, not physically lesbian, but very intense.' Her mother, she added, was 'very flirtatious' with both men and women, and especially 'attractive' to women. 'I can only think that maybe Catherine had written a mock love letter to her,' said Lady Selina.

But there was no pretence at all about Greene's impassioned longing. 'I've never dared to write like this to another person, or wanted to,' Greene ended his April 1950 letter that so powerfully links the image of Catherine to St Thérèse. 'Dear heart. I am all yours. I can only offer myself to God through you.' Not long after, he was saying that *twenty* times a day he now turned to the picture of St Thérèse by his bed. In art, St Thérèse is represented in a Carmelite nun's habit clutching a bunch of roses in memory of her promise to 'let fall a shower of roses' of miracles and other favours. Her feast is 1 October, the day before Greene's birthday. Whilst writing *The End of the Affair*, Greene often kept a photo of Catherine beside the image of St Thérèse.

In the same letter, his mind turned to thinking of lunching with Catherine, and the second glass of calvados, and he prayed: 'St Thérèse, pray for us – pray that I can live with Catherine for life and grow old with her and work with her. Nothing could take her place now. Even God.' 'I'm afraid that my prayer is always that God's will shall be in favour of our love,' he said in another letter. 'I feel no wrong in this love for you, I feel so often as though I'm married to you, only desperately sad sometimes at being separated from my wife (you, I mean).'

On the ferry over to Calais in May 1947, he scrawled her a love-note on the back of a letter from his bookseller friend David Low. 'It is after lunch and I love you more than I've ever loved you before [. . .] My dear you are definitely dear to me. You are a saint in love.'

In his introduction to *The End of the Affair*, Greene recalled that he had assumed the novel had been influenced by his reading in 1949–50 of the theological criticism of Baron von Hugel, especially – so he thought – passages from his study of St Catherine. But on re-reading the passages Greene had underlined – Greene always marked his books – he couldn't understand what possible relevance they had to the story that became *The End of the Affair*. Then he came across an underlined passage in another theological essay of Von Hugel that did make some sense: 'The purification and slow constitution of the Individual into a Person, by means of the Thing-element, the apparently blind Determinism of Natural Law and Natural Happenings . . . Nothing can be more certain than that we must admit and place this un-deniable, increasingly obtrusive, element and power somewhere in our lives: if we will not own it as a means, it will grip us as our end.'

During the impassioned and tortured periodic writing stints of *The End of the Affair* – in Capri, the Plaza Athénée Hotel and Ritz in Paris, London's St James's Street, weekends at Thriplow, on board the *Elsewhere* – Greene's imagination came to be seized by Catherine's influence in a way that threatened to almost drown him. Writing the novel became a personal obsession; his only hope of release from the pressure cooker of raw emotions that had been building up since 1947.

Although Catherine was clearly very beautiful, it was not her looks that Greene had become obsessed with. It was her complicated, ambiguous nature that he – the great architect of words – was powerless to control. In 1975, when *Observer Magazine* interviewer John Heilpern asked Greene what quality he most admired in women, he answered: 'Intelligence, I suppose.' In men? 'Sense of fun.' Heilpern then pressed him. Surely it is usually intelligence that women find attractive in men; and fun that men find appealing in women. Why did he admire intelligence in women? 'One doesn't *admire* an attractive woman.

Would you admire Marlene Dietrich for her looks? You can be attracted to the looks a woman is born with. What you admire is surely something that has developed.'

By the time he was writing *The End of the Affair*, Greene's own narrative had developed with Catherine's to the point where they used many of the same private expressions (i.e. 'book-hunt') and were writing double diaries together. But instead of steak and onion dinners at Rules, they now ate suppers of tinned ham and claret alone at No. 5 St James's Street. This was partly to avoid scenes in public. Greene had started to look at Catherine through the detached retina of his novelist's eye. He had greatly helped in Catherine's own development, but he became increasingly depressed as he felt the plot of his own life was being robbed of a happy conclusion. Between the end of March and early April 1950, Greene wrote 11,000 words of *The End of the Affair* in ten days. But no imaginative squalls existing between Bendrix and Sarah could compare to the bitter battle being fought in his real life. 'I do feel strongly for both our sakes that the hour has really struck for truth,' he wrote from Germany on 12 April 1950, exactly three years since they had first gone to Achill. 'The truth really does no harm to anyone.'

Catherine had Greene strapped to the rack. Had he really known the truth of what was going on back in London, one hates to imagine the consequences. Catherine's diary for 1950 shows that on Monday 3 April, with Greene conveniently abroad, her former American lover General Lowell Weicker arrived in England. The following day, after taking a morning train up to London, and having a cocktail with Greene's friend Christopher Sykes, she dined alone with Lowell at the Berkeley Hotel. The next morning Catherine made a point of attending the 8am Mass at Farm Street. Lowell and Catherine then drove up to Thriplow together. The following night she gave a cocktail party for him at which she got very drunk. The next day – in a rare display of guilt on Catherine's behalf – she drove back to London in a frantic search to find Father Dermott Mills at Farm Street. Presumably she wanted him to hear her confession. Afterwards, Catherine invited the Jesuit priest for a drink and a boiled egg at 6 St James's Street.

Early the next morning an anxious and deeply upset Greene called from Germany. In a rare use of the first person pronoun, Catherine confided in her diary that she was now seriously worried about the tightrope-wire situation between herself and Greene, and whether she could even go through with their impending trip to Italy. The day before Greene had left for Germany he had given her the original manuscript of *The Heart of the Matter*. They had planned on having a loving last day together. Catherine had a pre-lunch cocktail with Barbara Warner (as Lady Rothschild was now known) and then joined Greene, Rex Warner and Dick Stokes at Greene's flat in St James's Street. After a pub lunch, Catherine dragged her friend Margaret Huntingdon off to look at a parrot she was thinking of adding to the Walston family. She then had dinner with Graham and Father Philip Caraman at Overton's oyster bar just beneath Greene's flat. Yet the night ended with another vicious and brutal row.

Exactly the same thing had occurred the night before when Catherine gave a smart dinner party next-door at the Walstons' flat in St James's Street. Those invited, dressed in evening clothes and doubtless (if they had any) showing off their 'rocks', were clearly Catherine and Greene's 'set' as opposed to Harry's political cronies. The gathering included Greene, Harry, Frank and Elizabeth Longford, Margaret and Jack Huntingdon, Victor Gollancz, the left-wing publisher, Catholic Labour MP Dick Stokes, and Elizabeth Montagu (whom Greene had kept up with since visiting Vienna). Needless to say, it was a very different sort of dinner from Vivien's rations of canapés and 'snacks' at the Mauriac party at Beaumont Street. They had a huge jar of caviar from Paris, turtle soup with sherry, chilled Russian Imperial vodka, fresh salmon, sea-trout, and to drink, white burgundy and a magnum of Château Lafite Rothschild 1929. Harry flambéed a Thriplow turkey over a gas ring in the dining-room. To finish off, they had thirteen different fresh fruits, individually peeled grapes and fresh strawberries and cream.

One guest arrived late: the dashing Evelyn Shuckburgh (later Sir Evelyn), educated at Winchester, King's College Cambridge and a high flying British diplomat at the Foreign Office, with whom Catherine also had an involvement. His arrival at St James's Street seems to have turned Graham into a jealous wreck. Once again, the evening ended in an angry outburst of violent hostilities – it looks as though Catherine slept with Harry at No. 6. Other entries for April repeat the same story.

By now driven desperate, Greene clutched onto an unlikely idea. He asked his doctor brother Raymond to see Catherine – as if one of his own patients – and write up a clinical assessment of the rift between them. His brother's response to Greene read like an awful about-to-be-expelled end-of-year report. First, Catherine had decided she would never leave Harry. Second, she would have a 'much more peaceful and happy life', if she 'washed' Greene out of her life. Third, that although she 'loved' having Greene at Thriplow, his presence there 'always caused rows and gloom'. And last, that Catherine was concerned about his 'sexual energy', which Greene's brother said had become 'rather a nuisance' to her. Raymond later described her to Graham as a self-deluded liar.

'Now my dear for goodness sake tell me the truth,' Greene pleaded with her. He added – not very convincingly – that he would try and 'cut out altogether' the sex part if it really had become such a burden. How much truth there was in this devastating assessment of their relationship is hard to know. But, as he pushed on with the book that Bendrix calls 'this record of hate', there were certainly no shortage of explosive rows at Thriplow.

A four-page letter (sold at Sotheby's in 1994) that Catherine sent to her older sister Bonte details one of these rows in graphic detail. Harry was happy for Catherine to have affairs, but the terms of their arrangement was that she would always return home to him. Greene wanted to make her his legal wife, and told Harry as much. Harry Walston, in a rare show of emotion, stormed off to their bedroom with Catherine 'to have it out' with her. The next day, long walks were taken by all in the Cambridgeshire countryside. Harry Walston then refused point blank to talk about the subject again. Greene asked if he could borrow his wife for a trial of three months. Walston finally allowed three days in Paris (when they bought the huge jar of caviar for the 21 March dinner party; indeed it was so large that Catherine considered getting it insured before they travelled back to London).

Before the sale of the Sotheby's letters in 1994, a short extract of a letter from Catherine to her sister, explaining the difficulty of her ménage à trois, was published in the *Daily Telegraph*, along with other newspapers. She said Greene was a 'melancholic' by nature who had no plans, few friends, nothing to plan for, and only the frustration of his work to occupy him. She only made matters worse by her own fears of abandoning him. 'Were I really nice and good and brave I would walk out . . .'

Quite how stormy the 'rows and gloom' had now become is indicated in a letter Bonte Duran wrote to her husband in America, after staying with her sister Catherine when Greene was up for a weekend. 'Graham was in a good mood considering that the night before the sounds of irate quarrelling that came from Bobs' study made me feel sure he was about to commit murder.'

There is no 'After Three Years' poem. The '1950' diary that Greene gave Catherine (the inscription reads, 'with love from Graham at the end of 1949') is no longer a washed, Mediterranean sea-blue; it is a dark charcoal-grey hard-spined exercise book. There are fewer quotations in it and some entries are missing.

Writing in late January 1950, Greene began by apologising for the 'trouble' which had started again. 'Please remember that I love you entirely, with my brain, my heart and my body. And that I'm always there when you want me. I don't like or approve of Harry's judgements. When a man marries, he is like a Prime Minister – he has to accept responsibility for the acts of a colleague. My marriage failed (only God can know all the causes), but the *responsibility* for failure is mine. One can't lay blame on one's wife. Your marriage, intrinsically, had failed before I knew you, and the men must accept responsibility – which doesn't mean guilt. It had failed because marriage isn't just maintaining a friend, a housekeeper or even a lover.' Quoting the line he was to use again a few months later in the context of the divine flight plan of the Cambridge–Oxford flight, Greene added that the Catholic marriage service says 'with my body I thee worship'. Once that fails, he said, the heart has been ripped out of the marriage.

Far from thinking Harry one of the nicest people he had ever encountered, Greene's letters to Catherine now bristled with resentment towards her husband. In one letter he tries to casually pass on a secret told to him by Bonte, which he had promised he wouldn't tell her. Her sister liked 'us' (Greene and Catherine) better than she liked Catherine and Harry's marriage.

But Greene was losing, and he knew it. In another angry outburst Greene accused her of being calculating, self-centred, a liar and colossally selfish. Catherine (she was often candidly honest) admitted in her diary that he may well be right. And whilst he and Catherine tore at each other, emotion-free Harry emerged as a welcome rock of safety. For every miserable scene with Greene – 12 April 1950 saw several, with he and Catherine tearing into each other with equal force – there are now countless remarks about how nice Harry was being to her.

Time was against Greene. If she was ever going to leave Harry for him, it would be before she rooted herself at Newton Hall. But it's clear she couldn't wait to watch the furniture lorries pulling up. On 13 April, Catherine drove over to Newton Hall to measure up for new carpets and curtains and to pick out which bedroom (of twenty-eight) she wanted to share with Harry, as well as thinking about what colour scheme she wanted for the upstairs suite of rooms overlooking the west lawn that would be her private study and sitting-room. The children's bedrooms would all be out of sight on the third floor. As she knelt down with her tape-measure on Newton Hall's grand staircase – where a long Van Dyke portrait hung – anybody could have told Greene that Catherine did not look a woman about to give it all up for a restless, misanthropic, moody, obsessed, brilliant, but pathologically tormented novelist. Indeed, Catherine explained herself in a letter to Greene at this time. How, she said, can one put down the foundations for a life based on the complete abandonment of one's family?

Greene, perhaps wisely, decided to make an appointment to see Dr Eric Strauss, a Jungian psychiatrist upon whom he was to lean on heavily in the following years. Greene repeatedly asked for 'electric shock' treatment. The requests were refused. 'I like Strauss enormously,' Greene wrote from St James's Street on 4 May. Strauss also refused to 'deep-analyse' Greene, suggesting that his dark manic moods and tempers were probably integral to the conflict that lay at the heart of his creativity. Instead, Strauss advised his client (Greene uses the words 'forcing me') to write a long 'autobiographical screed'.

That Catherine's darkly complicated and contradictory nature represented a Medea-like sexual force, which Greene always found himself wrestling to get the better of, is suggested by his post-script following this session with Strauss: 'God bless you, my dear heart. I'm convinced that if I had a proper chance I could unravel you much better than any psychoanalyst. Love can cure most things & I love you an awful lot.'

Seeing Strauss seemed to help; almost immediately Greene appeared more cheerful. But he didn't like the way that Harry was now attempting to dictate when Catherine could see him. His letters are now full of Bendrix-like jibes (Greene draws the comparison himself in certain letters). They are also full of 'life plans' and tormented battle orders. One moment he is asking her to come away and live with him in Italy for a year; the next he is accusing himself of being a 'swindler' in love; the next he is blaming Vivien for his 'pseudo-marriage' that went wrong.

But it wasn't just poor Harry or Vivien; Greene turned his *contra mundum* resentment towards anybody within firing range. Success, he decided, was an 'unholy bore'. 'I've had it,' he said. 'I don't want it any more.' The slightest intrusion made him irritable: aircraft captains wanted to talk to him; hotel managers appeared with autograph albums; when he ordered a drink in a nightclub, the band would start to play the theme tune for *The Third Man*.

Greene was resorting to desperate measures. Back in the early spring, during their few days in Paris together (negotiated with Harry), staying at the Ritz, Greene had bought her a Jacques Faith couture dress and a Cartier double-band 'infinity' ring with a forget-me-not detail (now held at Georgetown). On 8 May, on a trip to Paris without her, he cut out of a glossy magazine a colour advertisement for Cartier 'Engagement Rings' and sent it to her.

Worse, in his notebook he had found a quotation from *The Tempest* – 'When I waked I cried to dream again' – that he had meant to put in her 1950 book. 'I wrote that down a long time ago and it had a different meaning then.'

Greene now tried to pretend, or at least convince himself, that he was capable of chucking in his hand and playing the honourable-lover-in-defeat card. He had a long talk with Father Caraman about writing a biography on the apostle St Thomas Didymus – a way of spiritual escape – as he thought it 'best for all of us' if he exiled himself from England for 'six months', holing up in Goa, probably in the autumn. St Thomas the apostle had offered to die with Christ on the way to Bethany but found himself uncertain of the way to get there. Throughout the Gospels he was often criticised for his lack of faith, although also commended for his confessions, in particular his confession of Christ's divinity. 'I feel very hopeless because now there's nothing whatever to hope for,' wrote Greene. 'God bless you. Pray for me. I always felt 1950 was going to be a bad year.'

Standing stooped and pummelled across the ropes, and staring bleakly into a middle-aged future alone, without a wife, a lover he could only see for occasional 'holidays', and a mistress (Dorothy) whom he no longer loved, Greene felt as if he needed a miracle to save him. Certainly, he would try anything. In the same letter he ended by dropping the suggestion that – having previously told her he didn't want his life to be changed by meeting a saint – 'maybe we'll see Padro Pio after all'.

Although in despair over Catherine, Greene – unlike Bendrix – does not seem to have turned his bitter anger towards God. Indeed, He was always his last hope. At the end of April 1950, Father Caraman invited Greene and Evelyn Waugh to a retreat at Stonyhurst College, the gloomy Jesuit public school, set behind dark woods in the remote Lancashire moorland countryside. Jesuit priest Gerard Manley Hopkins wrote his self-flagellating poems in the bleak grounds of the school.

Greene didn't seem to pay much attention to the Jesuits on his retreat, nor could he work on his novel. He found the set-up at Stonyhurst 'rather awful' as he could only think of Catherine as he knelt to pray. He was in no mood for Jesuit small talk. Instead, he fired off several long heart-of-the-matter letters (one is always later referred to as 'the Stonyhurst letter'), raising points that were to rear up again and again in the following months. Greene's thoughts were a whirling storm of questions and contradictions. As Catherine noted in her own diary, he seemed to be clinging onto a version of events that he hoped were true, rather than facing up to what perhaps was the case. His jealousy had indeed become a green-eyed monster. 'My dear, you can write things clearly,' he implored her from Stonyhurst. 'I feel hopeless. Suppose he had become Ambassador [referring to Lowell Weicker's visit to London]. This would have happened all the time [. . .] Would you have told me yourself? I'm lost. I don't know what to believe any more. Please pray for me as you've never done before.'

What Greene called the 'Lowell incident' of 24 April had somehow got back to him. Or perhaps Catherine had simply told him straight. 'I'm sorry dear. I took it very badly (I mean in a beastly way) & you were very good in telling me the truth,' he wrote at 10pm on Sunday evening from his bare retreat room at Stonyhurst. 'I was glad of my whisky when I got here.' Two days later, still at Stonyhurst, he wrote imploring her not to see Lowell (Greene was later to explode with jealous rage when he leant out of his sitting-room window at 5 St James's Street and saw Catherine actually kissing Evelyn Shuckburgh on the pavement below as he left her flat next door). 'Would you try not to have times alone with him? Or have you found that after all he is very important, more than we are?'

He had received two letters from her but they had only made him unable to sleep. He was taking sleeping pills and waking up to talk 'bitterly' with himself. If he was with her, he admitted, there might be an ugly scene. 'But the boil would burst & the poison drain away & we could be close again [. . .] My dear you'll have to be patient with me. Maybe you'll even have to seduce me – but for God's sake do it. We are lovers & we can't get right again & happy without the help of our bodies.'

Greene ended by saying that it had been a 'wretched' and 'hellish' two months. Two 'bad' quarrels, then Germany (the Lowell incident), the awful report from his brother Raymond, and then going to see Strauss. But worst of all was the Thriplow weekend when 'I made up your mind for you that there was to be no annulment and no marriage . . . Pray for us very hard. Please look forward to Italy. It will be all right when we get home to Anacapri and quiet.'

But 'holidays' with Greene had now become far from peaceful. Harry had originally banned her from going to Italy, and had only relented when Catherine said that he was failing to keep up his side of the 'arrangement'. Everybody was suffocating from the strains of the ménage à trois, not least Greene. Repeatedly in her diary, Catherine reveals that she was nervous about the trip. She didn't want to go, she says, but knows that she will anyway. Not even a private audience with the Pope at the Vatican in late May could quell Greene's mood of despair; afterwards, Catherine's diary for that night recorded another wretched scene.

On 23 May, Greene had written 1,000 words of his novel by midday, the first time since November. But two days later, after returning to the Villa Rosaio from a late lunch with a friend of Catherine, at which Greene had been bored by an old English colonel and his wife, he began mixing some of his lethal dry Martinis. The combination of the drink, the heat and Greene's frayed nerves resulted in an evening explosion at the villa that Catherine described in her diary as the worst they had ever had. The ferocity of Greene's hatred stunned her.

'I hate you,' he shouted. 'I hate your bloody friends. I hate what you stand for.' He even went so far as to yell that she was not a real Catholic and that he wouldn't be surprised if she traded in her Catholicism to become a Marxist. Greene stormed off to bed after swilling down a large tooth glass of whisky and a sleeping draft.

The next morning – a Monday – Greene was groggy and irritable. Unable to work, he sat in broody silence. The following day, Catherine worked on her own novel until 11.45am and then lunched with Norman Douglas in Capri town. It was very hot and everybody drank too much again. The long lunch was slept off on the roof terrace of Il Rosaio. One can surmise that they made love. According to Catherine's diary, Greene was now happy again.

But the novel that he pushed on with writing was no longer his 'Great Sex Novel'. Over evening cocktails at the Quisisana Hotel in Capri – the most luxurious hotel in Capri, where Oscar Wilde was once refused a room – and dinner at Gemma's pizzeria, Greene tried out other titles more appropriate to his book's themes of love and hate. After dinner he decided to revert back to 'Point of Departure'. He liked its French translation: *Point Depart*.

The next day they saw Korda's yacht, the *Elsewhere*, moored in Capri harbour when they took a boat trip to the neighbouring 'spa' island of Ischia. Ischia was where W.H. Auden had a little summer retreat, as well as being the home of composer Sir William Walton, whose villa is carved like a cave out of natural rock face. Two days later, on their return to Anacapri, Greene read bits from 'Point of Departure' on the roof terrace at the Villa Rosaio whilst Catherine sunbathed. Catherine was suitably impressed. But Greene remained despondent and edgy.

The holiday ground on. They walked over to the old Gracie Fields house, which had been turned into a ghastly new hotel. There was a break-in at the villa; her Leica was stolen, and Greene's Parker 51 fountain pen and a pencil – who would steal a pencil? – were also missing. The police came. Greene fired the maid because her fiancé had been sleeping in the villa whilst Greene was away.

They left Capri for Rome, where they stayed at the Grand Hotel and met up with Mario Soldati for drinks. The next day – searingly hot – they drove to Florence, to see Harold Acton and to meet up with Catherine's sister Bonte and her husband. They went for a steak and garlic dinner, followed by raspberries at a little trattoria. But Graham felt lousy. The combination of heat, work, wine, hayfever and travelling made him weary. In Capri, he had also lacerated his writing hand after smashing – possibly in a row – an ice thermos. Still, on the morning of 9 June 1950, drugged up with a Florence chemist's hayfever pills, he managed another 1,100 words in their suite at The Grand Hotel (paying 13,500 lire a day, and 'forced' to eat one meal).

Greene had now reached the end of 'Book III' of *The End of the Affair*; the end of Sarah's journal in which she has been dreaming that she is walking up the stairs of Bendrix's flat on the south side of Clapham Common, and she is happy because she is going to make love to him. But as she calls his name, it is not his voice that answers, but 'a stranger's that boomed like a fog-horn warning lost ships, and scared me'. Then she woke up. 'I'm not at peace any more. I just want him like I used to in the old days. I want to be eating sandwiches with him. I want to be drinking with him in a bar. I'm tired and I don't want any more pain. I want Maurice. I want ordinary corrupt human love.'

loser takes nothing

After Italy, Greene took off to France with Father Caraman, pushing on with *The End of the Affair* in between inexpensive but good French meals. Back in England, Catherine was also trying to finish her own novel. Like Greene she recorded in her diary the number of words written. There is no trace of the novel in the Greene–Walston collection at Georgetown; what she was writing about is anybody's guess. But in the absence of her own letters to Greene, most of which he burnt in the 1960s, her 'novel' may have provided a fascinating lens through which to understand Catherine's thinking just before she pulled down the 'iron curtain' on a future life with Greene. On the afternoon of Friday 23 June 1950, after picking strawberries in the kitchen garden at Newton Hall with her younger children Bill and Susan, Catherine rang the owner of the new Lefevre Gallery in Bruton Street to say she was buying 'the Renoir' they had for sale.

Before moving into Newton, she and her husband had begun picture shopping. On 19 April 1950, after lunching at Rules, Graham and Catherine had gone to the champagne 'opening' of the Lefevre Gallery and had seen a beautiful Renoir and a rich golden-yellow Degas nude of a ballerina washing her hair. The Degas also ended up at Newton Hall, although not without a passing flash of guilt over the size of Harry's bank cheque that acquired it. Not long afterwards, back to the more humble pursuit of 'book-hunting' with Greene, Catherine – it doubtless having crossed her mind that she should now learn about Degas – bought a complete set of Degas book plates for £50. As she did so she made a half-hearted self-promise to sell some of her other books to pay for the set.

On the last Thursday of June, Graham and Catherine were looking forward to seeing each other again at a 'Tackley week-end' at Barbara Warner's house, just north of Kidlington. Writing to Thriplow from the Pont Royal Hotel in Paris, Greene told Catherine that he felt 'a bit too sad' to write much. He said there was a 'curious lonely and empty feeling in Paris' without her. He added that Korda had sent him a cable: 'I WILL BE ON *ELSEWHERE* FROM END OF MONTH STOP WOULD YOU BOTH CARE JOIN ME LOVE KORDA.' Greene told her he had cabled back that he himself was sorely tempted, but that she couldn't manage it. 'What fun we could have if only we belonged to each other,' he lamented.

Shortly before seeing Catherine at Tackley, Greene wrote from the Hotel Terminos in Lyons to say he was bored and depressed, after a gruesome evening in which his London agent Laurence Pollinger and Jean Biche – the husband of his French agent – had tried to 'pimp' him off with an ugly over-painted mannequin. He didn't *like* it when women were provided for him on a plate. He was livid. But he had managed another 750 words of *The End of the Affair*. Today was very hard, however, as he felt so 'churned up with rage' about the night before. 'Do they do this for Mr Eliot when he goes abroad?' he protested. 'I wish I was with you. I could weep for longing to hear your voice. God bless you. You're the only thing I live for.'

Greene had written 5,000 words of *The End of the Affair* since their holiday in Italy. On 18 June, the quotation in Catherine's diary is from St Thérèse: 'I have nothing but God, alone, alone.' On 23 June, Greene got up at 6am and wrote 900 words before breakfast. At dinner that night he sat up with Father Caraman talking about the Goa book – his biography of the faith-challenged St Thomas the apostle – but he also said that he was 'depressed' by the idea of being away from Catherine for so long. He described his plan to quit England for six months as 'awfully drastic medicine'.

'I want you so much, so often,' he wrote to Catherine, adding that he felt 'physically disturbed' at the prospect of her 'not being available' to make love (because of her period) after four weeks apart. 'But don't worry,' he added, 'There are no substitutes for you.' He was waiting to hear from Korda about the *Elsewhere*. Greene added that he wouldn't bother waiting for Korda if there was a chance of 'seeing you on your own.'

Thursday 29 June was a beautiful hot summer's day in Oxfordshire. Catherine drove up early in the morning to attend the reception into the Catholic Church of her daughter Anne, who had recently written from school saying she wanted to convert to Catholicism. When Catherine had received the letter she had prayed fervently to St Thérèse before telling Harry. He had no objection. After the service at St Juliana's Convent, they had a picnic at the Trout pub and swam in the river in the afternoon. Then Catherine went to pick Graham up from Oxford Station, and they drove along the narrow country lane to Tackley. They were happy again. One can imagine Greene eating strawberries with his fingers from the remains of the picnic in the back of the car. After dinner in the round dining-room, with the French windows open, Rex, Barbara, Graham and Catherine all sat outdoors by the front lawn of the house.

Tackley was clearly a special place for Greene and Catherine. Writing to her from France, when she had been staying there the week before, Greene made a reference to telling Barbara about the 'mirror room', and added that when they were 'alone' together they would 'act the rest'. This sounds like some fairly routine sexual adventurism on Graham and Catherine's behalf. Certainly Barbara Warner's huge guest-room double bed held an important significance for them both. When Greene came very close to buying Harston House in 1951, Catherine suggested that he buy Barbara's bed as well (she had since moved from Tackley).

The next day, Catherine dropped Greene off at a pub in

Oxford to allow him to work on 'Point of Departure', whilst Catherine did an hour or two of shopping. On her way back to collect Greene, she experienced a Bendrix-like moment of extraordinary coincidence. As she was driving along, her head turned towards an Oxford bus. Sitting at the back, on her own, her face turned to the window, was Vivien, Greene's wife.

Catherine's reaction is unknown, but the incident must have gnawed at Greene's conscience. Vivien told me that on one occasion when he met her at Ampleforth – where Francis went to school – for a prize day or something similar, they returned to London (or Oxford) on the same train. She remembered that Greene had been embarrassed and rather cross with her when it turned out that she was travelling third class, whilst he was going first. 'There were many things I wanted to do if I had the money,' Vivien told me. 'No picture I bought cost me more than about thirty pounds.' The gilt pictures of Indian tigers hanging in her dining-room – made from grated marble and sand – were bought at Sotheby's for £17. 'I came back with them all that night in the train,' she told me. 'Aren't they lovely?'

Greene didn't know quite what to do with Vivien. With Catherine, his eyes – and senses – were opened to a glittering new world; a world in which money bought possibilities, but there would also, he knew, be a price to pay. In one of his impassioned cards-on-the-table letters he had said that they were not 'Capri-lounge-lizard' types and wouldn't be satisfied with life if they tried to be. This was probably more true of Greene than Catherine, but it was an ocean apart from the world with Vivien – and Dorothy – that he had left behind. The evening after Catherine saw Vivien on the bus, Greene and herself went to dinner with Henry Moore and his wife at their house at Perry Green. Catherine later drove her Renoir back to Thriplow almost as casually as if it were a box of Fortnum's groceries sitting on the back seat of her car.

Just before Greene headed off for Stonyhurst, he was forced to confront the subject of Vivien inside the confessional. He had originally walked over to Farm Street (where there is a shrine to St Thérèse of Lisieux by the confessionals) from St James's Street, but couldn't find a priest to hear his confession. Reluctantly, he went over to Westminster Cathedral in Victoria where, kneeling down for three-quarters of an hour, he gave the 'works' to a Father Pilkington. Pilkington was not accommodating, telling Greene that he had to go back to Vivien and that it was a mortal sin to keep the 'separation' going, and that he had to 'promise from this moment' to give up seeing Catherine again . . . Finally, Greene stood up and said, 'I'm sorry Father I must find another confessor,' and walked out. As he wrote to Catherine about the experience, he felt as if he had to teach the priest an elementary fact of life: it was impossible to return to a woman without desire.

The Tackley weekend, with its relaxed laughter and onion sandwiches, was only a temporary private oasis as Greene approached the edge of the desert. By Monday 10 July 1950, Catherine was recording another series of dejected evenings with him. On the evening of 11 July, after giving a cocktail party for her elder sister Bonte, Catherine got home to St James's Street at midnight to experience a Worst Ever Scene, adding, with an exclamation mark, that she felt very scared. The following Sunday, Catherine's diary quotation is from St Thérèse: 'My only weapon is *love* and suffering.' Greene has underlined the word love.

The following week Catherine attended Heinemann's twenty-first anniversary party for *The Man Within*. During the party Catherine met Dorothy Glover for the first time; the pair were later to become the most unlikely of friends. Vivien was not invited. The next morning Greene was up early to work on his novel before the 8.30am Mass at Farm Street. During the Mass, thunderous rain pounded down on the Mayfair church, leaking through the roof onto the wooden seats and pews of the poorly attended church. Afterwards, Catherine bought Greene a raincoat at Harrods.

The weather also didn't help Catherine's increasingly bad cough. This is certainly one aspect of Sarah's characterisation in *The End of the Affair* that was borrowed from Catherine. In the novel, when Sarah and Bendrix decided to switch restaurants, going back to Rules for the first time in two years, Sarah is suddenly 'taken' by a bad coughing fit.

'That's nasty,' says Bendrix.

'Oh, it's nothing,' Sarah replies. After their rather tense lunch, they leave Rules and walk towards the doorway on Maiden Lane where they first kissed. Sarah stands by the doorway in the empty street.

'I'll say good-bye here. It was nice seeing you.'

'Yes.'

'Call me any time you are free.'

I moved towards her: I could feel the grating under my feet. 'Sarah,' I said. She turned her head sharply away, as though she were looking to see if anyone were coming, to see if there was time . . . but when she turned again the cough took her. She doubled up in the doorway and coughed and coughed. Her eyes were red with it. In her fur coat she looked like a small animal cornered.

'I'm sorry.'

I said with bitterness, as though I had been robbed of something. 'That needs attending to.'

Sarah's unattended cough – not helped by her walks across the Common in the dark, 'slanting' January rain – results in her death.

Whilst in Paris on 14 May, Catherine and Greene had gone to Mass but had had to walk out because Catherine was coughing so much. On Monday 25 September 1950 – a howling, wet night – Catherine wrote in her diary that she had bad chest pains when breathing, worse when she coughed. The following day, after flying to Rome with Greene, she felt ill to the point of collapse. The next night, back at the villa in Capri where Greene was working on corrections to *The End of the Affair*, she had yet another coughing attack in the night.

On the evening of Monday 24 July – that afternoon Catherine had splashed out for the Degas book – Greene hosted a smart Catholic-literary-mafia drinks party at St James's Street before the group moved on to a large party being given for Father Martin D'Arcy. At the cocktails were Greene's psychiatrist Dr Eric Strauss, Dick Stokes MP, Evelyn Waugh (who was 'beastly' to Father Caraman), T.S. Eliot, Victor Gollancz and John Rothenstein. At dinner Catherine found herself and husband Harry sitting at Evelyn Waugh's table. As a letter that Waugh wrote to his wife about 'Father D'Arcy's orgy' makes clear, Catherine had come a very long way in upper-class Catholic circles since asking John Rothenstein to explain the point of genuflecting in a church. T.S. Eliot was dull and glum, Waugh noted, as he had been 'shanghaied into the thing believing it was a small intimate affair'. He went on to describe the evening:

> I thought it all pretty beastly but then I was already in a general despair. No one seemed to realise that wine was not included in the price of the dinner and I found myself a grudging host to many thirsty papists. I brought (Lady) Anne Rothermere (later married to Ian Fleming) & Randolph & June (son of Winston Churchill and his wife) & put at my table them & Eddy Sackville-West, a pansy I didn't know who was the only chap to offer a contribution towards the wine bill, Mr & Mrs Walston . . .

The following day Catherine lunched again with Greene, Eddy Sackville-West and Waugh. Having been acutely perceptive in his 'Electric Hare' essay about the relationship between Greene's personality and art, Eddy was also aware of the relationship between Greene and Catherine. In the early 1950s they often came to stay at his beautiful home, Long Crichel House, which he shared with three other intellectual 'pansy' friends. And whenever Greene was *persona non grata* at Newton in the

1950s, it became like a second Tackley. He and Catherine also stayed for the weekend of 6–9 July 1951, shortly before *The End of the Affair* was published. An entry in Eddy's diary following a 1951 visit by Greene shows how he clearly had sympathy for Catherine's predicament in becoming so intensely entangled with such a tortured, tormented, manic genius:

> Graham Greene has been here. Evident need for incessant conversation, veering round always to Catholicism [indeed Raymond Mortimer, one of the co-owners of Long Crichel, complained to a friend that during the weekend '*nothing* was talked about except religion']. He thinks Heaven may be the union of body & soul in a single point of love. Odd how every place he talks of seems sinister or squalid. Told me an extraordinary story of equivocal episodes in Lyons, with a louche businessman & a mistress & a rich widow. Also that the police prison contains a large rosary of leaden beads with which a renegade priest (c.1890) used to murder people. I fancy that Catherine's insistent favouring of my friendship with G is partly – but only partly – because of a desire to be relieved of some of this burden! Not that I mind. I am slightly in love with her myself.

Waugh and Greene had forged a very close friendship by July 1950. When Waugh died at his home in Somerset on Easter Day in 1966, after receiving communion at Mass from Father Caraman, Greene wrote in *The Times* that his friend was the 'finest novelist of his generation'. A fortnight before the D'Arcy dinner of July 1950, Waugh had written a postcard to Greene from Piers Court: 'I hear you have consented to write script for film of *Brideshead Revisited*. If true, thanks most awfully. It is more than I ever thought possible.'

Greene never did write the *Brideshead Revisited* screenplay, after the Hays Office – the Hollywood censorship office run by a pious Catholic called Joseph Bream – opined that many of the adulterous (but crucial) scenes and discussions about divorce in the novel would have to be eliminated in the cause of public decency. A few years later, exactly the same reasons were given for the heavy censorship of the original 1955 Hollywood version of *The End of the Affair*, with Deborah Kerr as Sarah Miles and Van Johnson as an Americanised Bendrix. The film was so abysmal, partly as a result of the moral censorship, that when its director Edward Dmytryk – one of the so-called 'Hollywood 10', jailed for contempt of Congress in 1950 after refusing to confirm his former communist sympathies – died in July 1999, many of his lengthy newspaper obituaries did not even bother to mention it.

Being seen with Catherine Walston at literary society dinners such as the Father D'Arcy event (there were about 160 guests), ensured that their relationship was an open secret long before *The End of the Affair* was published in September 1951 with its cryptic dedication 'To C'. The extent to which Greene drew on his illicit affair with Catherine whilst he was writing 'Point of Departure' has long been a contentious issue. Certainly their close circle of friends could not fail to notice many similarities between the novel and what had been acted out before them in real life. In Evelyn Waugh's published diaries, for example, his entry for Thursday 7 July, 1955 records:

> A sultry day heavy with elderflower. I went to the cinema and saw again the film of Graham's *End of the Affair* – most of it, that is to say. I could not face the detective a second time. Then I came home and read the book. Hardly a sentence from it occurs in the film. It has the obvious faults of elevating the social status of the characters and losing the inimitable Clapham drabness of the original. It also misses the entire point of the story – the events which follow Sarah's death are the real end of the affair. The heroine alone was moving. After the film a visit to the church.

Yet whilst trawling through the original hand-written manuscript of Waugh's diaries at the Harry Ransom Humanities

Research Center, I discovered that Michael Davie omitted (I assume deliberately, since the diaries were published in 1976 when Catherine was still alive) an interesting sentence with which Waugh had ended his journal entry about the film: 'Oddly enough', Waugh wrote, 'she and the hero had at moments a look of Katherine and Graham.' Later, when he knew her better, he spelt her name correctly.

'We've added about ten feet to give it a rounded stern so it will be about one hundred feet long and we'll put bulwarks up . . . so it will be more elegant,' boasted Korda of the *Elsewhere*. Greene managed to persuade Catherine to join him on board for a few days at the beginning of August 1950.

They flew to Nice from Northolt airport on Saturday 29 July. After drinks at La Bonne Auberge, they had their first dinner on board. Others in the party were Michael Korda, Sir Alexander Korda's young nephew, Carol Reed and his wife Penelope ('Pempy'). Michael Korda later described his memories of Greene on board the *Elsewhere* in his autobiography *Charmed Lives*. He was to become Greene's American publisher (he became chairman of Simon & Schuster) after making his old yachting companion an offer that it would have been rude to refuse. In a letter to Catherine after she left the boat, Greene admits to having a great fondness for Michael ('I've never liked a boy as much'), whose company Catherine had also enjoyed.

It was never certain how Alex would spend the day when he was on the *Elsewhere*. There was a restless quality to his life in the South of France which came from the simple fact that he himself did not know where he was going. Some mornings he would rise late and do nothing, happy enough to sit in the sun and make plans for an excursion to St Paul de Vence to have dinner at La Colombe d'Or, other mornings he would sit at Chez Felix au Port and make endless telephone calls to London, or have himself driven to Cannes or Nice to meet

with David O. Selznick, or Darryl F. Zanuck or Sam Goldwyn.
[*Charmed Lives*]

They stopped off in Monte Carlo, where Catherine bought some shorts. Greene usually wore a navy-blue sea-cotton open shirt. They had dinner on board whilst Korda gave the captain the order to sail directly along the path of the moonlight as it fell across the dark ocean. During the day, Korda would wear an old yachting cap and direct operations from the bridge, never wasting an opportunity to explain the 'proper technique' for anchoring. In Greene's 1955 novella *Loser Takes All*, the Pernod-drinking, unshaven tycoon character Dreuther, who speaks fluent French and decks himself out in an 'old sweat shirt' and 'baggy pair of blue trousers' as he bosses around his guests like an old admiral, is an affectionate but thinly disguised portrait of Sir Alexander Korda. This 'entertainment' was written following a 1952 cruise Greene took with Korda in the Aegean. Whilst on this trip, a *Daily Express* paparazzo snapped a tanned-looking Greene standing on deck with a glass of wine in hand, talking to Korda (one imagines an underling may have been instructed to tip off the photographer). The 'crew' aboard his 'cargo of talent', as the paper quipped, included ballerina Margot Fonteyn, Sir Laurence Olivier and Vivien Leigh, Ingrid Bergman and her husband Roberto Rossellini.

Although Korda was always announcing plans to sail around the world, or to India, or – as was the case early on in this August 1950 trip – to Spain, his more ambitious nautical plans rarely materialised. Most days were spent 'cruising' from one chic little Riviera harbour or port to another. A popular destination was a little island of Cannes, which had the only nudist beach on the Cote D'Azur. Guests on the *Elsewhere* – Michael Korda describes Greene as 'always Alex's favourite companion' – would ogle at the naked bodies through binoculars. Other 'voyages' were made to Calvi Bay off Corsica, eastward to Iles D'Hyeres off Toulon, down the coast to Monaco, and to Portofino, off Italy's Ligurian coast.

On Wednesday 2 August 1950, off Calvi Bay, Greene was up early and had written another 400 words of *The End of the Affair* by lunch. Catherine's reading had moved on from St Thérèse to St Benedict. He read passages aloud to her as she sunbathed at the front of the yacht. The following day the wind blew up. A storm was on its way. Dinners had to be taken at the Eden Roc hotel, as the crystal glasses and wine would have smashed on the deck.

On the Sunday, Greene narrowly escaped never finishing his novel at all after going for noon drinks with a friend in Antibes. On arrival, he and Catherine were poured out two large pink gins. They were just about to gulp their cocktails down when their host suddenly remembered that he had actually filled his Gordon's gin bottle with methylated spirits. The afternoon was spent watching actor Stewart Grainger showing off in his small black sea-plane which repeatedly circled the *Elsewhere*. Grainger came to dinner but neither Greene nor Catherine cared for him. Whilst the 'party' aboard the *Elsewhere* went on until 3am, they slipped off to their cabin early.

The next day was to be Catherine's last. Greene was fraught, moody and sad. A few hours after she left, he took a piece of Thriplow Farm headed stationery out of his briefcase, picked up his fat black Parker fountain pen and wrote: 'Antibes, 5.10pm, on the dreary day you left in August 1950.' 'Dear Heart,' he wrote, 'I've loved the time with you so much. You've been very sweet and dear to me up to the last kiss over the hedge at Nice Airport. How did the customs know that diamonds were not in my mouth?'

After Catherine left, Greene was downgraded to a cramped and rather hot bachelor cabin. He filled her in on his visit to the Prince of Monaco's yacht, which he had seen with Alexander Korda that afternoon, and told her that Michael had bought an eighteenth-century pistol. They weren't going anywhere – other than the casino in Monte Carlo – because another heavy storm had been forecast. He gossiped about the Guinness yacht, *Sea Huntress*, that had pulled up alongside, spilling over with wives and happy children. It was time for a drink, although he didn't feel like one without her. 'There are so many traces of you on board. Even the silences are full of you.'

Clear-headed the next morning, he was up early to work. Wonderful, hot, cruising weather, reported Greene. They headed to Bandol, where they drank crisp, dry rosé. The work went 'slowly', although he was soundly beating Korda at canasta. On 11 August, after stopping off in Marseilles, he reported that the work 'plods' on. He was up to 58,580 words; and 11,000 points up on Korda at canasta. 'We all miss you so much, especially Michael and me,' Greene wrote.

By 16 August, the Feast of the Assumption, they were off the coast of San Remo, near Portofino. Greene had been depressed by the arrival of two letters – from Vivien and Dorothy separately – forwarded on to him from London by his secretary Mrs Young. His spirits lifted, however, when he stood on deck watching the terrific Assumption Day firework display on the waterfront in honour of the Virgin Mary. 'Great flaming crosses, huge domes of fire dissolving in gold and silver rain, all the noises of the Blitz including the whistling of falling bombs.' How he 'longed' for her, he said, because *she* was the only person on board who would have understood the relevance to 'Point of Departure'.

After another few hundred words on the novel that morning he had made a 'rather feeble attempt' to go to Mass, but had been thwarted by a procession of little boats going out to bless the sea. Then he couldn't find a taxi, so he bought two peaches and a wine decanter instead. That night, after the fireworks, Greene dreamt his brother Hugh, who was off to Malaysia, was dead, and woke up in tears. He was glad to be away from Antibes, he wrote to Catherine, 'I missed you too badly there.'

He had now written 61,000 words. He had no definite plans once the novel was over. 'Except for yesterday morning, I've been very happy and peaceful on the whole except for sudden jabs of this or that, and I've worked steadily,' he wrote. 'God knows if the book's worth anything though! The greater part has been written very quickly', he said, although he added that 'I' (i.e. Bendrix) had not been behaving or thinking as he ought. 'I can't switch him rapidly and have to task him like a sailboat in the hope of getting him to the devised harbour.'

After lunch – and a 'fierce' game of canasta with Alexander – Greene finished the letter. A tall, dashing French army general called Edouard Corniglion-Molinier, known as 'Eddie', had come aboard. Off-duty, he was a middle-aged playboy whom Greene found 'very nice – dirty and amusing'. He had a rakish military moustache and usually wore a large-brimmed white hat. Eddie had surprised Greene the night before when they were alone on deck under the clear stars.

'You have a great influence on Alex.'

'How?'

'You're pulling him towards Catholicism.'

'It's very odd, isn't it, how the bad Catholic is used or may be used!' Greene added in his letter. 'Today, tomorrow, or Thursday, c'est fini. I love you. I wish you were here to drink the last word. How I love you.'

At about 4pm on Friday 18 August, Greene placed a call from Portofino, through the international operator, to Fowlmere 217 in England (the phone number at Thriplow). Catherine was working in the kitchen, preparing to roast a turkey for a small supper party she was giving that evening. Greene told her he was nearly done. He was flying back to London tomorrow. When could he see her?

Catherine spent the following morning at Newton Hall with Lady Walston, Harry's mother, rummaging through dozens of old silver-foil-lined tea-chests crammed full of old Chinese and Japanese pottery, porcelain and bronzes that Sir Charles Walston had brought back from his archaeological travels. Before Catherine and Harry moved into the family seat, the collection was being sold off – apparently it wasn't worth a lot – at Sotheby's.

Greene, meanwhile, had got up very early, just after dawn broke through the small curtained port-hole of his cabin. His fountain pen ink ran as dark blue as the cold morning sea. In the

final paragraph of *The End of the Affair*, Bendrix stands stub-
bornly on the edge, lacking the courage to leap into the
unknown waters of faith. Although the last words of the novel are
slightly different, this is what Greene originally wrote:

> I found the only prayer that seemed to serve the winter mood:
> 'O God. You've done enough, my mind is broken like steps.
> I can't jump. I can't get beyond human love. O God I hate
> myself. Don't bother me any more. Leave me alone forever.'
>   (no of words 63,162)
>
>   August 19, NY Elsewhere

Alexander Korda did not convert to Catholicism, but it is clear
that Greene's influence – and he could be a very persuasive
talker – was to cause him plenty of personal unease. On the ropes
himself, being squeezed by tough bankers and lawyers after over-
extending himself, Korda seems to have genuinely revered him.
Greene himself was anxiously waiting to be paid by Korda and
had taken out an 'enormous' overdraft after making some hefty
stock investments. But he still regarded him almost like a brother
(as he did his 1950s companion Michael Meyer). 'Poor Alex,'
Greene wrote to Catherine, 'He really is nearly defeated. And I
love him in my drunken way, and he loves us and I'm damned if
his lawyers are going to stand between us.' Greene added that
before having dinner with him, Korda's first words were about the
'Jesuit statement' about the Assumption in *The Times*. 'He is genuinely worried and washed up about Christianity,' added Greene.
If he listed the people in the world that he really 'loved', Greene
continued, the list would only include her, 'Hugh [his brother]
and Alex', and 'my girl' (Dorothy). He did not include Vivien or
his children (he became closer to them as they got older). 'The
odd thing is that when I feel I love anybody – God or man, then
suddenly I feel more love for you – as now. The trouble is the
times when one feels no love for God or anybody.' He added a
post-script: 'Written in drink. Sad at going away. You've been so
far off – only one word in a fortnight. Iron curtain? S.I.M.B.'

This was one of a long and complicated series of secret lovers' codes used by Greene and Catherine in letters. Greene had S.I.M.B. monogrammed on the cream silk pyjamas with navy blue piping that he gave her. Not even Sherry had been able to work out what it means, or others such as R.O.F. or P.Y.T.U.M. Other codes such as I.W.T.M.C. ('I want to marry Catherine'?), F.M.C. ('Fuck me Catherine'?) and K.M.C. ('Kiss me Catherine'?) seem easier to crack.

In late November 1950, a week or so before the furniture lorries pulled up outside Newton Hall, Catherine and Greene dined in Paris with Korda, at a restaurant near the Palais Royal. There is a tincture of smugness to Catherine's record of the occasion. Korda seems to have floundered rather embarrassingly when he attempted to take on Greene over religion by appealing to the A.J. Ayer school of scientific logic. Catherine had no head for rational positivism, or complex theology for that matter, but she always felt enraptured hearing Greene calmly pummelling the argument of science with his dispassionate but highly intellectual brand of 'sinner manqué' faith. He had the ability to make everything suddenly seem so obvious. As the 1949 *Observer* profile had memorably put it (Catherine had cut it out), 'Mr Greene has the most sensitive nose of all contemporary writers for the odour of spiritual decay.' When Catherine Walston had asked John Rothenstein what was the difference between Catholicism and Protestantism, he should have referred her to a 1930 article in the *Daily Express* ('Why It Has Happened To Me') that Evelyn Waugh wrote after converting following his wife's infidelity. 'You never see in Roman Catholics going to Mass, as one sees on the faces of many people going to Chapel, that look of being rather better than their neighbours. The Protestant attitude seems to be, "I am good, therefore I go to church", while the Catholic's is, "I am very far from good: therefore I go to church".'

When the *Time* correspondent in London showed up at Greene's St James's flat in 1951 in order to interview him for their cover story on *The End of the Affair* and Greene's rapid ascent through the ranks of the literary hemisphere, Greene apologised for having a bad hangover. He had been up late drinking with his priest. But although Greene was still drinking plenty of Scotch with Father Caraman, the priest he turned to for theological and spiritual guidance was the tough Jesuit intellectual Father Martindale.

No biography of Greene has dealt satisfactorily with the critically important question of the sources of his moral and religious thinking. Throughout his life – and especially as he got older – many of Greene's closest friends were priests. Back in the 1950s, Farm Street in Mayfair operated like a fashionable literary salon. The idea of today's top literary authors decking themselves out in their dinner jackets and paying to attend a party such as the 'Father D'Arcy orgy' that Waugh described is risible. But back in the fifties, with *The Month* as its intellectual flagship, Farm Street was a very real literary force.

Dozens of touching and moving letters from Caraman and Martindale to Greene are held in Boston; in one, dated 1954, Martindale is upset, on moving to a farmhouse retreat at Hinchingbrooke Home Farm, near Huntingdon (c/o Mrs Walston), to find that he has lost an old black and white publicity photo of Greene. 'Have you another to spare? Father Philip [Caraman] swears he hasn't any of my stuff that he oughtn't to have.' Another Martindale letter is dated 24 January 1952: 'Father Philip well but older and very self-possessed.' Caraman was later to write a biography of Father Martindale.

Another of Greene's close friends was Father Gervase Matthew at Blackfriars in Oxford. But there is little point in denying that during the 1950s both Farm Street and Stonyhurst also suffered from a climate of deep repression. There was nothing remotely new or surprising about this.

In today's open climate, the strait-jacketed sexual culture that existed throughout the Church (both Catholic and Protestant) before the 1960s may be difficult to grasp. The strictly disciplined Jesuit order, in particular, was still suffering from a pre-war hangover.

Actually, this suited Greene rather well. As Piers Paul Read explained over lunch at his house in Holland Park, Greene's concept of faith contained a paradox within a paradox. What was unusual about the Greene–Walston affair, he maintained, was not the stories of burning cigarettes or the exotic locations in which they chose to enjoy sex, but the 'intense religiosity' that went with it. He quoted the line of a priest in *Brighton Rock*: 'A Catholic is more capable of evil than anyone. I think perhaps – because we believe in him – we are more in touch with the Devil than other people.'

Writing about the Greene–Walston affair in 1994, Piers Paul Read argued that Greene's brand of Catholicism – 'gloomy, paradoxical, existentialist' – was what made him popular with Catholics like Pope Paul VI, who were urgently trying to drag the Church into the post-war era. Certainly the priests at Farm Street probably looked at Greene as a means of helping them, as much as the other way round. It was a mutual combination that worked well. Although Greene was intellectually progressive and radical in certain ways, the universe of his novels remained very much back in the gloomy pre-Vatican II kingdom of good and evil. Paul Read is insightful on this subject:

> Greene's view of sin was symptomatic of the Catholic thinking that saw the struggle between good and evil as simply a drama acted out between God and the individual, readily resolved in the confessional. Too little thought was given to the effects of the sin on others – in particular on the families of those involved but also on the wider world by scandalous example. Also Greene's cult of the sinner seems at times to come perilously close to the snobbish view found frequently among aristocratic Catholics that chastity, particularly conjugal fidelity, is a 'bourgeois' virtue while adultery is the sport of kings.

The very close intellectual friendships that certain Jesuits forged with leading Catholic intelligentsia like Greene, Waugh and Eddy Sackville-West, were, arguably, an emotional outlet for some of this repression. Priests are human, after all. Clearly something went wrong in the Jesuit ranks in the 1950s. It is significant, for example, that although Greene and Waugh spent much of their social life with Jesuits, neither of them sent their own sons to Stonyhurst. Nor did Catherine Walston send any of her four sons there.

Michael Shelden's often quoted line that Greene used the confessional as a venue for playing practical jokes on Jesuit priests seems unlikely. 'The thrill he got out of his affair with Catherine was the opportunity it gave him to mock the Church,' Shelden informed *The Mail on Sunday* in the summer of 1999.

Martindale was certainly one priest who Greene regularly saw for confession; there is certainly no suggestion of any foolery between them. Before a dejected Greene headed off to Indo-China in 1951, searching for danger in order to bury his despair over his failure – despite a brutal and wretched fight – to make Catherine the second Mrs Greene, Martindale gave him some friendly advice. 'You must not give too many handles to your critics. Say and get what you want, but not provocatively. You must not hamstring yourself at the outset as a Catholic force. Before you go [to Indo-China], you will make sure of being all square, won't you?'

The trip to Indo-China was important on several counts. It was there, just before her thirty-fifth birthday – so that it would reach her at Newton Hall by airmail from Saigon – that he wrote his sad poem, 'After Four Years'.

To Catherine, 6 February 1951 in the plane from Indo-China to Paris

> *I went as far as China to forget you,*
> *But in the razed village on the plain,*
> *In a car-track, on the latenite, I met you*
> *So it's no good going there again.*

> *In the marshes south of Saigon I lost you,*
> *Till a half-caste colonel stuns*

Me with his theory of grace and tossed you
Like a gage among the guns.

I had lost you in the body for a moment,
But the spirit made its reply,
I could lose you in the spirit, and the ferment
Of the body refused you to die.

I dulled my brain deliberate to forget
Our arguments over the glass
On Dominican views of Grace when you let
Ignatius give me the counter-pass

Deliberate I dulled my body to lose
Dew on fingers, toughness of hair.
I have struggled to find the final ruse
For forgetting, and found you everywhere.

Greene's friendship with Martindale lasted for many years. On 4 October 1960, for example, Greene wrote to Martindale thanking him for remembering his birthday. The letter is certainly touching and warm. Greene describes how he spent his fifty-sixth birthday on a train to Nottingham with his close friend John Sutro, taking 'my own wine' for the journey. Once again, he was revisiting the past to charge up his creative batteries. 'I had no business in Nottingham but was just revisiting old haunts – the Cathedral where I was received, the dreary newspaper with its bust of Gladstone over the door and the terrible house in All Saints Terrace where I had my lodging.' He added that he was off to Jamaica in a month and had a new novel called *A Burnt-Out Case* coming out on 16 January 1961 (in which the famous architect Querry is recognised in the Congo after appearing, like Greene, on the cover of *Time*). 'I don't know how it will be received by fellow Catholics!' ended Greene. The year before, on 23 March 1959, Greene had written to him from the leper colony where he was doing his research: 'The weather was so hot one could only write half a page at a time or the paper would be soaked in sweat'.

The extent to which Greene and Martindale respected each other's judgement is evident from a revealing letter the Jesuit sent Greene in August 1951 concerning the theology behind *The End of the Affair*, which Martindale was reviewing for *The Universe* (the leading Catholic newspaper). It is clear they had already discussed the book at length in private discussions.

> I want to be sure I get your idea right – you did tell me the 'point' of it and the jacket makes it almost too explicit when it says you have tried to express through a character who 'believes' he feels only hate. Starting at my end, I feel sure a man at whom God's love and grace were tugging, and therefore would be yielding a *little* bit, would be very angry, especially if he thought he didn't believe in God. He would then 'hate' God, and hate him the more he felt he was slipping towards him. Then I suppose he would hate any version of God – claiming love on a 'lower' scale, e.g. a friend or mistress. So (as I think you said) hate was a mask of love at various levels . . .

In the letter Martindale likens Bendrix to St Paul, to whom Christ said, 'It is hard for you to kick against the good.' When St Paul is stoned, his 'defences' collapse, says Martindale . . . 'possibly that happened to your Bendrix, though he didn't (in the book) get beyond asking to be left alone.'

Martindale's Jesuitical repression then leaks out all over the page.

> I now become spinsterish and impertinent. I think you have a good many allusions to physical details of love-making which are distractions and inartistic in as much as they interfere with the general flow of the story . . .

Greene said that he always sent his manuscripts to Caraman before publication. But the relationship between the two turned

252 the third woman

sour after Greene got back from Indo-China. One of the most curious aspects of the Greene–Walston affair is that it was conducted in full view of Father Caraman. He was a regular visitor to both No. 5 and No. 6 St James's Street; he even went on holiday to Achill with Greene and Catherine, and was a regular guest at the smart London restaurants they frequented. Yet Caraman was a Jesuit priest. It was bad enough for Greene to say, 'I have my ways,' when asked how he could reconcile his Catholic conscience with his brothel visiting. But how could Caraman reconcile his Jesuit conscience? In effect, by accepting an invitation to stay at Newton Hall he was validating their illicit affair in the eyes of God.

It's important not to understate this point. Things were very different when Catherine and Greene went to stay with Evelyn Waugh. In August 1951, a month before *The End of the Affair* was published, Evelyn had invited Greene to stay for the weekend of 12–13 September at Piers Court (known as 'Stinkers'). His wife Laura was on holiday with their children in Italy. 'Catherine, of course, welcome but warn her of Swiss Family Robinson Life,' Waugh added as a post-script. He was referring to the fact that the cook was away and his butler ill.

It was a timely invitation. The imminent publication of *The End of the Affair* had caused a series of scenes with Harry, and Greene was not welcome at Newton Hall. Catherine's younger sister Belinda had also taken offence, writing sharply to her sister that her allowing the novel to be published amounted to a betrayal of Harry, and revealed far more about the Walston family than anybody needed to know. Certainly some personal details had been shamelessly plundered. Greene even went so far as to borrow the 'squeaking floorboard' on the oak coffin staircase in the Walston flat above Lock's hat shop at No. 6 St James's Street. In the novel, Bendrix makes love to Sarah whilst her husband is in bed with flu upstairs.

Greene replied to Waugh that he liked living off boiled and scrambled eggs and wasn't too bothered by not being able to bath in hot water. Nor did he mind wearing a dinner jacket. Indeed, he had a new one. Before the smart dinner party with the magnum of 1929 Chateau Lafite in March 1950 at 6 St James's Street, Catherine had forced Greene to buy a dinner jacket, after Greene decided he couldn't face renting one from Moss Bros. 'We are both drinkers rather than eaters,' Greene wrote to Waugh, adding that 'Swiss Family Robinson Life is exactly what Catherine and I used to live when the world allowed us to.' He hoped that the visit might help get him back to work.

When Waugh biographer Martin Stannard wrote to Greene asking him about the visit, he replied that he wasn't a bit worried about being 'non-communicant' at the time (i.e. not taking communion), because he was, unlike Waugh, always a 'doubter'. He added that it was only those who have a 'real and dogmatic belief' who suffer from a crisis of faith.

Although the weekend at Stinkers did not solve any of Catherine and Greene's long-term problems, it was a happy time. As Waugh reported to Nancy Mitford:

> G. Greene behaved well & dressed for dinner every night. Mrs Walston had never seen him in a dinner jacket before [untrue] and was enchanted and will make him wear one always. G. Greene spent his days patrolling the built up areas round Dursley noting the numbers of motor-cars. He takes omens from them.

Bendrix, of course, does the same in *The End of the Affair*. The hobby 'teaches you about coincidences'. But what is most interesting about the visit is that a week before, on 24 August 1951, Catherine had taken the very real trouble to write to Waugh, in effect to ask if it was all right for her to sleep in the same bed as Greene in his house. She said she would not be upset if he said that he had a problem with her visit. She said she was used to the difficulty amongst their friends and that she would hate to cause any embarrassment. She asked Waugh not to mention to Greene that she had written.

Waugh replied:

Of course I won't tell Graham. I met you first as a friend of
Graham's, but I hope I can now look on you as my friend in
my own right. Please believe me I am far too depressed by my
own odious, if unromantic, sins to have any concern for other
people's . . . But when you say that Graham is sometimes
happier without you that is another matter . . .

Catherine certainly did not go to such trouble when Caraman
came to stay. Had he become merely a 'tame' priest; a Jesuit
equivalent of the obsequious Mr Samgrass always lurking around
the drawing-room at *Brideshead Revisited*? Certainly, by the end of
1951, Caraman was concerned to hear reports that Greene's faith
was wavering. When later Greene remarked over lunch at
White's that he was thinking of making his next book 'non-reli-
gious', Waugh retorted: 'I wouldn't give up on God quite yet if
I were you. It would be like P.G. Wodehouse giving up on Jeeves
halfway through.' In 1961, when Waugh was asked to review *A
Burnt-Out Case*, he returned his copy with sadness, saying that he
could not review it because of its apostasy.

But Caraman had been delighted when he received Waugh's
review of *The End of the Affair* for *The Month*. 'I thought [the
novel] beautifully written and a great technical achievement, but
I read it with sadness,' he had written to Evelyn. Whilst Greene
was away in Indo-China in 1951, Caraman's conscience finally
got the better of him. One of the most angry letters Greene ever
wrote to Catherine was concerning a story that he had been seen
in Paris with another woman. Greene emphatically denied it. He
also complained that she hadn't been writing. Had she not got his
letters? This was the same letter ('I can't get your letter out of my
head') in which he confessed to kissing Margaret Lane.

According to Lady Selina Hastings, privately Caraman very
much disapproved of Greene's affair with Catherine. When she
came to see him – distraught after not hearing from Greene
when he was in the Far East – Caraman decided to act.

'I'm absolutely desperate. I don't know why I haven't had any
letters from Graham,' Catherine said.

'The reason you haven't had any letters,' replied Caraman, 'is because your affair is over and he's at last decided to do the right thing and finish it.'

Lady Selina added that on hearing this Catherine 'went practically out of her mind, and believed him totally and wrote to Greene saying that if it was true, her heart would be absolutely broken and so on . . .' In fact, the reason the letters had not arrived was because of a postal strike in France. When Greene received this letter he went beserk. The moment he got back to England he stormed around to Catherine's flat.

'We're going straight to see that little shit Philip Caraman,' Greene said.

He marched into Caraman's office with Catherine and said: 'I hope you will be on your knees begging for absolution for the rest of your life for what you've tried to do.'

A tense Caraman replied: 'I was trying to do the wrong thing for the right reason which is to save both your souls.'

They tried to patch things up but, according to Hastings, Caraman was 'always frightened of him since that moment. Graham said he never forgave him.'

Certainly, paradoxically, Catherine seemed to be attracted to this angry side of Greene. Her husband rarely reacted to anything. The Earl of Huntingdon, Selina's father, thought that Harry 'was the sort of man who would be impotent with this gorgeous, sexy, hard-drinking, hard-talking wife. This wife that everyone knew was unfaithful to him. He thought that a real man would put his foot down and do something.'

The crucial difference between Sarah and Catherine is that whilst Sarah leaves Bendrix because she makes a pact with God over the bomb blast that nearly kills him, Catherine abandoned Greene (or at least his hopes of marrying her) because – in the last resort – she wasn't willing to give up her family, or the wealthy security of Newton Hall. It was still a time of austerity. Few people had any capital to spend. Catherine loved Greene dearly, but he was a nomad, whose future was as uncertain as his moods.

The affair continued, of course, for years, with many breaks and separations on both sides. Pat Frere, a close friend of Greene's and also a confidante of Catherine, told Lady Selina Hastings that one of the major break-ups came when Greene returned from another trip to Indo-China, this time with a Vietnamese girl-friend, a 'most exquisite little creature, like bringing back a kitten in a basket'. Pat Frere said that she had seen Catherine at a drinks party at their Albany flat (where Greene also later had a set of rooms), and she was standing alone by the window. Not talking to anyone. Pat asked her what was wrong.

'I've never been so unhappy in my whole life,' she replied. 'I would do *anything* to get Graham back.'

'From what Pat said, Graham left her,' added Lady Selina, 'but maybe she left him and then terribly regretted it.' Both of them, it seems, were totally heartbroken.

Once his affair with Catherine seemed doomed, his Catholicism certainly waned. In 1956, when Martindale was writing a piece about Greene, he asked him for some back-ground on his conversion to Catholicism. Greene replied that he was received into the Church in February 1926, 'and at a later period I became genuinely interested in Catholicism through the medium of books. My reception simply followed conviction during an instruction.'

Genuinely interested? That is not a very full admission of faith. Back in January 1948 – at the height of his tormented love for Catherine – Greene was very much more impassioned. At the 12pm Mass at Farm Street on Sunday 11 January 1948, Evelyn Waugh had encountered 'the shambling, unshaven and as it hap-pened quite penniless [Greene was always much richer than Waugh] figure of Graham Greene. Took him to the Ritz for a cocktail and gave him 6d for his hat. He had suddenly been moved by love of Africa and emptied his pockets into the box for Africa missions.'

But Greene's Catholicism did not adhere with the same sever-ity to the lines drawn by his friend. As Waugh eloquently put it in his review of *The End of the Affair*.

No one but Graham Greene could have written his latest novel; his unique personality is apparent on every page. All the qualities which we think of as being his own are here in abundance; his dark and tender acceptance of the inevitability of suffering; his conviction, which lies at the root of all morality, that the consequences of every human act for good or ill are an endless progression; and that human beings, especially men and women in their sexual relationship, are ceaselessly working on one another, reforming or corrupting . . .

Newton Hall certainly had a 'unique' personality too. Indeed, that was exactly the word that Harry Walston often used when asked to describe his house. After Greene returned from the *Elsewhere* in August 1950, he continued to hang around Thriplow, feeling increasingly uneasy, as he watched Catherine making preparations for her new life at Newton Hall. Although sad about Greene she was also in festive spirits. When Dick Stokes turned up at Thriplow at 10am on Thursday 24 August, champagne was immediately served. At 11am he joined Catherine and Greene as they went over to Newton to get some quotes from the decorators. Doubtless fed up with looking at paint and wallpaper samples, Greene slunk off with Stokes to drink at the Old English Gentleman in Harston. A few days later Greene took Catherine over to the house that had been so important to him to see his uncle, Sir William Greene, and his aunt.

In the afternoon, Greene was dispatched by Catherine to a Cambridge chiropodist to have some nasty thorns removed from his feet. One can only speculate as to the reason why he suddenly needed the emergency appointment.

That evening Greene and Catherine were querulous. Greene had accused her of being peevish. 'You are never very interested in the truth are you?' he snapped. 'You just can't *face* hearing it; or talking about it. You just aren't bloody interested in anybody but yourself!'

It probably wasn't Catherine's fault. After finishing a book Greene was always restless and indolent; 'The Point of Departure' was no exception. On the Tuesday after finishing the novel, he took Catherine to an 11.30am showing in London of Billy Wilder's *Sunset Boulevard*, starring Gloria Swanson, followed by lunch at Rules.

It is not known exactly when they exchanged a private form of secret marriage vows at St Augustine's in Tunbridge Wells, whether a priest was present, or whether they followed the Roman model, upon which a marriage existed by mutual consent. The first reference to their 'marriage' agreement comes in late 1950, around the time the novel was finally completed. One assumes that the Cartier ring that Greene had bought Catherine in Paris played a part in the exchange of vows. She wore it for the rest of her life. The engraved inscription reads 'C and G'.

After reading the proofs of *The End of the Affair*, we know that Greene sent Catherine the manuscript of the novel. In the enclosed letter he wrote that he wanted to give her a sentimental present: 'Because I hate myself today, because all the best part was written with you (I remember coming out of my workroom while you were washing up & reading one sentence & saying "isn't that good" – "virtue tempted him in the dark like a sin") and because I love you & bastard as I am, I'm married to you by this ms. Graham.'

Writing from the Hotel Metropole in Hanoi, Vietnam, in November 1951, Greene appeared apathetic to the international success of *The End of the Affair*. He was more worried about the six-month trial separation that had been imposed. He could not face returning to England, he said, if it only meant sitting alone, waiting for the phone to ring. He begged her not to throw away their 'marriage', which began one morning at Mass in 'Tunbridge Wells' (an event that he repeatedly reminded her of in his letters for the rest of her life). He added that he wasn't much inclined to return to England if things were truly over between them. He implored her to write to him from the depths of her heart. He was no longer afraid. He admitted, sadly, that he didn't think he had the self-control to be anything but her lover if they were ever to see each other again. He was simply still too much in love with her. 'Stick to me as you always said you would if the iron curtain fell. Nobody can make a curtain between us but you.' The phrase 'Iron Curtain' was first popularised by Winston Churchill in 1949: 'From the Baltic . . . to the Adriatic, an Iron Curtain has descended across the Continent.' So had it also for Greene.

Before Piers Paul Read and Greene became involved in a feud, Greene once told him, in the course of a discussion about whether novels could be 'prophetic', that the 'greatest passion of his life' had died with the writing of *The End of the Affair*. On 3 December 1950, the day after Catherine moved in to Newton Hall, the diary quote that Greene had hand-written into the exercise book well over a year before, was from St Thérèse of Lisieux. 'Life is very mysterious. But in the depths of the soul one feels an infinite distance which will make us forget for ever the sadness of desert and exile.'

red mischief

On the inside page of Catherine's 1951 diary – a hard-backed green school exercise book with a maroon strip along the spine – Greene pasted in a picture of St Caterina da Siena. The inscription reads: 'For Catherine from Graham with love and Adorazione. At the Ritz (happily) before Malaya (sadly). In the hope that there will be . . . in Anacapri, Achill, Paris, during the fifth year.'

On the day *The End of the Affair* was published in London on Monday 3 September, 1951, Catherine was back at The Old Head Hotel near Westport. But instead of staying there with Ernie O'Malley, or owning it with Greene, as they had once dreamed, sitting up late at the bar with Alec Wallace, she was holidaying in Ireland with Father Caraman and Father O'Sullivan (she would later take O'Sullivan to the Gritti Palace in Venice). Nor was she propped up in bed with *Madame Bovary*; she didn't need to read the novel any more. Her own passion for adultery far out-classed Flaubert's original heroine.

The day before Greene's novel was published, they had gone to 8.30am Sunday Mass at a local convent, followed by a visit to artist Evie Hone, who had a cottage at Lough Leane. The graceful designer of some of Ireland's most beautiful stained glass church windows now looked worn out by life. Catherine, as usual, was behind the wheel of her old Ford as it bumped along the pot-holed Old West Road towards Killarney Bay. Before they arrived at the Lakes of Killarney – whose 'luxuriant scenery' was praised by Sir Walter Scott and Thackeray – she stopped the car. Her two Jesuit companions climbed out of the car, pulled off their Sunday Mass dog-collars and cassocks and changed into thick Aran sweaters and corduroys. To reach the cottage by the lake where they were staying the night, they had to wade into the water carrying old sleeping bags, blankets and (doubtless) wine, beer, or perhaps just a bottle of Irish whiskey. Everybody got soaked and laughed so much that they nearly lost the blankets in the water. A fun and happy night for them all; Alec Wallace joined them for supper, bringing a fresh sea-trout.

Greene had been seeing Dorothy again, and cruising off Skyria in Greece on the *Elsewhere*. Writing to Catherine at The Old Head Hotel on 31 August 1951, he said he was 'scared' of spending two days alone with Waugh before her (hoped-for) arrival at Piers Court. He and Korda might have had a better time on the *Elsewhere* if they both hadn't been 'a bit dead of heart, but we drank a lot and played hard at canasta'. He added that to distract himself, he had begun recalling their 'memories . . . but by breakfast time one feels pretty tired with the effort and it seems so sad that one has to treat the best memories I have of life in that way'. He ended, 'God bless you my dear. I do hope you will come to Evelyn's.' He enclosed a 'nice note' he had received from Father Gervase Matthew at Blackfriars in Oxford. Greene had sent him a copy of *The End of the Affair*, with some self-effacing mark of disparagement. 'How much I disagree with your judgement,' Matthew said, saying the book worked on a very 'real level . . . I think that the conception of God that underlies that reality is the truest of all your books, and you said so much that I have seen so often in life but never in print.' A few days before Greene had written to Catherine, 'Remember, I'd always, if you needed me, come back at a moment's notice from anywhere. Your lover whatever happens, G.'

But Greene was now up against a very real new difficulty.

Catherine, it seems, wanted to see Greene but no longer sleep with him. At Newton Hall, she had been talking a lot with her new best priest friend Thomas Gilby – not to be confused with Monsignor Alfred Gilbey, who was the Catholic chaplain at Cambridge. Gilby, known as 'Father Thomas', was a Dominican theologian, and novelist, who had written a book called *Morals and Marriage: The Catholic Background to Sex*. Before heading off to Achill with Caraman and O'Sullivan, Greene had written to her, carping that she was spending too much time with 'Thomas', who, he added, wasn't a harmless 'distraction' like 'my girl' because he was always going on about Newton Hall, Harry and her children.

Father Thomas and Catherine had clearly discussed Greene in depth. He seems to have told her that since January 1947 she had been living out a 'fairy-tale'. It was time to get back to her responsibilities as a Catholic mother and wife. Greene replied that Gilby's solution was only a substitute fairy-tale 'in which one will be afraid to come into the same bedroom, afraid to kiss, afraid to touch you, when we shall be so self-conscious that the body will be always in one's mind because never at peace. I don't know what kind of "intellectual companionship" we shall get out of that.'

Finally, Greene, like Dostoevsky's desperate gambler, resorted to a last play involving the writing of numbers on bits of paper. On 10 August 1951, ten days after *The End of the Affair* was published – it sold very briskly – Greene drew up an ultimatum. He said he couldn't 'stand' the situation any longer. He hadn't the strength to go on. The night before, it seems, Catherine had tried to put the Gilby 'solution' into action.

The choices Greene laid on the table were as follows:

1. Come away with him to Italy and start 'annulment' proceedings. She could see her children in the holidays, they would 'marry', and try for a child of their own.
2. Return to the way they were before 'Newton' entered the equation. They could take occasional holidays. They could

remain 'in the Church', going to confession or taking communion when they wanted. 'But in between be lovers,'
Greene added.

3. He cleared off out of the country and her life from 'tomorrow'. The night before had well illustrated how he was
incapable of being with her and not being her lover. He was
'too in love' for it to be reduced to that.

I'd just ask one thing & that's for you to take my bureau key
& take away your letters in the top right hand drawer. I tried
the other day to destroy them, but it meant seeing them & I
couldn't.

Our love's been a good love . . . I have been your husband.
Please put 1, 2, or 3, on a piece of paper. It won't be 1, but if
it's 3 I think I must go away tomorrow . . . Your lover – probably for the last time of writing it.

★

Greene did not have to travel anywhere quite so romantically far
flung as Goa, Indo-China or Malaya to find a possible substitute
for Catherine. In February 1951, he only had to take his raincoat
off his St James's Street door-peg, walk up onto Piccadilly, amble
past the Ritz, and turn right into Dover Street where, as part of
the opening of the Festival of Britain, the National Book League
was hosting a party to mark the 100 Best Books of the Century.
Greene was represented at the National Book League exhibition
and had been asked to loan a manuscript. Vivien recalls Greene
ringing her up about 'borrowing back' his old manuscript of *The
Man Within*, and – she thinks – *The Power and the Glory*, that he
had once given her. 'So I sent them of course as I was told,' she
said. 'But I never got them back.'

The Festival of Britain, occupying twenty-seven acres of
derelict and bomb-cratered land on the South Bank of the
Thames, had been launched by the new Labour government,
who scraped in during the 1950 election (Harry Walston failed to
win a seat) to raise the post-war national spirits, ushering Britain

forward into a new, shiny, futuristic design age. 'This is no time for despondency,' said the King at the Festival opening. It was goodbye to Beaumont Street's drab utility beds and welcome to the great 'beached spaceship', as commentators called it, of the Dome of Discovery. A bulbous, phallic sculpture by Henry Moore was displayed along the Thames, along with the new Festival Hall. The idea was to mark the 100th anniversary of the Great Exhibition of 1851 at Crystal Palace which Greene had seen burning from his Clapham Common glass dome roof when it went up in flames. Such was the demand to taste exotic foods like 'spaghetti' served in cafés full of shiny and spiky new pink- and citrus-coloured wobbly Teflon furniture that the old Clapham air-raid shelters were converted into temporary bed and breakfast underground accommodation.

One can be fairly sure that the Festival of Britain stood for pretty much everything that Greene despised – from the 300-foot aluminium 'Skylon' to the tiny glow-worm lights embedded in the concrete crazy paving. He was catholic in aesthetic taste and hated garish, progressive, Disney-brand synthetic optimism. He always said that walks at night with Dorothy around Tottenham Court Road as bombs fell nearby were amongst the happiest memories of his life. 'I loved the Blitz. It was wonderful to wake up and know you were still alive and hear glass being swept up in the street. It was marvellous to walk down Oxford Street in the blackout and see the stars. I enjoyed the buzz bombs because you could hear them coming. I didn't like the V2s so much,' Greene later told playwright John Mortimer.

Still, Greene decided to show up to the National Book League party. Stooped, in his raincoat, unable to face fighting for a glass of cheap wine at the 'bar', he stood by the door on the off-chance of seeing some friends who had said they might be coming. At that moment an Australian painter, who was philosopher Freddie Ayer's girlfriend, saw Greene 'standing alone at the entrance as though trying to absent himself from his surroundings,' as she later recalled.

'Hullo Graham,' said Freddie, who was not one of the friends Greene had been half-hoping to meet. He introduced Greene to his vivacious young bohemian companion, who had a cherubic face, boyish brunette crop of hair and large pixie eyes. She was called Jocelyn Rickards. As the diminutive Ayer advanced into the heaving scrum of party guests, Greene explained to Jocelyn why he was standing alone by the door, looking as if he wanted to leave.

'I only came to ward off the boredom of dining alone with an expected Austrian I'm supposed to meet.'

Ayer and Greene both belonged to the inner sanctum of London's intellectual elite. They met from time to time at the Gargoyle Club, London's avant-garde nightclub founded by aristocrat David Tennant in 1925 for literati, bohemian toffs, louche politicians, spies (Greene's friend and MI6 colleague Philby was a member), and any 'artists' with a few basic social credentials. It operated on three floors of a house in Soho. On one occasion Peter Watson – the well heeled American backer of Cyril Connolly's *Horizon* – was sitting at the same table as Greene and Ayer whilst kitschy cabaret music floated around them. According to Gargoyle historian Michael Luke, Watson recalled Greene 'challenging' atheist Ayer to demolish his beliefs, or even half-beliefs.

'Talk me out of it,' Greene had urged. 'De-Catholicise me with your logical positivism.'

Ayer seems to have failed. They both had books represented at the National Book League exhibition, and a similar show put on by the Victoria & Albert Museum. But, so Rickards recalled, by the time the taxi pulled up at Dover Street, Ayer had succeeded in irritating her by the number of times he had told her 'how lucky I was to be his chosen consort'.

Rickards observed that Greene's glass was empty. 'If you promise not to move,' she said, 'I'll fill your glass.'

Already, she said later, she felt electrified by Greene's 'carnal presence', as John Le Carré once put it. 'I wanted him so much there were little red spikes on my hands.'

After the party, Rickards, Ayer, Greene and the anonymous Austrian crammed into a friend's car and went off to look at the lights at the opening of the Festival Exhibition on the South Bank. Then they all had dinner and moved back to Graham's St James's Street flat. By the time Rickards and Ayer left in the early hours, she was in love. 'There was such electricity between us [Greene and herself] but Freddie wouldn't have noticed,' Rickards later said, 'if I'd taken all my clothes off and paraded naked in front of the two of them. He was so secure and certain of me. He was also having affairs with seven other ladies at the time.'

Despite their religious differences, both Greene and Ayer had plenty in common. Not least, they were both serial adultery addicts. As was Catherine, who like Ayer seemed to use sex as a way of attempting to heal deep familial wounds of self-doubt and insecurity. Ben Rogers notes in his excellent Ayer biography that he once boasted that he would 'sacrifice all my friends for the most ephemeral love affair'. And he had many. Ayer was a happy hedonist, representing an Oxford intellectual version – especially in regards to women – that Greene may have become, were he not so plagued by his Catholic guilt.

The book that made Ayer famous was published in 1936, the year thirty-two-year-old Greene published *Journey Without Maps*. Ayer had been the star of the 1930s generation that came up to Oxford just after the Harold Acton aesthete set had left, but in many ways Ayer was even more arrogant than fellow Old Etonian Acton. When Lady Elizabeth Longford (who had been at Oxford in the 1920s) met Freddie shortly after *Language, Truth and Logic* came out in a whirl of controversy (amongst its most ardent critics was Father Martin D'Arcy of Campion Hall), she recalled asking him, 'Freddie, what comes next?' He replied, without a trace of modesty, 'There's no next. Philosophy has come to an end. Finished.'

But Greene was never seduced by a philosophy of nihilism. When he was once asked by his friend V.S. Pritchett how he felt about always failing to win the Nobel Prize for Literature, he replied that he was looking forward to a much greater prize: 'Death'. Controversy still continues over Ayer's claims of a death-bed change-of-heart after a near-death experience. But back in his prime he was a lethal opponent. D'Arcy – whom Waugh described as having 'a fine slippery mind' – once paid the back-handed compliment of saying that Ayer was 'the most dangerous man in Oxford'. D'Arcy had studied and later taught philosophy at Oxford before the war. Ayer used to vocally disrupt D'Arcy's seminars on Thomas Aquinas, turning them into an intellectual slanging match about the meaning of God. During the intellectual battle, Greene and Waugh sat dutifully in the D'Arcy corner.

After Greene lost his 'fight' with Harry Walston for Catherine, Ayer proved to be a walk-over. He was too self-absorbed in both himself and 'winning' other women (who included the wife of poet e.e. cummings and the beautiful, sexually charismatic American journalist Sheilah Graham, who had been Scott Fitzgerald's last love).

Like so many of the women that Greene was attracted to, Rickards seems to have had a feisty, almost masculine nature, and – probably a welcome change – was not a Catholic. Rogers' description of Ayer's attraction to Rickards also probably applies to Greene: 'Rickards was a foreigner, with few of the doubts, fears and scruples of English women of her class.' Rickards was born in 1924, brought up in an upper-middle-class Melbourne family similar in background to Catherine's family in Rye. 'She was alert, open minded, outspoken and ambitious, almost domineering in fact.' Greene used to call Rickards 'Pixie'. Although she may have been willing to dance naked down St James's Street – 'Graham saw me as a kind of happy savage whom he did not want changed' – it actually took a while before they slept together. 'Because his other mistress bloody Catherine Walston kept getting in the way,' as Rickards put it.

In a letter to Rickards I asked her if, when she read *The End of the Affair* in 1951, she had worried that Greene was lugging around a lot of personal emotional baggage with him with regards to Mrs Walston. I also asked why she thought Catherine exerted such a strong pull over Greene from 1947 until the early 1960s, even beyond.

> First of all I must say that I don't think any one woman had any part to play in this work, not even Catherine Walston, and I know on a first reading of *The End of the Affair* one is likely to assume that Sarah and Catherine are the same person, but with time I came to realise they are not and never were, nor did Graham intend that they should appear so. I don't know why she had such a hold over him particularly as they spent a great deal of time apart. I never found him obsessive.

Like everybody else I asked, Rickards did not know when Greene's 'affair' with Catherine finally stopped.

> My own feeling about Graham's, what I suppose must be considered as infidelities to Catherine, are that he was desperately trying to shake himself free from her, first with me and then Anita Bjork. It is true that we discussed marriage but as I said I didn't need the security of marriage, that I loved him and that was it. I suppose my feelings about Catherine Walston have mellowed over the interminable years, however, I still feel she was a grasping bitch who resented any part of himself that Graham gave to anyone else.

In Boston College, I came across a letter from Greene to Caraman after a close friend of Rickards had committed suicide by putting her head in a gas oven. I was curious to know if she had known that Greene had written to Caraman asking the priest to say 'masses' for her friend. That she didn't suggests Greene's Catholicism had sincerity to it in the early 1950s.

Rickards offers important evidence that Greene treated his own ex-girlfriends well, which makes his treatment of Vivien something of a mystery. In the last resort, guilt certainly had a lot to do with his attitude towards Vivien (she was very upset not to have been invited to the lunch party at All Souls when Greene was given an honorary doctorate by the university). He was angry with himself for having made such a mistake. But then perhaps the impressionable young Balliol man had just read too much D.H. Lawrence as an undergraduate. Lawrence famously declared that the requisite for a satisfactory marriage is that bride and groom are as different as two people can be.

Greene and Rickards did not begin their affair until 1953, because of their entanglements with 'other' people in their lives. On a cold, bright April morning that year, two intellectually pushy young writers from *The Paris Review* came to interview Graham Greene at his smart first floor flat at No. 5 St James's Street. It was the week before the London opening of his first play, *The Living Room*. Every aspect of Greene's surroundings was carefully noted – from the 'sad classicism' of the red pastel Henry Moore drawing on a wall, to a sombre Jack Yeats painting over the chimney-piece. An unremarkable lamp of Scandinavian design stood by the window. The only 'suggestion of an obsession' was his collection of seventy-four miniature whisky bottles above a book case.

Yet I cannot imagine any clever literary journalist today blundering quite so badly as to fail to finish their elegant set description (entitled 'Scene') properly.

The eighteenth century succeeds to the twentieth on the ground floors at the bottom of St James's Street. The gloss and the cellophane of oyster bars and travel agencies are wrapped incongruously round the leg of the dignified houses. Graham Greene lives here at the commercial end of this throughfare in a flat on the first floor of a narrow house sandwiched between the clubs of the aristocracy and St James's Palace. Above him, General Auchinleck, the soldier who was beaten by Rommel; below him, the smartest oyster bar in Europe; opposite the second smartest.

Of course, the high-brow *Paris Review* interviewers would think themselves above mentioning the fact that Greene's mistress lived next door. Still, had they dared to ask Greene about the significance of Catherine Walston at all, his gas-blue eyes would almost certainly have shot them back a blank, hostile glare.

His melodramatic letter of 1951 which ended 'for the last time, your lover . . .' was nothing of the sort, of course. They were to continue their affair – on and off – until the early 1960s. At Boston College there are a number of amorous love notes from Margot Fonteyn in the early to mid-1950s. They suggest Greene probably walked away from what seems like the offer of a serious affair with the world's most famous ballerina.

Dear Graham, Now that you seem to be living in space, it is very difficult to contact you by phone. I have made several unsuccessful attempts to catch you in Albany. Our season finishes in two weeks . . . and I fly off to Spain early the next morning. I'm not really sure of my holiday plans but if I don't see you before I leave I will ring as soon as I am back – by which time you will probably have gone to Indo-China. When I think of it, it is probably just as well that we never started that affair as we would have had very little chance to continue it. Love Margot

Another letter from Fonteyn refers to his play *The Complaisant Lover*, which she hadn't seen but was going to read. 'All I know is that 2 people did something 27 times in 3 weeks.' A friend of hers, she added teasingly, 'was very impressed with that'. Fonteyn clearly did not lack sex drive, or athletic energy, but despite her repeated notes – 'Dear Graham, I have been trying to phone you but guess you must be away or just out' – Greene actually wrote to Catherine that he couldn't start up with Margot because he was still too much in love with her. She ended up marrying Peter Moore.

But whilst Greene found escape by spending more and more

time abroad – Indo-China, Kenya, Vietnam – Catherine adopted a truly novel solution. She found the 'intellectual companion-ship' of Father Thomas so invigorating that he became almost a live-in priest at Newton Hall. Certainly, as with O'Sullivan in Dublin, Shelden seems to be right in suggesting that Catherine and Father Thomas were probably lovers. A close confidant of Catherine's confirmed to me that she was involved with Father Thomas, in addition to Father O'Sullivan. Clearly more went on behind the locked study door than simply drinking whisky and talking theology.

Oliver Walston admitted as much in *The Spectator*, when he said that certain priests at Newton Hall yielded to temptations for which their training had not prepared them. Harry Walston appears to have put up with Thomas Gilby but 'really hated' Father O'Sullivan. According to a former staff member at Newton Hall, there was another priest who often came to stay, whose room the maids were under strict instructions not to enter to make his bed. Catherine made it herself as there was usually a half drunk bottle of whisky under his pillow every morning.

Certainly, from Catherine's diaries, it is extraordinary how often Father Thomas was present at Newton Hall, along with Father Caraman (whom she was not involved with). It is mildly surprising that these priests – who both seem to have been on call twenty-four hours a day as her 'personal theologian' – could-n't find slightly more needy cases of spiritual help.

Lady Longford, who used to stay at Newton Hall in the 1950s, clearly remembers Father Gilby sitting at the head of the table and dominating proceedings at Sunday lunch. He was, 'very, very much more worldly than most priests I know'. She said a novel he had written she had found 'extraordinary, wonderful'. She commented that Father Caraman was a very 'human, loving character', adding, 'I don't know whether he really ought to have been a priest.'

Brian Wormald, the former Anglican priest who also became Catherine's lover in the 1950s, said that Gilby was 'one of the priests she collected; but he was rather special, yes. She never told me and I never speculated. He was nearly always there.' A letter from Catherine's sister Bonte Duran to her husband further suggests the oddity of the relationship between Catherine, Gilby and the rest of the Walston family.

> I have made several light hints about the character of Thomas Gilby, for I have tried without much success to see him as an intelligent, worldly, well-meaning individual. But his behaviour is so extraordinary that it is hard to be neutral and slightly indifferent. Not only does he behave in the most possessive manner with Bobs, but he behaves *sexually* in the most possessive manner, & she is entirely absorbed in him to the exclusion of everything else & everybody else.

Following John Rothenstein and Greene, Gilby clearly became another personal religious and literary 'tutor' figure. But with Gilby it seems to have been taken to an alarming new level of master to acolyte slave.

> All morning they remain in her study together reading and writing. At lunch he sits at the head of the table (as Harry is away again) and is deferred to on every question . . . Conversation is quite dead because a series of innuendoes which I don't understand covers most of his talk. Sometimes he makes a remark which hurts her feelings, and then she bows her head & won't say a word for some time, much to everybody's embarrassment . . . His behaviour shows a lack of dignity, coupled with a masked brutality. You feel he owns poor Bobs body & soul, and that he wants you to know it.

★

In Waugh's 1959 preface to *Brideshead Revisited*, he wrote that, 'It was impossible to forsee, in the spring of 1944, the present cult of the country house. It seemed then that the ancestral seats which were our chief national artistic achievement were doomed to decay and spoilation like the monasteries in the sixteenth century.'

By 1959 Waugh had visited Newton Hall on several occasions. In 1961, the year Catherine became Lady Walston, Cliveden famously became the focus of the great political scandal of the decade when John Profumo, Secretary of State for War, and his actress wife Valerie Hobson, spent the weekend at Lord Astor's Buckinghamshire country estate. He met model Christine Keeler at a cocktail party around the swimming pool, when she showed up as a guest of Stephen Ward, a part-time photographer who rented a cottage on the estate. At Newton Hall guests slept with the staff. Years before sex and sin became a public obsession in the sixties, Newton Hall was in many ways the prototype Cliveden, the unofficial Red Mischief playground for the left-wing smart weekend set. Labour minister Richard Crossman writes in his diary of a visit to Newton Hall in 1953:

Walston's wife, an American, is the heroine of Graham Greene's *The End of the Affair*. No one dares to ask Walston what he feels about this novel, which is all the more embarrassing since Mrs Walston talks all the time about Graham Greene. During the afternoon, while the others played croquet, she rather ostentatiously immersed herself in reading a translation of St Thomas Aquinas, which is being produced by her house guest, a Dominican, Father Gilby. Looking up, she said to me, 'Strange how, "the heart of the matter" has become a cliché since Graham's novel'. I said it was a cliché long before – and then I knew she didn't like me.

Brian Wormald remembers the same preoccupation with Greene in Catherine's conversation, even when their affair was smashed against the rocks in the mid-1950s. 'Constant talk,' he said. 'I mean you can *always* tell whether people still love each other . . .'

But Harry Walston's gambit to clutch onto the political shirt-tails of George Brown (twenty-two-year-old Oliver Walston

worked as his speech-writer) was not, perhaps, an inspired choice
of political thinking. In *Tired and Emotional: The Life of George
Brown*, Peter Preston gives a glimpse of a would-be high-society
weekend at Newton Hall just before Christmas in 1957. The
problem was that – unlike rich Tory grandees at Cliveden – certain Labour politicians felt acutely uncomfortable being greeted
by a footman, being waited on by a butler, and sitting at dinner
discussing mining conditions as the smoke from a dozen
Churchill Havana cigars swirled in a cloud above a set of ivory
candles in George III chamber candlesticks, or, as the political
talk moved onto Suez or agricultural policy, drinking a glass of
Hock served from a decanter with a William IV shaped oblong
wine label.

'Tired and Emotional' is, of course, the famous libel-avoiding
euphemism that *Private Eye* invented in the 1960s to describe a
hi-jinx (or more likely low-jinx) escapade caused by serious ine-
bration. And there was no shortage of alcohol at Newton Hall.
When Lady Walston became an alcoholic later in life, staff would
find bottles of Jameson's hidden in the pockets of her mink coats.
At opening time at the Queen's Head pub in Newton,
Catherine would slap down her solid gold cigarette case on the
bar and ask for a large Irish whiskey. Indeed, 'And, don't make it
stingy', Catherine liked to say with a good-humoured laugh
when somebody was pouring out a drink for her, former staff
still remember today. Harry had to eventually tell the butler to
lock up the drinks cabinet. Her empty bottles of Irish whiskey
were 'thrown' into a copse by the Newton church when it
became too embarrassing to have them stacking up in the bins at
the hall. Cases – never just a bottle – of Jameson's whiskey would
arrive in delivery vans. When the Shah of Persia came to stay in
the 1960s, Catherine was apparently too 'tired and emotional' to
make it downstairs before dinner. After Harry finally suggested
she went to a clinic, Catherine replied: 'Harry, I will never go to
a clinic. How can you expect me to . . . to just *give up* . . . after
drinking all your wonderful wine for so many years?'

Newton Hall was run like a hotel. When George Brown and

his wife Sophie came to stay, the staff set up a private mini-cock-tail bar in the bathroom adjoining his first-floor bedroom. For Sophie Brown, Newton Hall was an invitation to social hell. She refused to go down to dinner on the first night, bursting into tears because she wasn't allowed to bring the children. The Deputy Leader of the Labour Party had been too afraid to 'ask' Catherine if the children were invited. 'I knew this side of George's life was necessary, that the other guests, newspaper editors, writers, senior civil servants, were important, but I was shy, nervous, out of my depth,' Sophie told Preston. She had no idea what to bring as a present for Catherine, settling on a box of chocolates, and then 'found extreme difficulty in isolating her hostess to hand them to her'. Hugh Dalton, the Eton and Cambridge-educated Labour Chancellor from 1947–49, had also been staying for the weekend. Dalton had clenched his teeth when he heard Brown sidling up to Catherine and telling her: 'I'm only a lorry driver's son: not rich like you.'

Lady Longford, who spent weekends at both Cliveden and Newton Hall, said Newton Hall wasn't the sort of house you would leave after a weekend thinking that you had improved your career. Her husband had spent his youth 'rollicking about in Cliveden where Cabinet ministers were falling over each other'. The difference was that at Newton Hall she couldn't remember ever having 'a real political discussion, with several people at once. One played bridge quite a lot, which, I mean at Cliveden, that *wasn't* what you came to do.'

Lady Frances Donaldson, Evelyn Waugh's country neighbour in Somerset, also became friends with the Walstons in the 1950s. In *A Twentieth Century Life*, Donaldson explains how difficult it was when Catherine said something like 'when we were in Paris' to know whether she was referring to being with Graham or Harry. As a social hostess, 'Catherine was exceptionally beautiful, slightly dotty and more adept at discouraging her guests than Harry, and I always thought less kind.'

When they moved to Newton Hall, Catherine would enjoy cocking a snook at Cabinet ministers' wives who bought new evening clothes to wear for dinner on the Friday night. 'Catherine would appear in jeans. Accordingly the guests would go down the next night in day clothes to find Catherine in a long evening dress. Probably she had done this to keep them company, but it was very disconcerting.' When Donaldson once inquired why Greene never seemed to be around any more, Harry Walston told her that Greene had finally been forbidden into the house because 'he would criticise the food'.

In 1971, Newton Hall was sold for around £50,000. 'There's not an actual price fixed for a thing like this. We'll just get what we can and if we can't get rid of it, we'll just have to keep it,' Lord Walston said at the time. 'The trouble is, it's not a house that anybody wants because it's too big. It can only be used for some other thing than just living in – for offices, or a conference centre, or something.'

A three-day estate sale, flogging off the contents of the house, was organised by Knight, Frank & Rutley, starting at 11am on 23 June 1970. The sale brochure explained: 'At present Newton Hall is a family house but well suited for use as a residential training college or for other educational purposes, or as a nursing home, sanatorium, rehabilitation centre, museum or gallery, health centre, convent, hotel or other institutional purposes, subject to the necessary changes.'

'Notes for mansion-hunters,' wrote a local Cambridge paper on 23 November 1969, 'there are 28 bedrooms, eight bathrooms, six reception rooms, stables, garages and a lodge cottage.' After it was finally sold it was taken over as the headquarters of the National Seeds Development Organisation (a seed-breeding company). By the front entrance a series of ugly, vast hangar-like warehouses for storing seeds were built. They are now used to store and restore classic cars. Walking in on a Saturday morning, a yellow Lancia Delta turbo – all four doors open – with German plates had hip-hop music blaring. Inside, dozens of red Jaguars, Ferraris, Dodges, E-Types, every type of rare and collectible car, sat silently, covered in blankets, waiting to be used.

Like almost everything else associated with their long affair the house is now a forgotten, abandoned relic, owned by two local businessmen and leased out for office space. Long gone are the silver trolleys delivering breakfast to adulterous couples; its carpets are now grubby office brown, its corridors littered with giant humming Konica photo-copying machines, their green and red eyes flashing in a state of permanent readiness.

If you park outside the main entrance – a line of 'Reserved For' parking signs now stand in what was once a well-kept flower bed – and walk into the black and white marble hallway, you are greeted by a 'No Smoking' sign and a thin plastic tree in a black pot. A secretary sits at a cheap black office desk answering the switchboard and clicking away at a computer, above her, on a now empty grey-white wall, hang the old heavy copper hooks from which the Van Dyke used to cast his eye on arriving guests.

In his essay 'Henry James: The Private Universe', Greene twice returns to *The Ivory Tower* and James's fascination with 'the black and merciless things that are behind great possessions'. Newton Hall is the opposite to Greene's modest flat in Antibes. Walk all the way around to the main Edwardian 'South Front' lawn of the house, covered in ivy – a pile of old planks and abandoned scaffolding lay on the stone front terrace where guests like the Shah of Persia would be served drinks and cocktails – you can see the old Victorian ha-ha has long been dug in. The lawn is now roughly cut, for the sake of basic appearances. Hidden, to the left, by a line of old trees, the large outdoor swimming pool has long since been filled in. All that now remains is a large bulge, like a medieval burial ground.

Look behind you and there are a set of large bay windows on the first floor. From her window on the 'West Front', Catherine Walston used to sit at her type-writer whilst Greene would stretch out his long legs on the sofa, correcting his manuscripts, writing his journal, knocking off a frivolous or mischievous letter to *The Times*, trying out a love poem, planning their next 'holiday'. According to a former member of staff, Catherine's parrot (which she thought was called Catullus), used to be able to actually mimic the soft glug, glug, glugging sound of a large Irish whiskey being poured from a bottle of Jameson's into a crystal glass. In this room Catherine kept her priceless collection of Henry Moore drawings, sculptures and paintings, along with her collection of Greene's novels and manuscripts (including *The End of the Affair*, *The Heart of the Matter*, *The Third Man*, *The Quiet American*, *The Complaisant Lover* and *The Living Room*).

And what of Catherine's study today? Her parrot has long vanished. One of the few old newspaper clippings on Catherine that exist refers to the parrot's escape from the gilded cage of Newton Hall, a news diary story that Greene read about in an English newspaper in France (a Greene quirk was always insisting on having a 'fresh' newspaper). The former Newton Hall staff member who showed me round one weekend explained that, in addition to being able to imitate the sound of whiskey being poured into a glass, Catherine's parrot had a habit of saying 'To Hell with the Pope,' apparently picking up the phrase from Father Thomas Gilby. When the local bishop once came to Newton, the parrot had to be kept out of sight in a staff member's bedroom.

Catherine's study today is a drab executive office with a black glass coffee table in the centre of the room and brown beige carpet floor. The finely corniced walls are painted violet. Half-drunk plastic coffee cups stood on the desk. Cheap spot-lights are mounted in the corner of the ceiling. Flies buzz angrily around the bright glare. Instead of Greene's collection of first editions and manuscripts (kept in special boxes with blue silk ribbons) and her library of theology, the bookcases are now stacked with engineering account files. A few books are littered about on the shelves, rubbing spines with empty computer packaging boxes for modems or software. *The 1994 Voltage Regulator Handbook*; *1978 Michelin Guide to France*; *Advanced Level Physics*; Instead of *The Heart of the Matter*, a physics text book called *The General Properties of Matter*.

Like many wealthy Catholics, Catherine decided Newton

Hall should have its own Catholic chapel. In its prime one could walk along the balustraded first-floor corridor overlooking the marble entrance hall, and take the beautiful mahogany-panelled Edwardian lift down to the ground floor. By the entrance to the lift is the door that leads into what used to be the private chapel. Today it has a coffee-vending machine beside it and the room is a filing room for the SG Controls purchase orders and invoices. In place of the altar is a 1999 Sasco Year Planner. On a desk is a calendar featuring a naked man's bottom for each day of the year. Above it, hanging on the flaking white wall, is 'An Office Prayer': 'We are the unwilling led by the unknowing, doing the impossible for the ungrateful.' When Newton Hall had its estate sale in 1971, the old altar in front of which Greene, Catherine, Father Caraman, Father Gilby and the Walston children used to kneel, was bought for £22 by the Newton village pub owner, David Short.

When I began this book, a theme I intended to pursue was that whilst so many of the houses and places of the Greene–Walston affair were either now relics up for sale, or about to be bulldozed or boarded up, the one architectural constant would be the churches in which they prayed, confessed and took the sacraments. This was mostly true. Farm Street remains unchanged, along with its statue of St Thérèse (the roof has been fixed); the private chapel at Tackley is still well kept. But Newton Hall, having survived being turned into a training camp for the Women's Land Army during the war, proved the exception. As Waugh's Captain Ryder narrates after re-visiting the Marchmain family chapel on a frosty winter's morning:

> The builders did not know the uses to which their work would descend; they made a new house with the stones of the old castle; year by year, generation after generation, they enriched it and extended it; year by year the great harvest of timber in the park grew to ripeness; until, in sudden frost, came the age of Hooper: the place was desolate and deserted

and the work all brought to nothing. *Quomodo sedet sola civitas*. Vanity of vanities, all is vanity.

The old altar at Newton is now used as the Queen's Head private dining-room table.

Ibsen scholar Michael Meyer introduced Anita Bjork to Greene on a semi-blind dinner date in November 1955 (they had met briefly once before at the Stockholm première of Greene's play, *The Living Room*). Greene was giving a small dinner at a restaurant in Stockholm for his publisher Ragnar Svanstrom and his wife, and had asked Meyer along. When Meyer replied that he already had a 'date' that night, Greene replied: 'Perhaps you can find one for me.' He immediately added: 'No. I was joking!' Greene hated blind dates. Meyer brought Anita along anyway.

Part of Anita's attraction seems to have been her foreign, damaged, complicated nature, whose secrets Greene could never hope to 'unravel'. Her life had also been scarred by tragedy. A year before she met Greene, her husband Stig Dagerman, a brilliant but manic depressive Swedish playwright, had committed suicide. He was found dead in his garage after the car engine was left running. When Greene later employed exactly the same method of suicide in his 1959 'comedy' *The Complaisant Lover* – which borrows many elements from the bizarre ménage between not only Harry, Catherine and Greene, but Greene and Anita – the Swedish literary community felt insulted; indeed, Greene's ruthless 'borrowing' – which he denied – was thought to be a factor in why he never received the Nobel Prize for Literature.

After Noël Coward went to see *The Living Room*, he wrote in his diary: 'I cannot feel that Catholicism has made him very happy. The conflict between sex and religion is to me fairly unnecessary and extremely irritating.' The play deals with another complicated adulteress, Rose, who flaunts herself in front of a priest friend the night before she commits suicide by gulping down an overdose of sleeping tablets that belong to the wife of her married lover (Michael). Afterwards, the priest confronts Michael as to why he was attracted to her: 'You loved the tension in her.'

But tension – especially the wilful brand practised by Catherine – can be very tiring. The women that Greene pursued as a substitute for Catherine certainly had complicated natures, but they were never quite as emotionally exhausting. At the end of *The Complaisant Lover*, Clive Boot, who runs an antiquarian bookshop (Greene always fantasised about giving up writing to enter this profession), explains the 'sad truth' of why, although he's never loved anyone as much as he has Mary, he cannot go on sharing her with her 'complaisant' husband Victor. Clive says one day he shall get 'tired' of going home at night and leaving them together; tired of arranging holidays to suit her convenience; tired of cancelling holidays at the last moment; tired of waiting outside the shops in Paris whilst she steps in to buy shoes for her children.

Mary: And then you'll leave me?
Clive: No. Then, when you see how tired I am, you will leave me. That's what I dread.

Greene and Anita began their affair shortly before Christmas in 1955, on the first night that she came to London with Meyer to see him. Over the next four years, Greene shuffled back and forth from London to Sweden. He spoke little or no Swedish, but could not persuade Anita to leave Stockholm to live with him in France or England. 'I am sure she was as much in love with Graham as he was with her,' Meyer later recalled. Meyer, for one, certainly didn't care for Catherine, describing her in the BBC *Arena* documentary on Greene as 'a bit of a preying mantis. Somebody that likes to eat its victims.'

Shortly before Greene and Meyer set off for Tahiti in 1959, where they were spending Christmas as part of a long round the world trip together, Catherine took Meyer to one side. 'She was cold, hard and bossy,' he says. 'She wanted to brief me. I'd known him then fifteen years you see . . . and she said, "Now, you've got to remember . . ." – very much as though I was not far off a servant – ". . . now, you've got to remember that Graham needs to be alone a lot" [he was writing *A Burnt-Out Case*]. And I thought I'm sure there are some things she knows about Graham and I don't, but I'm bloody certain there are a hell of a lot of things I know about Graham that I don't think she does.'

In Georgetown, I read through dozens of letters Greene wrote to Catherine from Tahiti and other places on this exotic trip. Yet Meyer said her name hardly came up over the months they were together. Is he surprised to learn that Greene was writing Catherine passionate love letters at the time?

'Not in the least,' he said, 'I mean it's what I did; you had two affairs going on at the same time probably and wrote passionate letters to both ladies and hoped they never met. No, I think that's part of the course . . . We were good experienced immoral seducers.'

Yet on the Tahiti trip Greene did not, says Meyer, show any interest in the Tahitian natives that had so inspired Gauguin. In fact, he showed no interest in anybody, aside from one luridly Boswellian attempt to seduce a married older English woman after the 'dangerous third Martini'. The next morning, having invited her around to their beach bungalow for Planter's Punch, he quickly realised his mistake. 'She was very much below Graham's usual standard,' recalls Meyer. 'She was very ordinary, plumpish and then she turned up full of excitement. Graham was not exactly rude but was rather unwelcoming and didn't encourage her to stay and then afterwards he said, "She seemed all right in the candle light . . ." '

In an angry outburst to Vivien, Greene once claimed that he had 'had thirty-two other women'. But, in truth, although he felt it was perfectly normal to love two women at the same time, he was not the callow, immoral serial philanderer that he liked to pretend. Many of his 'conquests' were of the professional variety. As he got older, he couldn't bear the pain that he caused when he got bored or disillusioned by new 'adventures'. Meyer backs this up, saying that whereas he himself was always 'promiscuous' – on the Tahiti trip he bedded their chambermaid – Greene only had about five or six major relationships in his life. 'They were all long lasting and he never boasted about them.'

Greene was discreet partly because he was adept at seeing various of his women at the same time. When I asked Yvonne Cloetta if she knew of any other 'women' in Greene's life in the late 1950s, she mentioned an exotic Oriental woman called 'Mercia'. 'It was after the affair with Anita, he was so fed up with everything. How they met I don't know but they went together and stayed for some days and night in Brussels, they made love and I don't know what happened next, but she disappeared . . .'

But although Greene had his secrets from Catherine, he still wrote to her from wherever he was around the world. In one letter written from Canada on 30 December 1956, just before going to Mass and with his Stockholm affair with Anita very much established, Greene describes how Catherine continues to haunt him: 'Away from everyone I realise how everything belongs to you – my briefcase with R.O.F., my pyjamas, Scrabble, words in a book, even my shaving box. I am breaking up everything else . . . All last night I dreamt of you. You were wearing the ring and I felt it on your finger. It's seldom one feels in a dream. Every dream is a wish fulfilment. Please come back to me. I've come back to you.'

It was in Tahiti (and Fiji) that Greene first became a snorkelling fanatic. *A Burnt-Out Case* proved a stubborn and slow novel to write. In his Congo African journal, *In Search of Character*, Greene wrote that never before had a novel proved more 'recalcitrant or depressing'. As Meyer recalls, Greene used to try and find inspiration for the novel by putting on his rubber mask and flippers and floating in the Tahiti ocean. For hours, he would stare down into the water, looking for aquamarine life, and also hoping to release the depths of his unconscious. Occasionally he would surface, pull off his mask and ask Meyer for help over some plot point concerning Querry that was refusing to be solved.

As somebody who received letters from both Greene and Anita in the mid- to late 1950s, Meyer was uniquely placed to observe their affair from both sides. Along with the letters to Catherine, written at the same time, it quickly becomes apparent that extreme caution is required in believing everything that Greene writes to both Catherine and Anita. In his memoirs, *Not Prince Hamlet*, Meyer quotes a letter that Greene wrote to him on 24 October 1958. Greene had just got back from Havana, where he had been doing some 'research' before writing the script of *Our Man in Havana* for Carol Reed (starring his friend Alec Guinness). He had originally asked Meyer to accompany him to Cuba. Meyer later regretted declining the invitation to help provide colour background for his script, especially after reading Greene's nostalgic account of the Batista's 'louche' dictatorship in *Ways of Escape* ('. . . the brothel life, the roulette in every hotel').

Three hours after getting back from Havana, Greene told Meyer that he was 'very tired' and 'depressed'. After all the weeks away, he found himself 'just as much in love with Anita as ever – can't get her out of the system. Give me news of her,' he begged. 'I wish to God that she'd live half her time here – then I could stand half in Sweden.' But he was afraid the affair had 'gone flat' for her.

The letters Greene wrote to Catherine present a slightly different version of events, however. On 9 October 1958, he wrote that 'I love you very very much, dearest Catherine'. Although they had been out of touch, Greene longed for her news. Less than a month later, on 20 November, he wrote to her at the Walston Caribbean estate in St Lucia, to say that he was dreaming of her often, was wondering where she was, and that he was praying for her every night. He doubted whether his prayers achieved very much. He felt an 'awful vacuum' and that she was the 'most important thing in *this* man's life.'

On 25 August 1958, writing to her from Stockholm, Greene described the end of his affair with Anita, mournfully relating how it was a 'dreary' day, pouring with rain. She had been off filming at 7am and wasn't back until 7.30pm, and he had hung around all day trying to 'fix' some things at her house. It is an indication of just how serious Greene was about Anita, and further evidence of how well he looked after his women, that Greene had given her the house as a 'present', after deciding that her former husband's house – in particular the garage, because that was where her husband had committed suicide – had too many unwanted memories. That's the way the 'world' ends, wrote Greene, not with a 'bang' but with a whimper.

Twisting the knife a little, he added that the end came when Anita had the 'curse', saying this was an 'added advantage, of course'. A week before, he had written from Stockholm to say he had begun to 'half-believe' again in the sacraments, and reminded her – as he so often did – that 'I married you one morning in Tunbridge Wells'.

During the mid- to late 1950s, Greene never wasted an opportunity to let Catherine know that he was playing the field. Airplanes continued to present agreeable opportunities with other rich and sexy women. En route to New York from Havana in October 1958, Greene had an encounter with a 'very mysterious' and pretty English girl in a mink and sable coat and chauffeur-driven Rolls who was reading *Our Man in Havana* at the airport bar. The girl in question ('Patricia') shared Greene's taste for blue films and brothels. When they met up for a drink at the Algonquin Hotel bar in New York later that night, their conversation quickly turned to sex, just as it had done with Catherine over their first drink in 1946 when they had talked about the strip dancers at the Windmill Theatre. Only this time Patricia was telling Greene how, on her last trip to Havana, the landlord from whom she borrowed her apartment had developed a fetish for washing her feet in champagne and then licking them clean . . .

'With that fetish I suppose you felt . . . safe?' said Greene.

'Oh, he wanted to go further than *here*,' Patricia replied cooly, brushing her knees. 'I was terribly in love . . in Havana – I'm always in love with someone. But I thought it was rather squalid when I found that he had a kink. Wanted me to go to a brothel where he knew the madame and have the first six men who showed up. One of them had to be a negro. He was going to watch and I had to take money from them. He didn't like it when I said I wouldn't. Taking the money was *very* important. Wanted to humiliate me, I suppose.'

Whether a casual hotel room affair resulted from this piano bar chat with a fellow stranger is unknown. If nothing else, Patricia at least provided another character for his book, *110 Airports*. But more important than whether she joined him in his Algonquin suite is how the details in his letter to Catherine reveal that Greene was now playing a vicarious version of the Truth Game with his old mistress. The motive behind such revelations seems to have been to beat Catherine at her own sexual poker game. Back on 8 August 1958, Greene had written an oblique note, in response to what appears to be her request for a meeting, to say surely it was better to wait until she was 'free' and didn't have any 'secrets'? After all, his 'secrets' (probably a reference to his liaison with Anita) had been what had got them into such a mess. Now he passed the ball to her court; she could choose to stroke it back when she liked – in a week, a month, a year.

This *Liaisons Dangereuses* aspect to the later years of their affair is certainly confirmed by Yvonne Cloetta, who said that it was a quite deliberate game Greene played with Catherine before he met Yvonne in the Congo in 1959, and a game that he continued to play with Catherine after they began seeing each other in 1961. 'That was a real problem between them because they were both jealous of each other.' She likened it to an almost sadistic version of *Tom and Jerry*.

'Did Greene lead Catherine on, or was it the other way round?' I asked Yvonne.

'Oh, he would do the same . . . but she was much stronger than him, she was much, much stronger and definitely perverse, you say perverse, *non*?'

'Kinky,' I replied.

'Kinky, *oui*. She was always in search of excitement therefore she would take this as an excitement but he was not strong enough to cope with that . . . and suffered a lot.'

When not snorkelling underwater, much of the holiday in Tahiti with Meyer was spent playing Scrabble, a game that Greene and Catherine enjoyed playing in Capri. Greene displayed a fiercely competitive streak, keeping a tally of their scores and reporting back to Catherine that although Michael was ahead in games, *he* was ahead in points. Michael's winning obviously irritated Greene (later Greene was also to lose regularly to Yvonne, despite her broken English).

'Well, I always beat him,' Meyer remembers. 'You know he really wasn't good at it and he wasn't interested in a crossword and you need the same type of mind and he just wasn't . . . I think he rather resented losing the whole time.'

Greene resented it so much in fact that he resorted to invention to try and make up his losses. Meyer continues his story: 'I remember he kept on claiming deeply dubious sounding words, one of which was zeb, Z-E-B, you know z counts a lot if you can fit it into a word. He said, "You've probably never heard of this," and I said, "I don't think anyone else has." "No," he said, "it's an Elizabethan word meaning cock and when we get back to London I'll show it to you in my big dictionary."'

Greene was also guilty of a similar game of invention and selective use of the truth in his private life. Based on what Greene had said about Anita and what he had also written to Catherine, Meyer doubts that Greene's letters to Catherine were always reliable. 'When you're writing to a loved one it never is,' Meyer said. 'That's one of the first things you have to learn, no good pouring out the truth.'

Indeed, Greene admitted as much in a letter to Catherine, written at 1.15am on 12 January 1957 from New York: 'Poor dear, you learned over the Lowell episode that the truth doesn't pay, and I've learned it over this [his affair with Anita]. We'd have been much happier now if I hadn't spoken.' But this double-game was one of high stakes; not only did he risk losing Catherine, but Anita too.

In an undated letter of 1956, a crisis point was reached. Feeling like someone who has a terminal fever, he faces the prospect of making a choice, and his delay may already have lost him Catherine: 'I think it would be worse to lose you (like losing a world) but I flinch too at losing her [Anita].' Enclosed in the same envelope was a letter from his French agent Marie Biche to Catherine, giving her view that 'the Stockholm affair is not going to be a lasting one'. Marie goes on to give credence to Greene's words to Catherine: 'As you say he has so very little in life and is so miserable at the thought of losing you – who has been for so many years his only mainstay.'

But Greene continued to waver. He writes that, 'I can't say I'm really content and I've done less work than I meant. It's not A's fault but mine. I have nothing to talk about and I long all the time to get away and read. I get bored for no reason – it's as if, having once had the perfect companion, one can't be satisfied with anything else.'

Yet his relationship with Anita offered him companionship and a sort of peace, although not 'Il pace': 'You [Catherine] – when we are together – give peace *for* work from worry, and so in a smaller way does Anita. Neither of you are emotional cocktails. Neither of you make demands. There is a big difference with you – peace comes in the centre of talk, making love, arguing about books and Catholicism and children: a stimulating peace. In her case the flavour is so different – more like a sedative perhaps but peace all the same.'

But the sedative was too often like boredom (Greene admitted he was almost impossible to please in this respect) and he was restless when Anita was away on location for long periods of time, or at the theatre in the evenings. Meyer described Greene's loneliness, living outside Stockholm, away from the city: 'Half an hour outside but you had to get there by train and Graham doesn't drive,' Meyer recalls. 'It was terribly isolated sitting there when she was at the theatre all evening and I was one of the only two or three . . . the only friends he had over there . . . so it was nice for me because I saw a lot of him but it very much limited him and you know there was no pub life and those winters are awfully depressed.'

Bored, depressed and lonely, Greene had no outlet for his pent-up emotions. He wrote to Catherine: 'I feel lost these days without you to talk to and discuss things with – Anita is not a letter writer. An occasional postcard or telegram is all. So one bottles one's problems more and more.'

But Greene knew that it had a time limit, and the clock was ticking. Repeatedly he suggests to Catherine that he will break with Anita: 'It wouldn't be fair to spend it [referring to the first night of a play] with Anita, getting her more involved and yet knowing I was going to leave her at the end of it,' he writes from New York on 1 April 1957. Earlier in the same year, on 26 February, he had promised the same thing, 'that even if you won't come back to me, I'd break with Sweden. The awful thing is I'm bored, so bored, and you've never bored me for ten minutes. I'm alive with you, but I'm pretending to be alive with Anita. So if I can't mend the damage I've done, I'll just have to go off by myself. Only let me try first.'

Meyer thought that: 'Anita never bored him, but he was so much on his own you see in Sweden and he couldn't go round the pubs because there weren't any in Sweden. Anita couldn't bore anyone for ten seconds.'

When, later in 1957, it looked as though a 'slip' might have made Greene a father once again, he pretended to Anita and to himself that he liked the idea. Only after it was clear that there was no baby did Greene admit to Catherine that he was trying to convince himself, while 'secretly I made a promise that if there was no baby I would consider going somewhere . . . There wasn't a baby and now I don't see how it's to be done.' The news that Anita was either pregnant or wanted to have a child with Greene had apparently devastated Catherine. She confided to a close friend that *she* wanted a child by Greene more than anything else in the world.

But Greene was still seriously affected by what he described as 'this quieter love' for Anita. His letters, although they occasionally complain of his boredom, are also warm about her 'honest and sweet' nature. Meyer agrees: 'She's the most unbitchy person imaginable, Anita. She's got enormous integrity as a person, always has.'

In the end, it appears that Greene's own melancholy and misanthropic nature proved too much for Anita. He said as much in a wounded letter of 15 November 1958, when he complained to Meyer that Anita was a 'strange girl' who hadn't even 'acknowledged' his play, *The Complaisant Lover*. In it, there is a line about how it is the 'good' who are always the most difficult to leave. Greene told Meyer that 'if' he spoke to Anita on the phone, or wrote to her, could he say that she was still very much – unfortunately – in 'the blood-stream' and that he was quite unable to look for a substitute; again, this is exactly the same line he used to repeat – indeed was *still* repeating – to Catherine. He added that Anita was one of the 'nicest' people he had ever met and 'my only regret is losing her'.

Not long afterwards, he wrote to Meyer to say that Anita had finally left him. In a later letter to Catherine, he added, 'I'm miserable about the mess I've made – I seem to have made so many messes – Anita is the only one who escaped scott-free'. By the autumn of 1959, Greene was certainly writing to Catherine about Anita very much in the past tense. In September 1959, he wrote from Paris to say that he was 'surprised and disturbed' to have received a letter from Anita, the first, he added, for a year. In New York in early October, when the unbearably hot weather forced him to spend much of his time in 'air conditioned' cinemas, Graham was looking forward to the 'peace' of a forthcoming holiday in Jamaica with Catherine. He was worried about her health which hadn't been helped by 'all this electioneering' she had done for the 1959 Labour campaign trail ('I can't think how Harry allows it . . .').

Marie Selznick held a fifty-fifth birthday supper party for Greene at which he met his old 'dream girl' Lauren Bacall, whom he used to liken Catherine to ('I am in love with a Bacall profile . . .'). She was a disappointment, as it turned out. Also at the party was Ingrid Bergman, who came to stay at Newton Hall, signing the visitors' book 'the real Ingrid Bergman' to ensure that she wasn't confused with any of John Rothenstein's fake VIP entries. Greene reported that he 'liked' Bergman's husband after he spoke 'very wearily' of Anita as a 'great' Swedish actress.

Greene's correspondence to Catherine concerning Anita also needs to be read with a certain scepticism. In the mid-1950s, Anita represented a very real and dangerous threat to Catherine's place in Greene's life. When he set off in a canoe up the Congo to a French-run leper colony in 1959 to research *A Burnt-Out Case*, his emotions were as much burnt out by his failed affair for Anita as for Catherine.

The year 1960 was clearly a watershed for Greene. Writing to Catherine from Albany in January 1961, he spoke of his profound melancholy at how she was really the only person he could 'talk to' – except for gossip or work. He felt as if he had come to the end of a 'long rope' with *A Burnt-Out Case* and that he would probably never succeed in getting any further away from the Catholic Church. It was like, he said, when one was younger and taking a long walk in the country, and one gets to a certain tree, or a certain gate, and one stops and thinks 'Now I must be returning home'.

I wrote to Anita Bjork in Sweden asking to see her 'in order to be accurate about your involvement with Greene', and added, 'I would also be fascinated to hear what Greene said to you about his relationship with Mrs Walston. I have no idea if you ever met her, but I would be very intrigued to know why she seemed to have such a hold over him. Did you feel he was "over" her?'

About a week later I received a faxed hand-written reply:

Dear Mr Cash
I have nothing to say on this subject.
Anita Bjork

It is 3.30 on a late September afternoon in 1999, at Le Glacier, a busy ice-cream bar/café in the bustling Place de Gaulle in the old town of Antibes. The season is over. Peugeots, Renaults and Citroëns are parked bumper to bumper by the canopy entrance. Yvonne Cloetta, dressed in chic white designer trousers and looking to be in her mid-fifties, with pale grey-blue watery eyes, is sitting in a booth in the back room of the café, smoking a cigarette. Beside her is a small English-French dictionary.

'Did Graham ever talk to you about *The End of the Affair*?'

'A lot . . . but it was very difficult where to start and what to say.'

I said she could start where she liked.

'Well, he said that the only way he could finish the book was that he decided that Sarah should die, then he could go on with the diary. The part he liked best was, that's very curious too, was the end, the conversation after the death of Sarah, the conversations with Henry, that he liked.' She added that she had refused to continue co-operating with Norman Sherry after he had drawn such a specific 'parallel' between Graham's affair with Catherine Walston and *The End of the Affair* in volume II of his official biography.

'And you're saying it's more complicated than that?'

'How shall I put this in English? It is so difficult . . . this mixture between his life and his work, it's a whole problem. I don't want to doubt about Norman Sherry's work, but Graham is not a man to say something to somebody and the opposite to someone else.' (She pronounces his name 'GRRam' with a thick accent.)

Yvonne had read *The End of the Affair* before she met Greene in the Congo in 1959. They talked about the novel partly because she – like Margaret Cambell – was interested in the extent to which 'the part of the writer is in what he writes'. Yvonne asked him about the difference between the two Sarahs – both unhappy in love – in *The Honorary Consul* and *The End of the Affair*. Greene admitted it was 'a real problem' because of the question of point of view. When he wrote he was not talking about his own ideas or his own thoughts, he said, but what the character or the narrator wants to say.

'When was the first time he mentioned the name Catherine Walston?'

'Oh, very early.'

'What did he say?'

She laughed, saying that they 'quarrelled right in the beginning' just after their affair had begun – at the end of June 1960 – and he suddenly turned to her and said that he had to go back to London. 'I wanted him to stay of course but he said, "I *have* to go," and I asked him, "What's so important you have to go," and then he said, "Well, because I promised Catherine to take her to a Picasso exhibition in London and that's . . . tomorrow."'

Yvonne felt as if she had been hit with a sledgehammer. They had been seeing each other less than a month. 'And I said, "Go, but before you come back you must make a promise. It will be either Catherine or me but not both, that for certain."' Yvonne had no intention of being like Sarah in *The End of the Affair*. Although her own husband Jacques may have been acquiescent, Yvonne gave Greene the ultimatum. 'I am not a jealous person, *non*, I certainly am not, but it doesn't mean that I was ready to share him with another.'

Greene did not react well. 'He was in despair and he said, "I will be back in two or three days," and, in fact, on the fourth day he came back and I asked him, "How did it work, your appointment, your Picasso exhibition with Catherine?" And he said, "We quarrelled and didn't go".'

To see what sort of multi-handed game Greene was playing in the early 1960s, one only has to look in his Hermès appointment diaries. On 3 June 1960, the entry reads: '*Complaisant Lover*, C'; 16 June: 'To C'; 25 June: 'Nice', where, he wrote, he lost a small fortune in French francs (presumably at the casino). On 26 June he had dinner with Yvonne. The next day he saw her at 3pm (two crosses are marked against this date). He saw her again at 9pm, and 4pm the following day. On 29 June the words '1st night with C' have been crossed out and replaced with 'Yvonne' at 9pm ('XXXX'). It is unclear what the crosses are a code for. On 2 July he lunched at one of his favourite Cote D'Azur restaurants, the Voile D'Or. He clearly seems to have been seeing Yvonne until 6 July when the diary reads: 'Return London,' where he had dinner with his close friend John Sutro.

On 26 June Greene had a long dinner with Yvonne in Beaulieu sur Mer. 'For him he said that it was a *coup de fou*, straight away; the first time he fell in love, I don't know why but so it was, but with me it didn't work at all that way; but after that dinner, that was the first time we were left alone and we talked . . .'

There is no mention of Catherine or any Picasso show in Greene's personal diary. He returned to Nice on 16 July 1960. By the summer of 1960, Greene's letters to Catherine are often no more than a few lines on the back of a postcard; in early June 1960, he wrote from Venice to say that he can't face Paris – where he had just bought a new flat – without her, just as he can't be in Venice. The brief postcards from Antibes to Newton Hall sent between 27 June and 4 July do not mention his dinners and lunches with Yvonne. Lunching with Yvonne at Chez Felix on 30 June, for example, he says only that Antibes is 'more attractive' than even they had time to discover. He told Catherine that on no account should she let anybody know that he was staying at the Hotel Royal. For good reason; he was now enjoying himself there with Yvonne.

Back in England on 16 July he wrote a 'mean letter' to Catherine from his C6 Albany flat, saying that he was sad that the pattern of their meetings was now reduced to just a few hours' 'rendezvous' in London, invariably resulting in his 'crying' after having hardly spent any time with her because of 'bathroom trouble' or drinks with people like Mrs Young (his secretary), whom Greene seems to suggest she now sees more of than her 'old lover'.

The next day he wrote to apologise for being 'sour', and added that he hoped her marriage with Harry was 'gay and happy'. A week later, obviously not having heard from her, the note of deep suspicion returns. He tried to say 'goodbye' on the phone but was told by a staff member at Newton Hall that she was 'somewhere in Ireland' (presumably with Father O'Sullivan), which he likened to her sudden disappearance the year before to the north of Italy. He couldn't see the point of writing again until he heard from her. Returning to London from Paris on 7 August, his diary is marked 'lunch? C'; on 9 August 1960, 'lunch C' again; at 5pm on the same day he saw his son Francis; the weekend of 12–14 August he spent at Newton Hall.

In the early months of their affair, Yvonne asked Greene to be honest about the importance of Catherine. 'He would never say anything bad or disagreeable about her, never,' said Yvonne. 'He was a passionate man and therefore all the women he loved in his life it was with passion.'

Yvonne had first met Greene in February 1959 in the French Cameroons. During the school term, Yvonne lived in Juan Les Pins with her children; in the holidays they went out to Douala with Yvonne to see their father. It was on one of these trips that Yvonne met Greene, after Greene said he wanted to investigate the 'night life'. They danced until 4am at a local nightclub. In his Hermès diary for 1959, her address and phone number in Juan Les Pins is written in ink on the last page. Greene had asked her to write it in his book the next day when she came over to his hotel to see him off. As he packed up his suitcase in his little room, he began talking to her about 'the big things in life', a conversation that, she later told Selina Hastings, made a very great impression on her.

Greene had said he was 'single'. When the talk turned 'philosophical', had he said anything about his relationships with either Catherine or Anita?

'*Non*, nothing, he didn't speak about his past.'

Unable to fathom out the ambiguous mysteries of Catherine or Anita, Greene seemed to have more success with Yvonne. After only meeting him twice, she recalled that she thought, 'My goodness, this man knows about myself more than I do'. When he was next in the south of France, he looked her up.

Yvonne first heard about the significance of Catherine Walston through Greene's close friends, Marie (his Paris literary agent) and Jean Biche. One day Jean turned to Yvonne and said, 'Have you heard about how serious Catherine was?' Yvonne replied, 'More or less.'

'What I want to tell you,' Jean Biche continued, 'is that if this turns into being a serious affair it will be the end for Catherine . . .'

It took a while, however, for Greene's relationship with Catherine to die out. The final death blow came when he began taking Yvonne to Capri, where some locals thought she was his new wife. When this got back to Catherine she was mortified. 'Everyone was astonished,' said Yvonne. 'Especially the Dottoressa . . . he was always afraid that I would find ghosts there, meaning the presence of Catherine in the walls and in the house. She was very attached to that house, which was charming; and for them, it was their place for holidays together and so on, like it became for us, after, you know.' By the 1970s, old friends like Italian film director, Mario Soldati, who always used to stay with Catherine and Greene, would be writing to 'Graham and Yvonne' as though Catherine was only a memory of the past.

One reason for Greene not taking Yvonne to Capri for several years is that he continued to take Catherine there. When I raised this delicate subject with Yvonne, she said she knew about it. Catherine had a series of operations in the early 1960s after a bad accident. Greene had said that Catherine had asked whether he could take her to Capri for her convalescence, and would Yvonne mind?

'Well, I said, "It's not what makes me most happy but I understand," and I have some letters he wrote to me whilst he was staying with Catherine, obviously these letters show much more concern than love. In fact, I thought it was a good thing to have done that, for a woman he had loved in the past, she asked him, she wanted to go back to Capri. I had never been there so I didn't know what it was, and if she wanted to go there, why not?'

Exactly when (if at all) Catherine became merely a ghost 'in the past' is a tricky question to answer. When did Yvonne think Greene's affair with Catherine Walston finally ended?

'It is very difficult to know . . .'

'Being frank.'

'Well, absolutely, I'm frank with you . . . the thing is, Harry had decided to compete to become a Lord, I don't know how it works . . .'

I replied that he was a generous benefactor of the Labour party.

'Yes, the affair was known and it was a serious handicap for him, therefore he said to both of them, "Now, what I ask you, at least during the period of the campaign, that Graham goes away or that you stop this affair."' Yvonne added that Greene went off to Vietnam to the French war in Indo-China in order to try and finish it. 'Harry didn't ask them to separate definitely but for a period and he put four months or something and this is the reason why he decided to go away.'

I asked Yvonne what she thought about Greene writing love letters to both Anita and Catherine at the same time? 'Yes, it was a very difficult period, he couldn't make up his mind, the problem was that he was in love with Anita and it was a passion like it was with Vivien, like it was with Dorothy Glover and all of them, but he just realised that he couldn't live in a country where he didn't speak the language and he quite liked Swedish women, but not the men.'

As a test of knowing what to believe in Greene's letters, I asked Yvonne if she remembered receiving any letters from Greene during the Six Day War in Israel?

'Of course.'

Clearly Greene had written a detailed letter to Yvonne as well. She could recall exactly what he said. 'His companion was wounded badly, and when he came back from that he said never, never again, I am too old now to be killed away from home.'

But in the version of the letter he had sent to Catherine, I said, he added several paragraphs about how nearly being killed had made him think about the most important people in his life, and he realised that he loved both Catherine and Yvonne. Did that seem true?

She nodded her head, adding, 'Because it was not the *same* love'.

In one of her letters to me, Jocelyn Rickards wrote, 'I thank God for the day that Graham met Yvonne Cloetta, she calmed his restless spirit for over 30 years and when he died it was with her at his side.' Indeed, it was to Yvonne that Greene breathed his dying words in Switzerland. 'I was left alone with him and he started to speak to me about himself already in the past and I said to him, "You are still there, we are still together," and I took his hand like this, but he pushed my hands and he said, "I want to go," firm like this, "I want to go." The next day he was in a coma.'

'In his final days, wasn't Catherine mentioned at all?'

'*Non*.'

Greene, of course, used to write to Catherine about how she gave him 'peace'. Considering the turmoil and pain – as well as joy – that she caused Greene over at least thirteen years, this may seem ironic. But there can be no doubt that Yvonne was also a very important influence, less so than Catherine in terms of his creativity; more in terms of Greene being at peace with himself for extended periods for perhaps the first time in his life. 'Absolutely,' Yvonne said, when I mentioned that several of his friends had observed this. 'I've got a letter where he says, "You are peace as well as excitement" – those were his exact words.'

Many of Greene's readers may argue, of course, that his best novels were written against a background of what one critic described as 'emotion recollected in hostility'. Yvonne remembers Greene clearly saying that the mid-1940s to the beginning of the 1950s was the most 'tormented and chaotic time of his life'.

'Do you think happiest?' I said.

'*Non*, tormented, torments are not happiness.'

Yet this contradicted what Greene had once said. A few days before flying to Antibes I had watched the BBC *Arena* Greene trilogy. At the very end of the last tape, an anonymous radio interviewer had asked Greene, late in his life, the same question.

Q: When were you most happy?
A: In terms of personal euphoria? Between 1945 and 1955, I suppose.

I pressed Yvonne again, referring to Greene's own answer.

'This is a problem, one can't compare feelings you see, and this is why it's so silly to say Catherine was the passion of his life; it was a passion but it was a passion with all the women in his life. Each love is different from the other, therefore one can't make a comparison between or establish an *ordre de grandeur*.' Catherine was with Greene for at least thirteen years. Yvonne was with him for thirty-one. She added that it 'hurts me terribly' when she reads or hears Catherine Walston being described as the greatest love of Greene's life.

We moved onto Catherine's series of health problems and illnesses. Yvonne said he felt 'very sorry of course'. Greene always made a point of saying to Catherine that he wanted to be 'of use' to the women he loved. After James Walston was born, Greene felt he had been of 'some use'. But with Catherine increasingly hospitalised in London and Dublin, he despaired of what he could do. I remarked to Yvonne that he was good at understanding people who suffered. 'That was not always the case with Catherine Walston,' she replied. 'When he met her she was healthy, she was wealthy.'

Greene and Yvonne had actually discussed *The End of the Affair* and the differences between Sarah and Catherine. 'Graham always agreed that the real problem was jealousy,' Yvonne said. 'One of the differences between Sarah and Bendrix, and Catherine and Graham, was that Bendrix was wrong to be jealous of Sarah, while Graham was right to be jealous of Catherine, that is a great difference. And of course, as I told you, they would say to each other what they were doing separately.'

I read out to Yvonne the carbon-copy of Greene's typed reply to Mrs Cambell in 1976, in which he said she 'misunderstood' the book if she thought it was really 'true'.

'Graham always denied to me that. Based on his affair with Catherine, definitely, but whilst he was writing it he didn't think of it.'

'Did he ever say anything about the novel being his private way of killing Catherine off?'

Yvonne said that Greene had told her that writing the book helped him to 'get rid of the jealousy he had suffered so much; and it worked, in fact'.

Yvonne and Catherine never met. Yet she said that she knew perfectly well he was seeing Catherine when he went back to England.

'What did you think was happening?'

Yvonne laughed. 'I couldn't say.'

I suggested that Greene was prone to complicate his private affairs.

'Yes, and no, because, of course, each affair overlaps. Oh, he went on seeing her.'

Didn't she ask if he was seeing Catherine Walston?

'*Non.*'

'Did it occur to you that they were continuing their affair?'

'I just couldn't believe it.'

Yvonne strikes one as a very direct woman.

'I told you, I'm not a jealous person, even in love, not that kind of jealousy which precedes the act, but if I'm put in front of betrayal, if I *had* the evidence, then finished . . . and that Graham knew.'

So Greene, it seems, was playing another dangerous game. Lacking the evidence to convict him of betrayal, she tolerated his visits to London and Newton.

'What about when they went to Paris together?'

'What he told me he was in a very, very difficult position,' said Yvonne.

I suggested that Greene found it very difficult to sever his

closest relationships; and that he almost seemed to enjoy the torment of being torn between different women.

'Yes, but he couldn't have two women at the same time.'

'He could, perhaps, if one was in England and one was in
France.'

'*Non, non*, because it was not in his character; when he was in
love, really in love with a woman, of course, he had to see the
other one, did they make love? Possibly, but he wouldn't have
enjoyed it.'

Greene took Yvonne to London in August 1963. By this
time, their love affair had certainly turned serious. Catherine
had been reduced to second-string status. But the first trip to
England was not a great success. Greene had arranged for
Yvonne's daughter Martine to go to a summer convent school
in Lechlade (where his daughter Lucy had been sent) to learn
English. After they dropped Martine off, Yvonne burst into
tears and Graham 'got angry with me and he said, "After all, my
daughter's been there, it's not a prison," but it was terrible;
then, next morning we went back to London to his flat in
Albany, and he wanted to show me the place and so on; he
opened the door of his bedroom: there was a huge bed, a table
and on it a big photo of Catherine. I thought, "Why did I
come here"?'

'How did he explain that?'

'Well, he said, "I'm sorry but I didn't know it was there,"' said
Yvonne, laughing. 'That didn't help.'

'Was this his big blue bed?'

'Yes, the room was not very big and the bed was huge, so we
could make love that way or that way, you see.'

'Did he remove Catherine's photograph?'

'Yes, and I still have got the photograph; it is in the flat in
Switzerland [which Greene left her after his death].'

'Did he ever say to you, "Do you want to meet her
[Catherine]?"'

'*Non*, she did not want to meet me. I was ready to.'

Yvonne did meet Anita at the Paris flat. 'I was staying with him in the flat and Anita came to Paris and Graham had invited her for lunch, and, of course, he said do you mind, I said, "No not at all." It was very nice . . . and more than that was very curious, as soon as I saw her I understood why he was in love with her. She was not one hundred per cent female, which was very important for him.'

'He didn't like little pretty bits of porcelain did he?'

'*Non*, he didn't like fat women, certainly, and he didn't like what he used to call hens, *les poules*, you know, *les coquettes*, very feminine.'

'Are you saying he didn't like to be completely in control?'

'*Non*, and he liked women who would make themselves in charge and wouldn't depend on him.'

Certainly this was true of Yvonne. When Greene and Yvonne used to go sailing with close friends, like the Freres, they apparently watched in disbelief as Yvonne, lazing on the deck, would ask the Grand Man of English letters to go downstairs to fetch her lighter. And Greene not only did so; he quite liked it.

'So Graham didn't like submissive women?'

'*Non*.'

'Maybe that was the problem with Vivien?'

'Certainly, but that was not the only problem with her.'

'What was the problem?'

'Really you can't imagine two people so different from each other living together, but then they were very, very young of course.'

'Did he feel guilty that he treated her badly?'

'Not because he treated her badly but he was angry against himself because he had married her and took all the responsibilities on himself.'

'What did he say about Vivien, that he made a mistake?'

'"I was a fool," he said.' She added, 'He knew they would live like a sister and brother, he should have known that he couldn't cope with that.'

'Did he ever talk about Dorothy Glover?'

'Mm, that was the pain in the neck, because he certainly had much more regrets and sorrow about her than any other one; and when she died he was absolutely in despair.'

Shortly before she died, Greene visited seventy-two-year-old Dorothy in Sussex, on one of his occasional visits to England. He wrote to Catherine about how she now looked 'older than her mother . . . one would have said 80. Sort of hunchbacked too and the house naturally run to dirt.' She had recently been in a skin graft hospital after being set alight when an electric fire fell on top of her. Her stomach and front were burnt 'quite black', Greene told Catherine. 'She's been in hospital for weeks in great agony . . . I'm sure she'd like a letter.' Greene went over to England for Dorothy's funeral. After he had left her, she had never found anybody else.

'What, he felt sad or guilty?'

'He cried, yes and I saw him crying only twice.'

'What was the other time?'

Yvonne laughed. 'It was towards the end of his life, and he then burst into tears. Just, you know, suddenly, he became like a child, frightened. He said now you know how much I love you and then he burst into tears like this.'

'But what was the reason?'

'Probably emotion and he was already too feeble to cope with it.'

'What about when Catherine died in 1978? What did he say about that?'

'Good for her, because in the state she was, he said, "It's a good thing for her."'

'Was Graham shaken by her death?'

'Not all that much, because he knew that it had to be and so he was prepared. He was sad altogether about her.'

'Did he discuss with you whether he should go to Catherine's funeral?'

'*Non* . . . anyway, he hated funerals.'

Shortly before Greene died in 1991, he asked Yvonne to edit his dream diary, an 800-page manuscript he had kept by his bedside for many years. Even after his affair with Catherine petered out physically, he continued to dream of her often, and recorded many of the dreams. Indeed, they were an essential source of his continuing creativity. On 14 October 1965, for example, Greene wrote to Catherine saying that his 'Dream Diary index' recorded twenty-two dreams of her already that year. I asked Yvonne what she had thought when she had read through the manuscript as editor and come across these repeated entries, some of which were presumably erotic?

'I never read them.'

'Sorry?'

'*Non*, he showed me the index, but then he didn't put everything in.'

Before his death Greene does indeed seem to have edited out the repeated references to Catherine in his dream diary. 'He probably destroyed them. Burnt them. Just like he burnt all the diaries from Catherine.'

'Letters, you mean?'

'*Non*, no, diaries, and letters.'

Yvonne explained. In November 1965, Greene decided to leave England altogether and live in France. 'I've got a letter where he says, "I have spent the day in the difficult, or painful task of destroying the diaries, letters of Catherine".'

'Did you feel that burning them was the real end of Catherine for him?'

'*Non*, because he had already told me that Catherine gave him the diaries and the letters but with the promise that they wouldn't be shown to anybody.'

'Why did he choose that date to destroy them?'

'Because he had decided to leave England and that part of them were in England in his flat, and part in his flat in Paris.'

'But why didn't he just bring them with him?'

'Because *she* wanted them to be destroyed.'

At Georgetown, the only diaries that survive are those for 1949, 1950, 1951 and parts of 1952 and 1955. Whilst the 1949 diary misses almost no entries and has a diverse range of quotes reflecting their shared religious and literary tastes, the 1952 diary is almost barren, containing only a few pages of completed entries. Although Greene has painstakingly written out quotes for every day, they look unread; some pages are still stuck together.

The inscription of the hard-spined maroon exercise book for 1952 reads that it was bought on 15 February 1951 after a 'chocolate lunch' at No. 5 St James's Street, having planned to go and see a film they never made it to. Catherine appears to have got her hair done instead at Elizabeth Arden. Greene finished writing up the quotes in December 1951 in Indo-China with her on 'forbidden' territory, referring to the ban imposed by Harry; he called the diary a 'Christmas present from exile'. The diaries that Greene burnt appear to be the set of their 'double' diaries that Catherine gave to him.

There is a touch of irony in the fact that Yvonne's own love letters from Greene (or at least around one hundred of them) are also in Georgetown University, filed away in acid-free folders and boxes close to those he sent Catherine. She has another 300 that have not been sold, or seen by anyone. The letters that were sold to Georgetown, says Yvonne, were done so without her permission by an unscrupulous London bookseller who had the letters 'on loan'. Greene had encouraged her to sell the letters, saying they would only be sold after her death, so why not get the money for them herself? Yvonne says she was double-crossed by the book dealer. 'He swore, this is what he said, that nobody would have access to the letters whilst we were alive.'

After seeing the one hundred or so letters that were sold to Georgetown, Norman Sherry wrote in *The Sunday Times* that they spoke 'of an intimacy far different from anything that went before'. Based on the few extracts that were published, one can fairly say that Greene's letters to Yvonne about 'buying her duty-free cigarettes', 'tending to her dog' ('*Mon* cocker, Sandy', the only dog he did not despise) and 'doing his shopping' are unlikely to earn him an entry in the *Oxford Book of Love Letters*. His letters to Catherine are another matter.

Still, it would be very wrong to dismiss the importance of Yvonne to Greene in the last thirty years of his life. On the back of a photo that she has of Greene, he has written, 'If I were to live my life again there is only one thing I would want to change, meeting you, knowing you, loving you'.

It has to be remembered, of course, that Yvonne was a rival mistress to Catherine. In this inquiry into the theme of unreliable narrators, Yvonne is herself another witness with her own version of events. 'It's obvious that it was a passion, but it was a passion with the other women because he was a passionate person. He had had *enough* of that game you know [referring to the sexual poker game he played out with Catherine], he had had enough definitely and because when I met him he was a burnt-out case himself and that was a result of all these failures one after another.' Like Bendrix, who discovers that even with love 'we get to the end of other people', so with Greene and Catherine. In the end, Greene simply lost her.

'What is the time?' Yvonne asked.

Not having a watch, I shrugged.

'Already quarter past six,' she said. 'Time for a whisky now.'

epilogue

the last word

The closest Greene came to committing suicide over Catherine was on the evening of 26 June 1951, after a desperate night of savage rows. The day began badly when, instead of spending some promised time with Greene, Catherine agreed to drive Father Caraman and Father D'Arcy to Wimbledon to watch the tennis. Her day was then fairly routine: a pub lunch in Mayfair with an Italian friend who gossiped about another Padre Pio miracle; an afternoon of gourmet shopping with Greene – she had an account at Fortnum & Masons – for food (salami, caviar, sausages, vodka); a cocktail party with Greene followed by dinner at their now favourite London restaurant, Prunier. By the time *The End of the Affair* was published, Rules, it seems, just had too many painful memories.

The row began either during or after dinner. Greene then stormed out, telling her he was going to take enough sleeping draft to kill himself he hoped. At 8am the following morning, Catherine went next-door to 5 St James's Street (she had her own key) to check on him. She found him slumped half-dead, a wreck of a man. He was still breathing but was only semi-con-scious. Very concerned, she spoke to Mrs Young, his secretary, whom she was driving up to Newton Hall. Bizarrely, Greene not only 'borrowed' Harry Walston's wife; the two men also shared the same secretary, an 'arrangement' that allowed Greene to secretly spy on Harry's diary when, during periods when he was *persona non grata* at Newton, he wanted to sneak in an illicit rendezvous with Catherine. A phone call from Catherine to the flat at 11am established that Greene was indeed alive, although so drugged that she could hardly understand a word he said. She reminded him he had to catch a train to York, to visit Francis for his school prize day at Ampleforth.

'What time's your train?'

'Two o'clock,' Greene slurred. Slowly, he put on a grey worsted suit, walked downstairs to the mahogany-panelled entrance hall with white marble mosaic floor, and stood on the St James's Street pavement between Lobb's, Lock & Co. and Berry Bros.

Today the creaking staircase that 'squeaked' when Catherine and Greene made love in the room below Harry's bedroom is hung with framed photos of actresses such as Kristin Scott Thomas modelling Lock & Co. hats in *Vogue*, *Tatler* and *Brides*. Its oak coffin floorboards are well polished and could belong to any old Oxford college. It remains very much in use, although serving a less romantic purpose. It is the staircase that hundreds of Lock & Co. customers tramp up every week to look in the 'ladies showroom': British 'county' set women splashing out on a new Sylvia Fletcher hat for a wedding; American wives of husbands wishing to dress up like Sherlock Holmes; Japanese women wanting an exotic feathery silk headdress.

Once on the train to York, he sat down in the first-class dining car. It was a four-hour trip, but Greene liked long train journeys. Staring through the window, he was overwhelmed by remorse and sadness. Greene could still somehow write even when badly hungover – aged forty-seven he had had years of training. He took out his fountain pen.

In the Restaurant Car
Written in the train to Ampleforth after treating you badly the night
before and writing under dope.
June 27, 1951

Suddenly last night
I wanted to die;

As he sat thinking, staring into the countryside, trying to make sense of the madness of last night – trying to *remember* what had happened – he cannot understand why anybody should ever be good to him. What has he ever done to merit it when he is so 'hopeless', 'angry' and 'bad'? Looking through the train window, his face pressed up against the glass as though peering into a fish tank, memories flash back to him. Random acts of charity . . .

Forgive me, dear, that I become bitter and angry
against those little things that sting
the sense of hopelessness, those words
'Never, never,'
that I can never make sing
'Ever, ever':
in spite of Father Pio
and the prayers I always pray
hopelessly, day by day,
expecting no reply,
that You stay You and I
forever
true to each other
as the rivers fill with the waterfalls
and the rivers fill the sea.

But we remain sixty miles away
and only the telephone calls.

Continuing to write this poem to the only woman he loves, he describes himself as 'doped and drowsy and weak', and unable to find the convincing words to say, 'I love, I love.' The waiter in the restaurant car, he says, seemed to know already he was a man 'in trouble', as the Pope later described him.

Catherine always used to whistle to Greene. His post-affair memories of Achill, and Italy, and sitting in her study at Newton, often link his desire to her whistling. Like opium and sex, it was another part of their 'private universe'. In the depths of his imaginative psyche, Catherine, more than any other woman in his life, represented the real-life embodiment of the Western myth of women as a powerful life-in-death sexual force, that since Homer has held up a dark mirror to the often contradictory forces of nature, being both a source of destruction and a source of creation.

Catherine's last letter to Graham was written on Wednesday 18 May, 1978. She died from a cancer-related haemorrhage, aged sixty-two, at Addenbrooke's Hospital in Cambridge. She was admitted after falling seriously ill in late August. At her hospital bedside, having stayed with her all night, were her husband of forty-two years, Harry, and son Oliver.

Greene was at his Paris flat. He heard of her death from Marie Biche. In Boston College is a letter she wrote from England two days after Catherine's funeral at St George's Church, Thriplow, on 7 September 1978. Greene did not attend.

Biche's letter to the seventy-four-year-old grand old man of English letters ('Dear Dear Graham') begins with an apology for 'barging into your flat' and interrupting his afternoon siesta. She had lost her diary and remembered last using it in his flat the day before (Marie Biche and Greene were close friends in Paris, but she had recently moved to a house in the country). She thought Greene had already left – he was off on a trip – and hadn't seen his bag and coat in the hallway. It is not clear whether Greene learnt of Catherine's death after being woken up as Biche clattered around, or whether she had previously rung to tell him. 'I hated having to be the one to break the news of Catherine's death to you,' she wrote. 'What is somewhat consoling is that everyone here says that she was on exceptionally fine form mentally for the last few weeks.'

That Greene was heading off to the airport when he heard about Catherine's death is certainly appropriate. But more darkly ironic was the fact that Catherine's 'painful decline', as Oliver Walston had put it, began with an accident; falling down some steps at Dublin Airport, of all places – the 'point of departure' for so many of their early trips to Achill. One can assume she had been seeing Father O'Sullivan; possibly she had been drinking (when together they always did). She broke her hip and was operated on by Dublin doctors who made a mess of the surgery. 'I was horrified to hear that you were back in hospital in Dublin. You seem to be given no rest at all – you really are doomed to be a saint,' Greene wrote to her.

Catherine had endless operations in London. But her hip never really recovered. Having become Lady Walston in 1961, she was never able to really enjoy it. Her looks began to fade, partly as a result of her increasing alcoholism. Yet Greene remained deeply loyal. He tried to reassure her that 'you are an angel in disguise and sometimes the disguise wears very thin'. On another occasion he wrote: 'I shall expect to see a halo round your head when I return.'

For all her devout reading of St Thérèse, Biche said that Catherine had at first been 'very frightened of death'. As it approached, however, she began to think of it in a 'peaceful' frame of mind, as 'something to come in the now distant future'.

This is certainly borne out by the very last letter she wrote to Greene, which – along with a few others written between 1976–78 – he did not burn. In his spidery hand, he has marked it at the top 'C's last letter'. In the early days of their love affair, Greene always used to comment not on her looks but on how 'beautiful' her hand-writing was. Her last letters to Greene are mostly typed. But not the very last, which is three pages long and impeccably neat. Thirty-two years after her first letter ('Dear Godfather'), her writing was still sensual, intelligent and elegant. It looks as if it was carefully written, possibly knowing it would be the last she would send to the man who was perhaps the greatest true love of her life.

She begins by referring to a letter she has just received from Greene, which followed a long silence after his last visit to

London (he always stayed at the Ritz) six months before in November 1977. She was happy to get his letter as she feared his silence was because of his being cross with her. During this visit, or a later one, Greene had wanted to see her for a last time.

The go-between from the Ritz to Town's End Springs (the name of the new house that Lord Walston built in Thriplow) was Mrs Dawes, Catherine's former housekeeper at Newton Hall. On hearing that Greene was in London, Mrs Dawes had taken the initiative to contact him. Lady Walston was at the London Clinic and probably didn't have too many months left. Greene thanked her and said yes, he would like to see Catherine. But Catherine, who had spent most of her recent life either in a wheelchair, operating room or convent hospital bed, said no. She wanted him to remember them as they were when they were so happy. Thus, it has been said that 'the real end of the affair' came when Greene stood alone in the rain outside the Ritz, watching a London taxi filled with flowers to Catherine driving away on a grey, wet afternoon into the red tail lights of the Piccadilly traffic.

But an item in Greene's 'Walston' file at Boston College reveals that this was not quite the finale.

Catherine's last letter is a brave attempt to leave the world on happy terms with Greene, despite their turbulent personal history. But how their worlds had now changed. The last few letters that Catherine wrote to him are a sad testimony to how her exuberance for life, sex, men, drink and cigarettes simply burnt her up. In the absence of shared gossip, she now confessed that she had become a TV addict and asked Greene if he was too. Typically, by her bed Catherine had one of the first remote control devices in Britain. On 18 October 1977, writing to confirm details of his visit to Cambridge on Saturday 13 November 1977 – which is possibly the last time they ever saw each other – Catherine says that she will send the chauffeur to pick him up from Royston or Audley End Station. She adds that she might try to pick him up herself (as she always used to from Shannon

Airport) only she can't drive again yet; rather sadly, she says that she hopes to one day. She never did.

Greene himself was shortly off to Capri with Yvonne Cloetta. With what could be read as a twinge of jealousy, she nostalgically reflects on *their* times together at the Villa Rosaio, even recalling the moment when they first swung open the iron gate on their visit in the early spring of 1948. Greene had referred to his 'yearly fortnight' in Spain with 'my only priest' friend Father Leopoldo Duran. Catherine had never heard of him, nor even knew that Greene spent any time in Spain (*Monsignor Quixote* was published in 1982). She inquired if he had any priest pals in Antibes, adding that she missed no longer having any priests around in her life. Father Thomas had recently died.

Catherine was always a snail-paced reader compared to Greene, but she remained an avid one, even towards the end of her life when her mind became slow. So many years after being given her 'reading list' by John Rothenstein, she was back to the Russians, dipping into Tolstoy's two volumes of letters when the mood took her. She remained appalled by her ignorance of so many Russian writers. Greene had sent her his most recent book (*The Human Factor* was published in 1978), and Catherine remarks that it looked perhaps the most difficult book he had ever written. Somehow I rather doubt it had drained him in the same way as *The End of the Affair*.

By spring 1978 Catherine hoped Greene might occasionally write, or ring her up, but she clearly does not want him to visit her. But she is not dejected. She gossips a bit about old friends who she has completely lost touch with: John Sutro, who was ill; and Greene's close Catholic friend Jeanne Stonor (later Camoys), of Stonor Park. Catherine had read in the paper that their enormous house near Henley was apparently impossible to sell (like Newton Hall), and that they had refused to allow their eldest son to buy it, which Catherine found strange (although not as strange as what happened to the estate at Newton Hall). When Greene came to England in the 1960s, weekends not spent at Newton Hall were usually spent at Stonor Park in Oxfordshire.

As one of Britain's oldest Catholic families, the Stonors were happy to have the well-known Catholic novelist to stay at Easter or Christmas. Greene donated a rosary he had been given by the Pope to the family chapel at Stonor. Jeanne also liked to flirt with Greene, which Catherine did not always appreciate. 'Fame,' Greene once told Meyer, 'is a great aphrodisiac.'

As Catherine entered her forties, she became increasingly jealous of any other women in Greene's life. Indeed, as her health deteriorated and she realised she could no longer 'turn heads' as she used to, she even began to get jealous of her husband Harry's women friends. Although their marital sex life had broken down hardly before it began, Harry had a steady stream of other women in his life himself, all of whom appear to have been quite domineering and matronly figures. When he became Lord Walston, there was a small queue of women who suddenly seemed to find him rather dashing. In fact one of his mistresses was Marie Biche. However, when Harry was free he married the deserted wife of a Catholic MP, Lady Scott, the wife of Sir Nicholas Scott, the former MP for Kensington and Chelsea.

Catherine's final letter is really a thank you letter to Greene for the happiness he brought her. But there is no mention of love, or of Harry. The letter has echoes of Greene's soul-pouring letter of 1967 written from the Dan Hotel in Tel Aviv during the Six Day War ('My darling with you I found a strange beautiful underwater world like Cousteau's and nothing can ever make me forget it'). Near death herself, she now writes of her vivid memory of Greene teaching *her* to swim underwater in Jamaica in the 1950s. On one Caribbean trip they stayed at Ian Fleming's house, Goldeneye, where Fleming wrote all his James Bond books.

In her own letter, Marie Biche explains that Catherine has been talking to members of staff, asking them what they plan to do after she is gone. She gave them suggestions. It was typical of Catherine to get her hair done before going into Addenbrooke's Hospital for what turned out to be the last time. 'Porter, the old chauffeur, you must remember, told me that when he drove her

to the hairdresser's (in Harston I believe) on the day before she
went in . . . she was particularly live and cheerful.' On Thursday
evening and Friday morning, all her 'entourage' came to see her
for 'good chats'. Then she had a haemorrhage and the doctors
decided it would be useless to operate. On Saturday morning,
when another X-ray was attempted, she passed out (as Marie
understood) at 10am. 'At last, so long, out of pain. The amount
of physical pain she had to endure over those innumerable years
since she broke her hip is beyond inhuman.'

Part of the reason for Catherine's drinking was because of her
physical suffering. Greene viewed her suffering as if she were a
martyr. 'You are really having your Purgatory here and now,' was
a typical remark; or he would say, 'I hate your being in pain and
me not there.'

Today there is only one hairdresser's in Harston. It's a modern
shop in a concrete bungalow right opposite the gate to Harston
House, Greene's uncle's old house, which had such an important
pull on his early creativity. When Sir William Greene finally
died in his nineties in 1951, Greene nearly bought the house that
he had always been so happy in. Catherine's diary for 25
February 1951 records how Greene gave the local Harston parish
priest £50 after inheriting some money from Sir William.
Catherine added that it was the first money he had ever inherited, as opposed to earned.

But in the end, Greene decided against buying Harston, not
because it was too large for a bachelor, as has been previously
said, but for exactly the opposite reason that he had originally
decided not to buy the Queen's House at Linton back in 1947:
he wanted Vivien as far away as possible. By 1951, his relationship
with Catherine was in ruins. The last thing Catherine wanted
was Greene living a mile away from her marble doorstep.

Catherine's funeral was on a suitably cool, grey, drizzly morning, wrote Marie Biche. The service was short but good. 'The
one person who was deeply missed by all was dear Father
Thomas Gilby (I know he wasn't a favourite of yours but he was
a universal favourite of all who were close to C).' Another

tragedy for Catherine had been the death of her eldest son David, who was killed in a car accident in Beirut in 1978.

Inevitably, Catherine's funeral had a touch of Greeneland comedy. 'No "words" if that's the term,' Biche informed Greene, 'because the one who should have had the "honour", the senior chap from Blackfriars, an excrutiating bore who had made the service for Father Thomas unbearable for C, was present. So Harry had to say "No thank you" when he offered to make a speech. "No words by anyone." Actually any words would have been superfluous.'

Bendrix and Henry become quite close after Sarah's death but it's difficult to gauge what sort of relationship Harry and Greene had, in view of the sensitive question of the letters resting in the Hoare's bank vault in Fleet Street. Greene wanted them back. But dying without a will, the 'chattels' of her estate – including her Cartier ring and all Greene's love letters – passed to Harry. 'I have not opened the boxes,' Harry wrote to Greene, advising him that he planned to sell them to an American university. Catherine's instructions were that the Black Box should be kept either in the bank or in a lawyer's safe until after her, Greene's and Lord Walston's death. At that time they were to be disposed of to a suitable institution/academic body (the University of Texas, Balliol Oxford or King's Cambridge) at the discretion of the lawyers after consenting with the children.

Oliver Walston, who for many years was not on speaking terms with his father – presumably because Harry was selling off Catherine's effects – wrote to Greene strongly protesting that the letters were being sold at all. He thought they should be given to the library. After acting as go-between, Oliver then later wrote to Greene in a personal capacity asking to see him in Antibes to talk about his mother, whom he felt he hadn't known at all well, during her prime, fun, years; he wanted to get a sense of what she was really like. Could he put something down on paper? 'Let us meet and talk,' Greene replied. 'Your mother and I were very close over ten years and I loved her a great deal.'

So had Harry, but that did not stop him marrying Elizabeth

Scott with deft speed following Catherine's death. All Catherine's Henry Moores, John Piper paintings and Lowrys were sold off for a fortune by the new Lady Walston. She and Harry moved from Town's End Springs to Frome. When asked by a journalist why she was selling off Catherine's fine private collection of modern art, the new Lady Walston replied, 'The reasons are too personal.'

Greene always said the bit he liked best in *The End of the Affair* was the bizarre bond that Bendrix formed with Henry after Sarah's death. Greene and Harry certainly ended up having an odd relationship. In the Walston file at Boston College, for example, there is a letter from Harry, written long after Catherine's death, asking Greene whether he is interested in investing with him in a low-budget film project he sounds excited about. I can't imagine anyone less suited to being a film producer than Lord Walston but Greene wrote back diligently, diplomatically pouring cold water on the idea. After Catherine's death, Harry left writing to thank Greene for his letter of condolence until last.

'Who can honestly say that he has gone through life without causing pain?' Harry wrote to Graham in Antibes. 'And you gave joy too.' He added that it was impossible to draw up a balance sheet of plusses and minuses in life. 'But you gave Catherine something (I don't know what) that no one else had given her.' He ended the letter suggesting they get together for lunch.

But there is one Henry Moore that Catherine will always have with her. If one visits St George's churchyard in Thriplow – as I did on a rainy Saturday morning in October, with the local church bell-ringers busily in action – the headstone of Catherine Walston's grave contains a beautiful Henry Moore relief bronze of a nude woman and child. Inscribed below her name is that of her husband, 'Henry David Walston 1912–1991'.

In *The End of the Affair* Bendrix is a man driven to the edge of faith by an unnatural series of coincidences. Greene and Lord Walston died within weeks of each other in the spring of 1991. What would Bendrix have made of the fact that their strange ménage à trois continued to the very end? At noon on 6 June 1991, at the same time as the great and the good of the literary world – led by Vivien Greene, Yvonne Cloetta, and the likes of Sir Alec Guinness and Cardinal Hume – shuffled into Westminster Cathedral to celebrate a Memorial Requiem Mass for Greene presided over by Father Leopoldo Duran, sixty miles away in Cambridgeshire, Lord Walston's ashes were being scattered on Catherine's grave.

Although Greene did not attend Catherine's funeral, he did make a solitary visit to her grave when he came over to England. In his papers at Boston is a postcard of St George's church with a black ink drawing on the front. It shows Thriplow's pretty medieval village church with the usual array of tombstones. Exactly where Catherine is buried, Greene has drawn in her gravestone, marking it with a cross in black ink, just as so many years before he would always mark the postcards he sent her from Rome, Venice and Vienna with a cross marking which balcony room he was in, or which old room they had been in before. At the bottom of the card he has written the initial C, circled it, and put the date 7 September 1978.

There were no eulogies at Catherine's funeral. But perhaps Greene should be allowed to say a final word. It is taken from a letter written on the roof of 'her house' on Capri, long after their affair ended. 'Darling, please get it firmly in your dear head (that I fell in love with you on a plane) that you are and always will be the most important and unchanging person in my life. The years with you have contained the greatest happiness (perhaps the greatest unhappiness for moments too – one can't have one without the other) in my life. You are always with me. Now I lead a very quiet life, not unhappy – but it's not the same. Even if I spend half the time away, the half I spend here is because of you. Let's see more of each other.'